Mountain
Feds

*Arkansas
Unionists
and the
Peace Society*

T0308739

Mountain Feds

Arkansas Unionists and the Peace Society

James J. Johnston

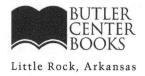

BUTLER CENTER BOOKS

Little Rock, Arkansas

The Butler Center for Arkansas Studies
Central Arkansas Library System
100 Rock Street
Little Rock, Arkansas 72201

www.butlercenter.org

First published September 2018
ISBN 978-1-945624-12-4 paperback
ISBN 978-1-945624-18-6 hardcover

Manager: Rod Lorenzen
Book design: Shelly Culbertson
Cover design: Mike Keckhaver
Copyeditor: Steven Teske

The painting that appears on the front cover of this book
is by Thereisa Housley and appears courtesy of the artist.

Cataloging-in-Publication data is on file at the Library of Congress

Butler Center Books, the publishing division of the Butler Center for Arkansas Studies, was made possible by the generosity of Dora Johnson Ragsdale and John G. Ragsdale Jr.

Printed in the United States of America

This book is printed on archival-quality paper that meets requirements of the American National Standard for Information Sciences, Permanence of Paper, Printed Library Materials, ANSI Z39.48-1984.

Contents

To Margaret,

who put up with my many

years of researching and talking

about the Mountain Feds

and the Peace Society

Acknowledgements

Daniel Sutherland, Brooks Blevins, and Mark Christ read the manuscript and offered positive comments and suggestions, many of which I followed. Of course, all problems are mine alone.

The sources are varied, and many institutions provided help: Special Collections at the Mullins Library at the University of Arkansas provided access to manuscripts and reports of the Arkansas General Assembly; the Arkansas State Archives helped with manuscripts for years and with access to the Thomas Boles photograph; the University of Arkansas at Little Rock Center for Arkansas History and Culture provided the John Rice Homer Scott Papers; and Nancy Smith of the Arkansas Archeological Survey and Hog County Media provided technical support. Thereisa Housley generously let me use her painting of the chain gang before they left the Burrowville courthouse on the book cover. Annette Hendrix Matthews and Doug Hendrix provided a copy of the painting of their ancestor John W. Morris as first lieutenant, First Arkansas Cavalry (U.S.)—probably a painting provided by a Union veterans' organization. Others who helped resolve knotty problems and gave information were Kathryn C. Fitzhugh, John Bradbury, Lynn Morrow, Roberta Watts Ferguson, Eddie Watts, Betty J. Harris—and others who are now deceased: Hattie Watts Treece and Orville J. McInturff.

This book benefited greatly from the assistance of Rod Lorenzen and Ali Welky of Butler Center Books at the Central Arkansas Library System and book designer Shelly Culbertson.

Introduction

In September 1941, Luther E. Warren (1883–1958)—a Tulsa newspaperman who grew up close to the Searcy–Stone County line—between Flag and Oxley in north-central Arkansas—wrote to Arkansas Secretary of State C. G. Hall explaining Searcy County's Republican bent. (Searcy County had voted for only two Democratic presidential candidates since the Civil War.) He said that the reason for this political tilt was sympathy for the Searcy County men who were marched away as a chain gang and forced into the Confederate army. These men were members of the secret pro-Union Peace Society.[1]

Such men were brothers Asa Watts (1831–1901) and Benjamin G. Watts (1833–1910), two of six sons of John Watts (1790–1865), who came to Searcy County about 1837 from Wayne County, Tennessee, through Hickman County, Kentucky. The family said that the John Watts family came to north-central Arkansas while Indians were still there. After first stopping in the Bear Creek valley, the Watts family moved on to Owls Fork of the Little Red River on the Van Buren County line. There John Watts obtained a military land warrant issued to Caleb Bates to purchase forty acres in Owls Cove, where he had lived for some years.

Asa, his fourth-eldest son, married Elizabeth Duck, sister of Peace Society member Timothy Arthur Duck, in 1852. They had four children by 1861. While his father John and three brothers remained on Little Red River, Asa moved to near Lebanon in Bear Creek valley by 1858 and was taxed for twenty acres adjoining his brother-in-law, one town lot in Burrowville, and $480 in personal estate. Asa and Benjamin G., like all the Watts men, were staunch Unionists. Sympathy for the Union was a family trait in Searcy County, and Unionist families supported each other across family lines. About May or June 1861 Asa joined the Peace Society, a secret organization with signs and passwords. The society's object was to oppose the Confederacy and aid the Union forces. In 1857 Asa's younger brother Benjamin G. Watts married Polly Ann Denton, daughter of Christopher Denton, a Peace Society recruiter from Van Buren County. He joined the Peace Society at a house-raising along with several others. In November the Peace Society was discovered by Searcy County Confederate officials. Asa and his younger brother Benjamin G. Watts, along with more than seventy others, were arrested by the Searcy County militia for belonging to a treasonous organization. They were confined in the Searcy County courthouse in Burrowville. Asa and Benjamin G.'s older half-brother John Harvey Watts was a member of that militia, because membership was mandatory for men.

After being confined for about two weeks—during which time measles broke out among the prisoners—the men were chained in pairs and marched 125 miles to Little Rock in early December. When the militia began to prepare the prisoners for their march to Little Rock, Clint Griffin—who was putting the chains around their necks—refused to chain Benjamin, because they had been boyhood friends. Nevertheless, Benjamin was chained to William F. Potter and marched to Little Rock. In Little Rock, Asa and the other prisoners were given a choice: enlist in the Confederate army or be tried for treason. They had no doubt that the authorities could prove what they pleased, so the prisoners enlisted in Company I, 18 (Marmaduke's) Arkansas Infantry. They were shipped to Bowling Green, Kentucky, in December 1861, and the chain gang members immediately began attempting to desert. In March 1862, Asa made his attempt. He walked away from his company without being challenged, but soon came upon soldiers digging graves. He had to pass through them to escape, so he pretended to be a local farmer looking for his hogs. Every once in a while, he would climb upon a log and call hogs until he had transited the burial detail.[2]

Benjamin G. Watts came down with the mumps and remained with Marmaduke's regiment until after the battle of Shiloh in April 1862. Because of his mumps he was furloughed home to Little Red River and arrived home in May.[3]

With Asa and Benjamin G. Watts marched off in the chain gang, Asa's family moved to Little Red River to be with Asa's father John Watts's family for protection and support. Benjamin G.'s family lived close by. Asa joined them there in April 1862, and Benjamin G. was home soon after. In late May or early June 1862, Confederate conscription officers came after them, and they had to hide in the woods. The brothers hid in a nearby cave with fellow Peace Society and chain gang neighbor Benjamin H. Gary, where Asa's ten-year-old son Benjamin Arthur delivered food to a nearby spring for them. Asa and Benjamin G. managed to avoid the conscription details and finally in October 1863, Peace Society member Benjamin F. Taylor recruited them into Company M, Third Arkansas Cavalry (U.S.). Benjamin G. Watts was regularly recruited as a private and served until he was discharged in May 1865. Asa, however, was not enrolled, but he was described as a refugee citizen, was issued ammunition, and did regular duty. He was not paid or issued clothing from October 1863 to April 1865. Asa thought he was rejected because of a sore leg.[4]

The Watts brothers learned that their youngest brother had been killed and that their seventy-five-year-old father John Watts had died on February 4, 1865. Both deaths were blamed on raiders who were terrorizing the countryside. John's house had been ransacked and John tortured to make him reveal hidden valuables. John died soon thereafter and was buried in the nearby family cemetery. Benjamin sought the murderers, but without success. He then learned that they had been raiding a house near Shirley when a young boy from the household returning from hunting came upon the raiders and killed the leader. The raiders scattered and never came together again. Benjamin felt that revenge had been done.[5]

The Arkansas Peace Society was one of several secret Unionist organizations throughout the South; it was the first to be discovered by Confederate authorities. There was Unionist sentiment throughout the South on the eve of secession among old Whigs, Northern and European immigrants, and mountain yeomen.

As was true throughout the South, Arkansans opposed to secession fell into three broad groups: old Whigs, who were mainly urban merchants, large rural landowners, and planters; recently arrived immigrants from the North or Europe; and yeoman farmers from the upland northwestern part of the state. In Arkansas old Whigs led the anti-secession movement. Although Northerners and the foreign-born played Unionist roles in many other Southern states and were topics of concern in Arkansas, their role in Arkansas was insignificant. The old Whigs provided the Unionist leadership until Lincoln's call for troops, but they then either aligned themselves with the state's southeastern lowland slaveholders or fled their homes to seek refuge with the federal army. The Whigs based their hopes for a peaceful resolution on cooperation with Border States to keep all the border states in the Union. They were called "cooperationists." Most Northern and European immigrants were Unionists, but their numbers were too small to give them any significant role. Indeed at least one German immigrant community—Hermannsburg in Washington County—abandoned Arkansas after being persecuted. The yeomen in the mountainous upland were the main strength of the Unionists after secession.

Much Unionist sentiment evaporated with President Abraham Lincoln's call for troops after the Confederates fired on Fort Sumter. Although opposed to secession, these Unionists saw Lincoln's action as aggression against the South, and they were Southerners. In Arkansas, Whigs quickly accommodated themselves to the Confederate government. Immigrants fled to the North. However, Unionist sympathy continued in the South after secession, especially in the mountains of the border states, which gave these men the epithet of "Mountain Feds" (Federals). In Arkansas, the men who remained to oppose the Confederate government were from the

Ozark and Ouachita mountains. They were largely yeoman farmers living in the poorest counties. They owned no slaves, and they were very conscious of the distinction between themselves and the slave-holders of the lowlands, whom they resented. The mountaineers had an inherent sympathy for the Union and a primary desire to protect their homes and families. They saw Confederate military service as a major obstacle to that end. "A rich man's war and a poor man's fight" was a phrase bandied about at the beginning of the secession crisis (and afterward) that expressed the sentiments of the Mountain Feds.[6]

The Arkansas State Convention in its first session—March 4 to 21, 1861—consistently defeated all secessionist efforts by a vote of 39 to 35. When it was recalled on May 6, 1861, the Convention voted the state out of the Union on the first day it met, began to raise troops, and prepared Arkansas for war. It took about six months for new Unionist leaders to respond and organize for their own protection, and these leaders were Arkansas's mountain-eers. For most Arkansans, whether secessionists or Unionists, the primary concern was to protect their homes against slave revolts, Northern invasion, Missouri refugees, and—for the Unionists—Confederate Arkansas authorities. These concerns gave birth to the Peace Society, and this book is the story of those loyal men.[7]

The preoccupation with local safety affected Arkansas's war efforts. The Arkansas 1861 State Convention found it difficult to raise troops for the Confederacy, or even for the state, because its members and their constituents were concerned with their own security. Strong pressure existed to create home guard units, and service in those units superseded service in state regiments. Some communities formed local vigilance committees and published their activities in the Little Rock press. The State Convention of 1861 created a Military Board that assumed the bothersome duties of raising military units to protect both Arkansas and the Confederacy. It, too, had difficulty putting the goals of the Confederacy or even of the state above local defense. The Board and Arkansas governor Henry M. Rector, after south Arkansas's initial rush to colors, found it difficult to meet the demands for troops by the Confederacy's secretary of war while also raising troops to defend Arkansas's border with Missouri.

Although there was no conscription act yet, pressure was put on men to enlist. Unionists who sought safety and security from military service by forming similar self-protection organizations could scarcely be open about it. Therefore, they began to form secret societies sometime during early 1861. Besides the Arkansas Peace Society, similar pro-Union organizations appeared in 1862 in Alabama, North Carolina, Georgia, Florida, Mississippi, and Virginia under the names Peace Society and Heroes of America (or Red Strings). There is a hint of a group in December 1861 in Virginia. Confederate authorities believed that these movements originated within the Union lines, but they did not take the organization seriously at first. Conscription invited men to defy the authorities and to band together for self-protection. Danger of arrest by Confederate authorities made them operate clandestinely. As with the Arkansas Peace Society, the origins of the eastern secret Unionist organizations are uncertain.[8]

Confederate strong-arm recruiting tactics caused the Arkansas Unionists' Peace Society to grow significantly. Later the same tactics led to its denouement by men sworn into its secrets. Secret organizations were not unique to the Southern uplands during the Civil War era. Masonic fraternities with their secret rituals had been in America since the eighteenth century, and some see its secret signs in Peace Society signals. Secret Greek-letter college fraternities dated to the 1820s. The most common and recognized Peace Society token, recognized by almost everyone in their neighborhood, was the yellow cloth displayed at their homes to identify themselves to fellow Peace Society men for mutual protection, and (some said) to identify the home to the Union army when it invaded. The yellow cloth was so widely known that those who displayed it were known as "Yellow Rags" or the "Yellow Rag Boys."

First betrayed by John Holmes—who informed the local authorities about the Peace Society on November 17, 1861, in Clinton—the fever of investigating, arresting, and suppressing this secret Unionist organization spread throughout north-central Arkansas. Confederate authorities thought they were dealing with a treasonous insurrection on the verge of revolt. Captured Izard County Peace Society members were forced into Confederate regiments on the spot to meet recruitment goals. Those that refused to enlist were sent to Little Rock for investigation and to stand trial. Unionists from Carroll, Fulton, Izard, Marion, Searcy, and Van Buren counties were marched as captives to Little Rock, and most were intimidated into enlisting in the army to meet Arkansas's need for recruits. Those who elected to be tried in lieu of enlistment were found not guilty and released in a couple of months because they had not actually committed any acts of rebellion. After secessionist candidates defeated cooperation candidates in the fall of 1861, a Washington, Arkansas, newspaper exulted that there was no longer a Union element in the state.[9]

Nothing could have been farther from the truth. The misapprehension illustrated the vast cultural divide between the upland and lowland parts of Arkansas. Not all the Unionist sympathizers had been captured. Some who felt most threatened fled to Union posts in Missouri. Others fled to the woods, and yet others just kept their heads down and their opinions to themselves. Union men who had been dragooned into Confederate service began deserting in early 1862. Many fled to Missouri or enlisted with General Samuel R. Curtis's Union command in Batesville, while some fled to hide in the woods.

When the Confederate Conscription Act began to be enforced in north Arkansas in June 1862, some Union men who had been in the Peace Society formed guerrilla bands to oppose Confederate authority—especially conscription. Eventually, as many bands were broken up, the men fled to federal lines to enlist, although some Unionist guerrilla units continued until the end of the war.

As the Confederate war effort became more demanding of men and resources in late 1862 and 1863, Unionists sought other Unionists and formed secret bonds with them in bands avoiding conscription officers. What had been known as the "Peace Society" or "Peace and Constitution Society" then styled itself the "Union League." There is evidence of it in south Arkansas before April 1862. As federal forces pressed farther into Arkansas, more Arkansans sought them out to enlist in federal military service. They not only joined designated Arkansas regiments, but they also enlisted by squads and even companies in Missouri regiments in eastern Arkansas and Kansas regiments in western Arkansas.

Not strong enough to return Arkansas to the Union before the 1864 election, Isaac Murphy and other Unionists—and maybe some opportunists—organized a state government loyal to the Union. Peace Society men were significant supporters. Murphy's government tried to seat Unionist senators and congressmen, but it was rebuffed by a Radical Republican Congress. As time went on, these wartime Unionists became the foundation of Arkansas's Republican Party.

Unionist sympathizers in the seceded South were neglected by historians of the Old South and rejected by the people in general prior to World War II. An exception was Georgia Lee Tatum's *Disloyalty in the Confederacy*, published in 1934, which was the first "attempt to portray the widespread disaffection in the Confederate states." Tatum commented, "Until recently, many historians, as well as people in general, have commonly accepted the idea that every man, woman and child in the South stood loyally behind Jefferson Davis and the Stars and Bars in support of the Confederacy." This assumption was certainly the case in Arkansas. Luther Warren's 1941 letter to Arkansas Secretary of State Hall about men in his neighborhood who had been captured by the Confederates, marched in chains to Little Rock, and forced into the Confederate army in 1861 led to a rebuttal by Arkansas History Commission Director Dallas T. Herndon. He did not believe Warren's account and refuted Warren's premise in the *Arkansas Gazette,* writing, "Things just weren't done that way. The Confederate States of America and Arkansas did not resort to such tactics."[10]

Not until after World War II did Southern historians began to investigate Southern Unionism. Ted R. Worley, director of the

Arkansas History Commission and Herndon's successor, published in the April 1958 *Arkansas Historical Quarterly* "Documents Relating to the Arkansas Peace Society of 1861," which he found in the Commission's archives. These documents supported Warren's narrative. Other states' historical journals also published articles about secret Unionist organizations, such as the Red Strings (or Heroes of America) in North Carolina and the Peace Society in Alabama.[11]

After Tatum's 1934 book, no further major works solely addressed Unionist sympathy in the Confederacy until 1981 with Phillip Shaw Paludan's *Victims: A True Story of the Civil War.* The pace picked up in the 1990s with other books about Southern Unionists, but no major work has covered the pro-Union Peace Society in Arkansas, although it was the first secret pro-Union group to be discovered in the Confederacy. These early Arkansas Unionists became the nucleus for Arkansas Union regiments and companies in other states' regiments. Arkansas produced more Union soldiers than any seceding state except Tennessee. Lightly treated by Arkansas Civil War historians, this facet of the Civil War in Arkansas deserves greater attention.[12]

Background: Arkansas in 1860

A line drawn diagonally across Arkansas from the northeast corner, through Little Rock, to the southwest corner—roughly following the old Southwest Trail from Illinois to Texas—would approximately divide the state into a rough mountainous upland northwest half and a lowland, often swampy, southeast half. On the eve of the Civil War this division also roughly divided the state into pro-secessionist and pro-Union halves. James M. Woods's *Rebellion and Realignment: Arkansas's Road to Secession* made this observation and provided a wealth of supporting data in the appendix's tables and figures. The northwest part, including the Ozark and Ouachita mountains, was largely pro-Union and relatively populous, with a preponderance of yeoman farmers, few slaves, and a subsistence economy based on grain and livestock. The mountainous upland's small farmers supplemented their corn and wheat crops with hunting and livestock. The upland creek and river bottoms and flat mountain tops were the first to be settled. Roads were trails, but only outsiders seemed to complain. In most upland counties yeoman farmers tilled small fields in the creek bottoms to grow grains, raised stock, and hunted. Livestock was their principal source of income. If they had any slaves, they usually had fewer than five. The lowlands were pro-secession and were level, with immensely fertile soil—although much of it was swampland.

The soil and landscape in each area determined the type of agriculture and thus the culture. Lowland counties were farmed by slave plantations to grow cotton, a money crop, to produce great wealth. The wealthier cotton-growing, market-oriented southeast was less heavily populated by white people, but it had many more slaves. The northwest drew immigrants from the upper South and border states of Tennessee, Kentucky, Missouri, and North Carolina, while southeast immigrants came from the Lower South, mostly Alabama, Mississippi, Georgia, and South Carolina. Although Arkansans considered themselves Southerners, the slavery issue was not important to the slave-less mountaineers. Even Arkansans dependent upon slavery for their well-being disagreed on how best to protect those assets. The predominantly yeoman mountaineers were small farmers—few owned even one or two slaves—while the lowland plantations were entirely dependent upon slave labor. Although Arkansas was still a frontier state in 1850, the disparate regional cultures had already established themselves into the yeoman uplands and plantation lowlands with their different economies and cultures. Seventy percent (37,339) of Arkansas's 47,100 slaves were in the lowland counties. Sixty percent of Arkansas's over 162,000 white population was concentrated in the uplands.[13]

The 1850s brought heavy immigration to Arkansas as it vigorously promoted itself. The state legislature passed a generous homestead law, and the federal government gave the state the swampland in the fertile delta, land which Arkansas then offered to anyone who would drain the swamps and protect the land from overflows. The cheap land provided by the provisions of the state and federal governments in the 1850s saw a massive influx of cotton planters and their slaves from Mississippi, Alabama, and Georgia into the lowlands. These actions brought wealthy planters to south Arkansas to create large slave-dependent cotton farms. By 1856, the price of cotton had jumped to over twelve cents a pound, making it the highest it had been since 1838. It remained above eleven cents for the rest of the decade. This increased the wealth and total population of the lowland counties which profited from the new cotton land. The upland counties also saw an increase in population—coming from Tennessee, Missouri and Kentucky—but the newcomers predominantly were white yeoman farmers seeking similar lands in Independence, Izard, and Searcy counties.[14]

From 1850 to 1860, the overall Arkansas population increased by 107.5% (209,897 to 435,450). The twenty-five upland counties had 58% of the white population (187,840) compared to the thirty lowland counties' 42% (136,351). However, the lowland counties had 52% of the total population, compared to the upland counties' 48%, if one counted slaves. This disparity in the slave population had more than doubled by 1860. Although all parts of the state grew in the 1850s, the lowland counties grew more rapidly than the upland counties, gaining on the upland counties by 2% in white population and 3.5% in slave population. The lowlands had 83.6% of the slave population to the uplands' 17.3%, which was mostly found in the Arkansas River Valley counties. The location of the slave population also indicated the source of wealth, since land and slaves represented the vast majority of Arkansas's wealth. Of the fifteen wealthiest counties, all were in the lowlands. The fifteen poorest counties, except for Craighead and Greene, were in the uplands. The three poorest were Newton, Searcy, and Van Buren, with Marion, Izard, and Carroll not far ahead. These six adjoining counties in north-central Arkansas astride the Boston Mountains—the watershed for the White and Arkansas rivers' drainage—provided the strongest opposition to the Confederacy.[15]

There were exceptions to this generalization, of course. Greene and Craighead counties in northeast Arkansas both adjoined prosperous Mississippi County, but they were plagued with overflows and swamps. The upland counties of Conway, Independence, Johnson, Pope, and Yell were riparian counties along significant waterways with ample bottom lands for cotton and a slave economy, but they still contained mountains and yeoman farmers.[16]

The politics of the state reflected its economy. Since Arkansas became a state in 1836, its yeoman, small-farmer culture had favored a Jacksonian egalitarian Democratic Party that dominated politics. A more elitist Whig Party, dependent upon urban businessmen and large plantation owners, almost always came in second. The Democratic Party early in Arkansas's history became controlled by "The Family" or "The Dynasty," a clique of

Conway-Johnson-Sevier relatives. They first came to power in the
1820s, when Henry W. Conway was elected territorial delegate. He
was followed by his cousin, Ambrose Sevier. Their strength lay in
their egalitarian appeal to the small farmers, and they regularly
carried the poorer mountain countries. However, as the lowland
counties grew, members of The Family paid more attention to
their needs. As early as 1850, Congressman Robert Ward Johnson
(brother-in-law of Ambrose Sevier) came out strongly for slavery,
even secession. Issuing an "Address to the People of Arkansas"
he spoke for "our rights under the constitution within or without
the Union." Arkansas governor John Selden Roane and the state's
two U.S. senators, William Sebastian and Solon Borland, supported
Johnson's views. Those views went against the sympathies of most
Arkansans, who were more interested in progress than secession.[17]

Newspapers played a major role in Arkansas politics. The
Family newspaper, the *Arkansas Banner*, became the *True Democrat*
in 1850 under Richard Mentor Johnson, Congressman Robert Ward
Johnson's younger brother. The opposition Whig Party newspaper,
the *Arkansas Whig*, died in 1855. However, the *Arkansas Gazette*,
the old anti-Family state newspaper, was acquired by Mexican War
veteran Captain C. C. Danley, described as a crypto-Whig. He soon
joined with Solon Borland and Albert Pike to take the *Arkansas
Gazette and Democrat* into support of the Know-Nothing (American)
Party, inheritors of the Whig mantle in Arkansas.[18]

The most influential Whigs in Arkansas were the plantation
owners of the lowlands and the businessmen of the urban areas:
Little Rock, Fort Smith, and Camden. Whigs elsewhere in the state
sometimes won local office, including Albert Pike (a Scottish Rite
Mason of Little Rock), Judge David Walker of Fayetteville, attorney
James Spring of Van Buren, and John Campbell of Searcy County.
A strong Masonic affiliation united some of these men. Pike was
an outstanding author of Masonic doctrine; John Campbell brought
the Masonic lodge to Searcy County after his 1852–53 stint in the
Arkansas legislature. The Whigs had practically no success winning
state offices—a notable exception being the twenty-five-day term of

Thomas Newton, successor to U.S. Representative Archibald Yell upon Yell's resignation to become colonel of an Arkansas regiment during the Mexican War. Nevertheless, the Whig Party became a catchall for opponents of The Family. Upon the party's death nationally in 1854, the old Whigs, supporting the Know-Nothing Party, continued to lose to The Family and the Democrats; but they continued to be the basket that held The Family's opponents.[19]

Paradoxically, the decline of The Family came from within. Thomas Carmichael Hindman—whom The Family supported at one time—was an ambitious Mississippi lawyer who settled in Helena in 1854 and married Mollie Watkins Biscoe, the daughter of economically and politically successful pioneer Henry Biscoe. A gifted public speaker and imaginative politician, Hindman contributed to the Democratic Party victory over the Know-Nothings by hosting a three-day rally that denigrated them. His effective Know-Nothing bashing ingratiated him with The Family, and in 1856 he demonstrated his political strength by almost defeating A. B. Greenwood, The Family's incumbent congressman for north Arkansas. In 1858, attempting to co-opt him, The Family supported him as he won the same north Arkansas representative seat. Hindman's ambition was not satisfied. In 1859 he began campaigning for the Senate seat held by Family member William King Sebastian, who was stepping down. Hindman founded his own newspaper in Little Rock, the *Old Line Democrat*. His newspaper attacked The Family's *True Democrat* and The Family's leadership as an oppressive aristocracy opposed to Jacksonian democracy. The Family changed the party's rules to allow Sebastian to be re-nominated as senator, and opposed Hindman's reelection, but Hindman handily won his congressional seat. The *Old Line Democrat* from its beginning supported the South and the right of secession, but its attacks on The Family's flawed Jacksonian principles won Hindman votes in the upland counties of north Arkansas. In the August election for state, local, and congressional offices, Hindman's victory in the northern upland counties was overwhelming.

District-wide he received 20,051 votes, with 5,479 coming from the poorer mountain counties of Carroll, Fulton, Izard, Madison, Marion, Newton, Searcy, and Van Buren. His opponent, Independent Jesse Cypert of White County, supported by The Family, garnered only 9,699 votes district-wide and 1,823 from the poorer mountain counties. In these counties Cypert did best in Izard and Searcy counties, almost tying Hindman, a reflection of The Family's lack of strength there.[20]

Another politician running against The Family in 1860 benefitted from Hindman's campaign resources. Henry Massie Rector—a first cousin of Governor Elias N. Conway—had enjoyed the support of The Family during a long career in Arkansas politics, including, in 1859, a seat on the state Supreme Court. This appointment did not satisfy him; to the consternation of The Family, he announced himself as a candidate for governor in May 1860. A plantation owner in Saline County and a Little Rock attorney, Rector campaigned as "a poor honest farmer of Saline County" against The Family's candidate Richard M. Johnson, younger brother of Senator Robert Ward Johnson and editor of the *True Democrat*. With the support of Hindman's newspaper, the *Old Line Democrat*, Rector decisively defeated Johnson 31,948 to 28,487. Rector carried eight of the fifteen poorest counties, including Pike, Fulton, Madison, Marion, Searcy, and Newton, all counties that would feature prominently as Unionist counties. His strength, as with Hindman, was in the poorer counties with the largest percentage of white population growth. He did not do as well as Hindman in those five counties, except for Searcy County, where he received more votes (492) than Hindman (368). To emphasize The Family's defeat, another Hindman ally, Edward Gantt, was elected representative from the southern congressional district.[21]

All The Family's opponents ran as Jacksonian Democrats opposing The Family's domineering behavior. But they were also strongly pro-slavery and pro-secessionist, positions they did not emphasize during the campaign. Slavery did become an issue during the 1860 presidential election. Stephen A. Douglas of Illinois, the leader of the national Democratic Party, had won the support of the Southern states with his Kansas-Nebraska Act, which promised to open the remainder of the Louisiana Purchase to slavery. He lost this support with his opposition to admitting Kansas under a pro-slavery constitution and later with his "Freeport Doctrine." Of Arkansas's eight delegates to the Democratic Convention in Charleston, South Carolina, six were Family supporters. Northern delegates were in the majority and most supported Douglas. The delegates from seven Southern states walked out when the free-state delegates would not agree to federal protection for slavery. Six of the Arkansas delegation, the Family supporters, joined the walkout.

Stymied, the convention agreed to reassemble in mid-June at Baltimore. There, again, the two sides could not work together, and the Lower South delegates walked out, followed by the Upper South; again, six Arkansas delegates joined the protest. The remaining delegates nominated Douglas. Southern delegates who had left the Democratic Convention met in Baltimore's Maynard Institute and nominated John C. Breckinridge of Kentucky, the sitting vice-president. Breckinridge's platform pledged federal protection for slavery. There were now Northern and Southern Democratic parties.[22] The Republicans, meeting in Chicago, nominated Abraham Lincoln and adopted a platform that appealed to a wide variety of free-state interests, including opposition to the expansion of slavery. However, their platform and Lincoln's statements accepted slavery where it already existed.

There were moderates in the United States that were fearful of the avenue they perceived the various political parties were taking and sought a middle ground. The former Whigs and Know-Nothings, particularly those of the Upper South, formed a fourth party, the Constitutional Union Party, and nominated John Bell of Tennessee (a former Whig and large slaveholder) as president and Edward Everett of Massachusetts as vice-president. They hoped to protect slavery and the Union under the banner "the Union as it is and the Constitution as it is."[23]

In Arkansas, The Family and Hindman factions supported John Breckinridge and the South. Douglas's Arkansas support was limited to Thompson Flournoy and John Stirman of Fayetteville (the only Arkansas delegates to the Democratic Convention who did not walk out), and Albert Rust, congressman from the Southern District. Although they established a campaign newspaper in Little Rock—the *National Democrat*—and had the support of the *Van Buren Press* and of former Governor Thomas Drew, Douglas's Arkansas campaign never had a chance. It did not have the funds for public festivities; nor did it have enough newspaper coverage to win the people's support from the Democratic Party machinery.[24]

John Bell's supporters did have funds, and the old Whig press that emphasized Bell's ticket was the only one that could defeat the Republicans and hold the Union together. The Constitutional Union supporters accused the Breckinridge people of being disunionists and pleaded for support from every Union man.[25]

Lincoln's name did not appear on the Arkansas ballot, and in the final count Douglas did not carry a single county. He was strongest in Jefferson and Crawford counties where newspapers supported him. Bell ran strongly in the old Whig counties of eastern and southern Arkansas and did well in the urban-commercial river towns. However, the old Democratic Party loyalty of the yeomen in the northern and western counties carried Arkansas for Breckinridge. He won clear majorities in five northwestern counties that would become centers of mountain Unionism.[26]

Arkansas's response to Lincoln's election was relatively mild, despite the immigration from the Lower South over the previous two decades to the rich alluvial lowlands of the south and east. This influx of pro-slavery, pro-Southern immigrants, with wealth in slaves and land acquired under the Swamp Lands Act, brought the Old South to Arkansas politically, culturally, and economically. Yet, despite this pro-slavery weight to Arkansas politics, Arkansans decided to wait to see what Lincoln's election would portend. The *Arkansas Gazette* and ex-Whig Albert Pike both advocated a wait-and-see approach; even The Family's *True Democrat*, a prominent Breckinridge newspaper, commented November 24, "[T]he South should not secede because Lincoln had been elected by only a minority of the people." On the same date, the Fayetteville *Arkansian*, another Family-controlled paper, counseled caution: "[W]ait until after his inaugural and see what course he will pursue."[27]

Arkansas secessionists—Hindman, Rector, and Edward Gantt—all began pressing the newly elected Thirteenth General Assembly to action on dissolution. The Assembly convened on November 5, 1860, the day before the presidential election. On November 19, Fulton County representative Jehoida J. Ware wrote to his wife Christiana Ware, "There is great excitement here and I am afraid that we cannot avoid a dissolution of the Union. Rector, Hindman, Gant [sic] and most of the leading men are in favor of a dissolution. Lincoln is elected without a doubt. Georgia has appropriated one million to arm the Militia. There will be resolution offered here for dissolution though I hope they will be kicked out of the House." Governor Rector addressed both houses of the legislature on November 15, followed by Hindman and Congressman-elect Gantt on November 24 and 25, all three advocating immediate secession. The Family, despite Robert Ward Johnson's long-time pro-slavery, pro-Southern, pro-disunion stand, initially continued to urge caution, but it did not take long for them to come around. Senator Johnson, leader of The Family, published a letter to his constituents in the December 22 issue of the *Arkansas Gazette*. In it he urged Arkansas to secede with the Southern states.[28]

Despite politicking by the winners of the August election, the inherent conservatism of the yeoman farmers in the north and west and the old Whigs in the lowlands kept the legislature from taking precipitate action. The legislature was predominantly pro-Unionist, and the first moves to take the state out of the Union failed. Eventually, the gathering strength of the pro-secession lowlands on the legislature produced a bill to allow a double referendum on the disunion issue. The citizens would vote whether to call a state convention and to select delegates for that convention. This left Unionists in a precarious position of voting against the convention, but for a Unionist delegate.[29]

John Campbell, Searcy County representative to the 1861 state convention.
(Courtesy of the author)

Chapter 1

Fight for the Union: Whigs and the Northern- and Foreign-Born

Abraham Lincoln's election to the presidency presented Arkansas with a new set of problems and divisions. The lowland southeast was rich ground for the old secessionists to cultivate, and they did it with zeal, eventually uniting the lowland cotton farmers into a bloc that saw secession and a place in the Confederacy as their only solution. The northwestern upland saw secession as ruinous. The old Whigs and the Douglas Democrats were the principal spokesmen against secession and led the fight for union under the old Constitution in hopes of a negotiated settlement between the North and the South. This meant the protection of slavery and rights of slaveholders throughout the United States and slavery's expansion into the territories guaranteed by the Constitution. As the political forces outside Arkansas played their game, the Arkansas Unionists found their options curtailed by constraints of their own making. Voted out of the Union, Arkansas's leaders of all stripes went easily into the Confederacy. Some of their followers did not agree on this course.

Lieutenant Colonel Albert W. Bishop, First Arkansas Cavalry (U.S.), wrote about the upland Arkansans' attitudes, "The old frontiersman, sitting musingly in his chimney corner, on the slope of a mountain spur, could not see wherein the election of Abraham Lincoln had injured him." However, it was not just old frontiersmen who did not immediately jump to break with the Union.

The Arkansas press, almost unanimously, urged caution and saw no immediate threat to the state's way of life or to slavery, unlike people in the Deep South. Little Rock's *Gazette* and the *Des Arc Constitutional Union*, which had supported Bell, led the call for caution after Lincoln's victory. The *Gazette* carried on a campaign of pacification by blaming politicians for the disunion sentiment. It predicted that, in a seceded South, rabid secessionists would hold the civil offices while the common folk did the fighting. The *Van Buren Press*, which had supported Douglas, urged calm and proper reflection. Even The Family's *True Democrat*, stalwart Breckinridge supporter, did not call for secession just because Lincoln was elected. Only Hindman's *Old Line Democrat* reacted shrilly by advocating an alliance with the Deep South, even in secession. Irrespective of some Arkansans' deep-seated fears, it took the actions of the fire-eating politicians to rouse the secessionists' cause to challenge inherent conservatism.[30]

Although concern for the implications of Lincoln's election was great, some Southerners hoped for a peaceful resolution within the Union. One wealthy slaveholder, thirty-two-year-old Alabama-born Nicholas V. Barnett of Smith Township, Bradley County—with $30,000 in real estate and $50,000 in personal property—wrote to Lincoln on November 30, 1860, recommending that Lincoln and his vice-president should resign or decline inauguration so that the country might still be preserved. Barnett said that "as a Union-loving and patriotic people, we are desirous of preserving our country as a unit, on just and equitable terms, both North & South."[31]

On the cusp of Southern secession—at Abraham Lincoln's election—there was anxiety among conservative Arkansans of all backgrounds about what Lincoln's policies would be and how they would be affected, so they wrote to ask him. Their letters reveal the concerns and interests of the state. Northern-born Unionists, especially, were concerned about the possibilities of secession in Arkansas. Some of them were pessimistic about the outcome, while others believed that Arkansas would stay in the Union. Samuel

B. Pinney, a thirty-two-year-old attorney from Pennsylvania, was pessimistic. He wrote Abraham Lincoln on December 10, 1860, from Little Rock to say the following:

> The excitement of Disunion is vastly increasing in this State Legislature and throughout the State[.] [T]he Governor of Miss has dispatched a messenger to this State to ascertain what it will do. We Still hope that our Legislature is conservative. 3 of the 5 of the Committee on Federal relations are known to be. Gloom is cast over this fair Land and Nation, and a Northern man Scarce knows or dares to give utterance to his patriotic pride in defense of our Constitution, the Palladium of our Liberty. In all of the Southern States it is not in my power to describe the feeling of envy, hate, and malice, as well as Settled determination to overthrow our Government. Publicly proclaimed by many quite able and Somewhat distinguished men in this State, (or rather wily Politicians).[32]

A far different view was taken by the activist Snow family, which came to Pine Bluff in the late summer of 1860. Josiah Snow, born about 1810 in Rhode Island, had interests in newspapers and the telegraph. About 1849 he established the *Detroit Tribune,* an anti-slavery newspaper. In 1851 he became involved with Anson Bangs, a civil engineer, land speculator, and entrepreneur involved with big construction works and with the Atlantic and Pacific Telegraph Company. The latter promoted a southern telegraph line from Natchez, Mississippi, through El Paso and Yuma, to San Diego, and along the coast to Monterey and San Francisco. The Snow patriarch was accompanied to Pine Bluff by his son William D. Snow, born 1832 in Massachusetts, and by an unnamed son-in-law. He set up a pro-Union newspaper, the *Pine Bluff News,* which he operated until about May 26, 1861. He also established the Pine Bluff Telegraph Company, with lines between Pine Bluff and Little Rock, including plans to run a line to Napoleon. Josiah Snow recalled that at the November 1860 presidential election his family made a Lincoln ticket of electors. Only he, his son, and son-in-law voted it, and he speculated that Lincoln got a mere ten votes in the whole state. Probably because of his pro-Union newspaper, his family was invited to leave town in twenty-four hours, urged on by a tin horn serenade. Still defiant, they did not immediately leave, but continued with the newspaper and telegraph company.[33]

As early as the election of November 6, Josiah's son, William D. Snow, reported to Lincoln on the Union sentiment in Arkansas. His letter at the time of the election said that there was strong Union sentiment in Arkansas and that the state would not secede. On November 16, he wrote from Madison, St. Francis County, that he had returned from Helena where he had witnessed the defeat of Congressman Thomas C. Hindman's efforts to raise a militia company, outweighed by Senator William K. Sebastian's counsels of moderation.

Another letter, dated November 28 from Pine Bluff, reported he had been through Monroe, Prairie, Arkansas, and Jefferson counties and observed strong Unionist sentiments of the Arkansans. He also commented on the state legislature's preoccupation with selecting a U.S. senator and felt that pro-Union S. H. Hempstead or Ben DuVal had the support of the Union members of the state Senate.[34]

As the newspapers reflected the conservatism of most Arkansans, the contest moved to the state legislature. The Thirteenth Arkansas General Assembly had just convened when Abraham Lincoln was elected and the election results became known. His election left most of Arkansas in limbo, but political fire-eaters Hindman, Senator Robert Ward Johnson, Governor-elect Henry M. Rector, and Representative-elect Edward Gantt began pushing for secession. In his November 15 inaugural speech, Governor Rector declared that the offenses of the Republican states and Lincoln's election were just cause for immediate secession. However, he also hinted that reconciliation remained a possibility, which created more confusion than clarity. Nonetheless, Fulton County representative J. J. Ware saw him definitely in the secessionist camp, and he wrote to his wife on November 19 that Rector was in favor of secession.[35]

Hindman jumped immediately to advocate secession. In early November he tried to organize a militia unit in Phillips County, but Senator William K. Sebastian contested the proposal at a meeting in Helena, and the meeting adjourned without taking action. Hindman's *Old Line Democrat* kept up a constant drumbeat emphasizing Arkansas's ties to the cotton South. On November 24, he made an inflammatory address to the General Assembly, followed the next day by a similar speech from congressman-elect Gantt. Following Hindman's speech, the legislature took up the question of secession.

A resolution to follow the Lower South in secession was countered by another resolution to consult with the Upper South states or not to secede at all. Only Hindman's followers were advocating secession during the month following Lincoln's election, and their moves in the General Assembly for secession were consistently defeated.[36]

In a slight change of tactics, Ben T. DuVal of Sebastian County submitted a bill for a state convention to consider secession. It was ignored; but immediately thereafter, on December 11, Governor Rector urged the legislature to advocate a convention that would pull the state out of the Union immediately. He saw the fast-approaching March 4 date for Lincoln's inauguration as a disaster that he had to avert. In Washington for a post-election congressional session, Hindman and Robert W. Johnson smothered old animosities on December 21, cabling a plea to the General Assembly for a state convention to consider secession. The next day, December 22, their joint message was published, and an earlier dated (December 1) letter from Johnson to his constituents firmly placed The Family with Hindman. This Hindman-Family coalition had carried Arkansas for Breckinridge and was now an almost insurmountable force for secession.[37]

However, the Thirteenth General Assembly was predominantly conservative and turned down all attempts at secession or a state convention to consider secession. To bring pressure on the legislature, in early December secessionists became active in lowland Arkansas, promoting county meetings to pass resolutions either for a state convention or secession. Senator L. H. Belser from cotton-growing and wealthy Chicot County presented his county's resolutions rejecting the Lincoln administration. This was followed by similar resolutions from Desha, Jefferson, Ouachita, Hempstead, and Clark counties. They were answered by anti-session resolutions from the upland counties: Sebastian, Sevier, Marion, Carroll, Newton, Searcy, Conway, Pike, Van Buren, Columbia, Clark, and Pope. The divisiveness of the situation is indicated by Clark County's two resolutions—expressing stands both for and against secession.[38]

The eventual strength of the two sides is indicated by each one's internal cohesiveness. Those resisting secession were divided between "Unionists," who wished to remain in the Union even under a Republican administration, and "cooperationists" who would cooperate with the Border and Upper South slave states to bring about a reconciliation with the Deep South. A profile of the March 1861 convention delegates by the *True Democrat* identified their politics.

Of thirty-nine non-secessionist delegates, nineteen identified as "Union," four as "Conservative," four as "Co-operationist," nine as "Anti-secessionist," one as "Anti-lmd't soc," one with no politics listed, and one "What is right." Of the thirty-five secessionists, twenty-eight were identified as "Secessionist," two as "Democrat," one "State rights," one "Southern rights," and one "Conditional Secessionist." Resolutions from the cotton-growing counties called for the legislature to work with the governor in calling a state convention to seek redress of their grievances, including secession. Unionist resolutions condemned disunion and sought compromise, but their resolutions differed from each other, perhaps even more than some differed from secessionists'. Sebastian and Conway counties deplored Lincoln's election but did not believe it justified secession. Sebastian, Conway, Pike, Johnson, Clark, and Van Buren counties spoke for defending slavery inside the Union. All preferred settling the problem without secession, although Johnson, Clark,

Sebastian, and Pike would consider secession or revolution as a last resort to protect slavery. Only the combined resolutions of Carroll, Marion, Newton, and Searcy counties were so wholeheartedly for the Union that they did not mention slavery as an issue. These counties would become a stronghold of post-secession Unionism and the Peace Society.[39]

On December 21, 1860, representatives of Carroll, Marion, Newton, and Searcy counties met at Bluff Springs in extreme southwestern Marion County. This would be the heart of the secret pro-Unionist Peace Society. In 1854, the Arkansas legislature had incorporated the Bluff Springs Male and Female Academy with John H. Marshall, William M. Davis, William Dugger, Jonathan A. Hicks, Jacob Glenn, Alexander Dugger, James Pershall, and William M. Wharton as trustees. These men were landowners in the immediate area, and most were ardent Unionists. Camp meetings and funerals were held at Bluff Springs, and it was a well-known, centrally located building for the four counties, which had an aggregate of 708 slaves and 23,523 white residents. The *Arkansas Gazette* does not report who or how many people attended, but the resolutions were the most pro-Union submitted to the General Assembly. They stated that through the Constitution "the people of the United States did enter into a bond of Union which has so far succeeded in the accomplishment of its objects in that, that we have grown to be a great and prosperous people." They acknowledged that Lincoln's election had "violently agitated the country and endangered the government, imperiled the country's peace and prosperity and involved the people's social relations in inextricable difficulties." They regarded the continuous agitation of the slavery question by partisan demagogues, both North and South, as a means of self- aggrandizement, unworthy of patriots and statesmen.

They stated that the perpetuity of the general government ought to be preserved and that the disruption of the United States would be one of the most dire calamities that could befall the American people. They believed that suspension of commerce with the North would imperil peace and prosperity; that the election of

Lincoln was not just cause for dissolution; and that the secession doctrine subverted the Articles of Confederation. They would abide by the Constitution and support the president in the discharge of all constitutional duties, and they were opposed to the present unconstitutional secession and regretted the position taken by Congressman Hindman in favor of immediate secession. Furthermore, they disapproved of the legislature's $250,000 appropriation to purchase arms and munitions of war, as recommended by Hindman.[40]

Upland counties opposed immediate secession, but caveats on what it would take to change their minds varied with their slave populations. Van Buren County—where the pro-Union Peace Society would be discovered first—held 200 slaves in the 1860 census and 5,157 whites. At a meeting in late December 1860, its citizens unanimously adopted resolutions that stated they stood to maintain and defend the Union, the Constitution, and the laws, and to reject secession or revolution. They spoke for Southern rights, however by stating, "No state has a right to pass a law or laws, impairing the right of recovery of property of citizens of sister states." If such a law was passed, the Constitution and laws should be enforced, but they voted to follow "no sectionalist—Yancy, Seward, Greely, Tom Hindman, nor any set of disunionists who have nothing in view but their own selfish and hellish designs."[41]

The citizens of Sebastian County met December 15, 1860, at Greenwood to agree on resolutions to send to the General Assembly. Sebastian was a Unionist county, and William M. Fishback—who was to play a major role in the State Convention—strongly supported the Unionist cause there. The county was in the middle third of Arkansas counties economically, with 680 slaves and a white population of 8,557. Its resolutions regretted the election of Lincoln, which had given "just cause of offense to the Southern States." Yet they accepted the results as entirely constitutional and saw no just grounds for revolution or secession.

The county's resolutions did not recognize a right of secession. "Revolution or resort to arms would be the greatest curse to befall our country," they said, and should only be "resorted to when every other honorable expedient fails." They did not believe the present was such an occasion, as the South had equal rights in the Union. They believed a Southern Confederacy was a chimera. Still they would watch the Lincoln administration and resist to the death any unconstitutional aggression on their rights or equal status in the Union. Sebastian and the other Unionist counties had more wealth than the hill counties of north Arkansas. They were willing, though reluctant, to consider a break with the Union if the situation warranted it. This situation would amount to—as Sebastian County stated—Northern "aggression."[42]

Conway County found Little Rock newspaper coverage for its meeting on December 15 difficult to obtain. By January 10, 1861, it finally received notice in the *Gazette* after first submitting the resolutions to Hindman's *Old Line Democrat*. The meeting's secretary, T. T. Henry, posed the question, "Why have they not been published?" and answered, "It is because the resolutions were conservative in their character, showed a devoted attachment to the Union, and a determination to contend for our rights under the constitution." He went on to declare that the resolutions had been passed by a large and respectable meeting of the citizens of Conway County, who came together irrespective of party. Among the members of the committee to draft the resolutions was the Reverend Thomas Jefferson Williams, later to recruit Company B, First Battalion Six-month Arkansas Infantry (U.S.) and to lead a Unionist guerrilla band operating with the Third Arkansas Cavalry (U.S.). The resolutions, as recalled by Henry, deplored Lincoln's election, but did not consider it grounds for secession. They condemned the inflammatory speeches and the fanatics of both the North and the South, and they recommended that Conway County's legislators not elect anyone who believed Lincoln's election cause for secession to fill the vacant U.S. Senate seat. The resolutions declared that the citizens would meet the issues, face the dangers that were upon them, and contend for their rights under the Constitution. Among those rights were slave ownership and the protection of slavery where it existed and in the territories.[43]

Representatives from the secessionist counties, armed with their counties' resolutions urging secession or some form of cooperation with other Southern states, made another push for a state convention to consider secession. South Carolina's secession on December 20 brought more vigor to the debate. Governor Rector advocated secession based on Arkansas's natural trade outlets, and Jefferson County's representative General James Yell followed with a strong secession speech that was enthusiastically received by a large audience. Pro-secession demonstrations and Hindman's and The Family's press created pressure that was too strong for the General Assembly to resist. The House of Representatives on December 22 passed a measure providing for an election for a state convention. The Senate balked but eventually passed a bill on January 15 that called for an election on February 18 to vote for or against a state convention and for representatives to such a convention.[44]

Although some county resolutions opposed secession, they also supported a state convention—perhaps hoping to lay the issue to rest, but also to ensure the representative voted in accordance with his constituents' wishes. Unionists were in a quandary because their best choice would be to defeat the convention and to choose a Unionist representative. Their predicament was expressed in Mark Bean's January 28 letter to David Walker. Writing from Cane Hill in Washington County, Bean reported that Cane Hill would send twenty delegates, who would rather die than see disunion, to a mass meeting to nominate a Union candidate to the convention. From what Walker had said about the Convention bill, Bean felt "like opposing a convention at all."[45]

At a January 26, 1861, meeting at the courthouse in Dover, Pope County, the people rejected resolutions previously prepared for them that were tinted with secessionism. Between five hundred and eight hundred citizens attended and listened to presentations by leading members of the county on the merits and faults of the secessionist proposals. A vote to approve the resolutions was called for by yeas and nays, but the crowd was so large and noisy that this was ineffectual. Then, those who were in favor were ordered to form on the left, and the opposition on the right. The resolutions were voted down by more than four to one. After the vote, the people marched around the public square under the "old Stars and Stripes" while thirty-three guns were fired for the Union. This meeting was organized to be an overwhelming vote for secession; instead it turned into a mass meeting for Unionism.[46]

At another pro-Union meeting held on February 2 at Russellville, the attendees from the surrounding counties were described as numerous, all regular Arkansas folk, and a very motley looking group. The event drew a group from Searcy County, including John Campbell, Samuel Leslie, and Dr. Andrew J. Stephenson, all of whom spoke against secession.[47]

Whatever their motives, the voters of Arkansas approved a state convention 27,412 to 15,826; but they elected more Unionists than secessionists 23,626 to 17,927 votes. This election demonstrated the upland-yeoman/lowland-cotton grower split that had developed in Arkansas over the secession issue. Northern and western Arkansas counties elected almost entirely Unionist candidates while the lowland counties voted almost entirely secessionist. The Southern secessionist drumbeat had not convinced all Arkansans that their fate lay with a slave-holding confederacy.

The border slave state legislatures in Maryland, Kentucky, and Delaware refused to call a state convention, or even to consider secession. Only in Missouri did the state legislature summon a state convention, which turned down secession on March 19, 89 to 1. Upper South legislatures in North Carolina and Tennessee let the people vote, as did Arkansas, whether to hold a state convention. Both states turned it down.[48]

Arkansas Unionists in the winter of 1860–1861 hoped for a peaceful reconciliation that would defend the rights and property of slaveholders within the Union protected by the Constitution. They had supported the Crittenden Compromise, a series of resolutions supporting slavery, which they hoped would hold the country together. On December 18, in the face of impending secession of

South Carolina and other Lower South states, the U.S. Senate had formed a thirteen-man committee to review compromise measures proposed by Senator John J. Crittenden of Kentucky to avoid the crisis. He proposed reestablishing the Missouri Compromise line to allow slavery below it and to protect constitutional slavery in the southern territories, to encourage American pro-slavery adventures in Latin America and the Caribbean, and to safeguard the rights of slaveholders in the free states. The Crittenden Compromise would have extended slavery to the territories, which was anathema to Lincoln and most Republicans. The compromise died in committee two months later.

A second compromise initiative launched by Virginia called for a Peace Conference in Washington to be held on February 8–27, 1861. It would be based on Crittenden's points, and Arkansas Unionists viewed this initiative with hope. Twenty-one states were represented by 133 delegates, but Arkansas was not among them. Governor Rector did not appoint an Arkansas delegation, but Arkansas Unionists were optimistic about a national compromise that could save slavery in the Union. The Conference met and debated secretly in Washington's Willard Hotel, but was interrupted mid-stride when Jefferson Davis assumed the presidency of the Southern Confederacy and declared that no changes to the Union would lure back the seceded states.

The Conference was now limited to keeping Virginia and the other Upper South states in the Union. Seven constitutional amendments similar to Crittenden's proposal were adopted by narrow majorities and submitted to Congress. Crittenden's recommendation that the Peace Conference propositions become amendments was defeated four to one. Only one amendment—that Congress could never interfere with slavery where it existed—was passed by the House of Representatives. Before they adjourned, members from the Upper South states agreed to meet on May 27 in Frankfort, Kentucky, to find a way to keep the slave states that had not seceded in the Union. This was the sole hope for Arkansas's Unionists and Cooperationists.[49]

Following the results of the February 18 election, Governor
Rector called for the State Convention to meet on March 4, 1861,
in Little Rock. In the organizational meeting, David Walker of
Washington County, a Unionist, defeated secessionist Benjamin
Totten of Prairie County for chairman of the convention by a vote
of forty to thirty-five. This first test of strength between Unionists
and secessionists continued throughout the March session of the
convention despite various pressures exerted by the secessionists.
It showed that Arkansas Unionists were yet Southerners, and the
caveats in their decisions reflected that background and eventually
decided the course they would ultimately take. In the meantime,
the Arkansas State Convention was importuned by both sides.[50]

William M. McPherson, an old Whig living in St. Louis who
had previously lived in Helena, informed his old compatriot David
Walker on March 19 that he had learned that Walker had been
elected president of the convention and was fighting for the Union.
McPherson said that he was delivering speeches for the Union
and awakening the populace. He urged Walker to stand firm and
commented that next to Missouri, Arkansas had more to lose by
seceding than any other state, because it would be on the border of a
free United States—with all the problems of runaway slaves that the
United States then had with slave-free Canada—and facing an inev-
itable civil war. He told Walker that he had a contact on Lincoln's
staff, who assured him that if the border states stood firm for the
Union that the free states would guarantee a solution to their basic
concerns.[51]

Spokesmen for secession came to Arkansas from the seceded
states to pressure the convention. Representatives from Georgia
and South Carolina were the first to arrive in the first week. Their
speeches did not change any votes, and South Carolina's imprudent
suggestion that Arkansas must heed its request to secede because
Arkansas owed its admission to the Union to South Carolina may
have hardened some Unionist votes.

Confederate president Davis sent his own representative,
William S. Oldham of Texas. He had been an anti-Family Democrat

from Fayetteville in the 1840s but had immigrated to Texas after a failed Arkansas career. None of these emissaries influenced the delegates. Nor did Governor Rector's address on March 8, urging secession because the North and South could not compromise over slavery, the real difference between them.[52]

The *Fayetteville Arkansian* published what was already common parlance among secessionists, accusations that Unionists were Black Republicans in favor of equality for African Americans. This topic must have given pause to many mountaineers and was an effective secessionist argument against Unionism. Albert W. Bishop in 1863 insisted that secessionists "were straining every nerve" and using the "most extravagant statements" to undermine Unionism. "Every supporter of the Administration was termed a Black Republican," he said and, "advocates of secession...found no subject so fertile of conversions among hard working farmers, as the absurd notion of negro equality....It was...well calculated to alienate the poorer classes."[53]

Despite the various secessionist efforts to siphon away Unionists, the forty to thirty-five Unionist majority stood firm, as did the thirty-five delegates who voted for secession in its several forms. On March 5, the convention's second day, William Grace of Jefferson County moved that the convention draw up an ordinance of secession. Rufus Garland of Hempstead County, a Cooperationist, replied with a motion to adjourn, which carried thirty-nine to thirty-five. The Unionist-Cooperationist majority of five votes, including Chairman Walker's, controlled the assembly and all major committees. Strong Unionists had joined with Cooperationists hoping to cooperate with border slave states to keep them in the Union. By mid-March the convention would neither secede nor submit the question for the people's vote. Becoming desperate, the secession-prone southeast talked of splitting the state.

This may have persuaded the Union-Cooperation party to acquiesce, but not before it had named delegates to a May 27 border states convention in Frankfort, Kentucky, and passed Crawford County delegate Hugh Thomason's bill to recommend changes similar to Senator Crittenden's proposal. T. B. Hanly of Phillips County made one last effort by substituting an ordinance of secession for Thomason's proposal to restore the Union to be ratified by the voters on the first Saturday in May. It failed on March 18 by thirty-nine to thirty-five. Historian James W. Woods's analysis of the votes for the Hanly motion found a clear pattern of slaveholding and wealth in the lowland counties, which voted for secession, and the poorer, non-slaveholding upland counties, which voted against.

Through March 18, the Union-Cooperation party had been able to keep the secession issue from a popular vote, but the next day Benjamin Totten of Prairie County proposed that a referendum on "secession" or "cooperation" be submitted to the voters the first Monday in August to determine the public's will. The Unionist-Cooperationists feared that the secessionists would find another way to secede and acquiesced in the August vote. Searcy County's John Campbell wrote a friend that the Unionists agreed to an August vote because they feared the governor would re-call the legislature, which might then vote the state out.[54]

The convention ended on March 21. The forty Unionists summarized the convention's accomplishments and stated their program in the "Union Address to the People of Arkansas," published in the April 6 *Arkansas Gazette*. The Unionist caucus's resolutions favored a national convention and set out the basis for a settlement: amend the Constitution so that the president and vice-president should be chosen alternatively from slaveholding and free states, but not both from the same; admit territories north of 36 degrees 30 minutes north as free states and territories south of that line as slave states; deny Congress all power over slavery except to protect it; recompense slaveholders when their slaves are taken by force; protect slaveholders and their slaves when traveling in the free states; allow only white people to vote. These amendments were not to be changed or abolished without the consent of all the states.

Other resolutions approved Virginia's call for the Border Slaveholding States Convention May 27 at Frankfort, Kentucky, and provided for submitting to the people on the first Monday of

August the question: "Shall Arkansas cooperate with the border or un-seceded slave states to secure a permanent and satisfactory adjustment of the sectional controversies disturbing the country, or immediately secede?" Other resolutions declared against coercion of the seceded states and protested quartering federal troops in United States' posts in the Southern states to coerce seceding states or to prevent secession. The address summarized the Unionists' principal thrust:

> Thus, it will be seen, that while Arkansas is not committed to the doctrine of secession, she condemns coercion by the Federal government, and recommends the removal of causes that might lead to a collision; and the adoption of constitutional means to restore peace and fraternal relations between the sections, and happiness and prosperity to our once united, but now distracted country. Four months will intervene before the election, affording ample time for reflection, and the formation of a just conclusion. None can complain that the people—the source of all power in this country—have not been consulted, or their voice stifled, and it is to be hoped that the expression thus fairly obtained will be respected, and the decision acquiesced in by all.[55]

With the adjournment of the State Convention, both sides returned home to begin campaigning for the referendum to be held on August 5. The Unionists' opposition to federal government coercion of Southern states would betray their hopes for the Border State Convention and national reconciliation.

The secessionists began active campaigning at once with radical secessionists Robert Johnson, Gantt, and Hindman taking the stump all over the state. Hindman's hegira was not to start until April 27 in St. Francis County, proceeding in May through the heart of Unionism: Fulton, Izard, Independence, White, Van Buren, Searcy, Marion, Newton, Carroll, Madison, Benton, Washington, Crawford, Sebastian, Franklin, Pope, and Conway counties, and ending in Little Rock on July 4. Hindman never made his canvass because events changed, but one wonders how he would have been received in the counties that fulminated against him in their December resolutions.

Shortly after the state convention adjourned on March 21, Albert Pike (the old Whig who had been pro-cooperationist) published a pamphlet entitled *State or Province? Bond or Free?* which justified secession based on states' rights. Secessionist newspapers advertised picnics and free barbecues to attract people to hear their message. On March 30, H. B. Allis of Pine Bluff wrote the following to David Walker:

> Col. R. W. Johnson opened at this place last Sat. assisted by Genl. Yell. The union men of the convention rec'd their share of **cusses** for the course Ark. pursued in not going out. The Col's brag argument now is 'that 7 states are out and **will never come back** home, Ark. ought to go with them, and **when she does go** a **majority** of the slave states being out the rest will be **compell** [*sic*] to **follow**,' the forcing process is to be tried upon the Border States."

Allis thought that Jefferson County would "send up such a vote as we may be proud of" and went on to give examples of secessionist activities that were alienating the public: musters becoming a burden, and the governor's recall of weapons distributed from the captured Little Rock Arsenal. "All these little things are telling here. Men are beginning to see thru them. The 'bone and sinew' of the county when they see **all** the lawyers of Pine Bluff and those who do not labor for a living on the side of secession are remarking it." Allis went on to urge Walker to speak out. "I hope my Dear sir that you, Gen'l Thompson, Jesse Turner & others, will meet Col. Johnson as oft as possible and give him a **warm** reception—Mr. Rogers sent my name to the President of Convention for delegate &c—I am flattered by the compliment—Mr. R & Judge Scull and myself have agreed to take the field here as often as necessary and do what we can—our history you know does not justify large expectations from us—we can only promise **true hearts** and willing hands."[56]

Other Unionists were actively opposing the secessionists. Lawyer James P. Spring of Fort Smith wrote to his old friend
and fellow Whig David Walker, thanking him for his efforts to
have Spring named a delegate to the Border States Convention in
Frankfort and stating that he was glad that Walker was considering
going. Spring wrote on April 4 from Carrollton while canvassing
northwestern counties before the August 5 referendum. He intended
to go next to Burrowville and Yellville, but he assured Walker,
"The union question is safe here now–*Cooperation* is the word and
I certainly think that when the question is put to Arkansas as to
whether she will go out alone on the [?] of uncertainty, or cooperate
with those noble states who stand fast to the union that the vote
will be *cooperation*."[57]

On April 10, W. M. Fishback (Sebastian County's representative on the Unionist ticket) wrote D. C. Williams (a merchant in Van
Buren) that he had enrolled sixteen subscribers to the *Van Buren
Press* and hoped the editor would spare no pains to give his paper
efficacy as a campaign paper. He wanted the paper to emphasize
that the secessionists wanted to break up the government and were
hostile to compromise. He wanted to organize Union Clubs in the
counties and make a great show of zeal. He had heard good Union
men say that the state would secede because secessionists were
making more efforts than Union men. The Union Clubs should meet
frequently and have addresses by men from other counties. Jesse
Turner and H. F. Thomason could speak in adjoining counties.[58]

All the planning and efforts to sway voters were overturned
by the Confederates' April 12 firing on the federal garrison in Fort
Sumter, South Carolina, the Union surrender two days later, and
President Lincoln's call for states to provide 75,000 troops to put
down the insurrection. Arkansas's quota was 780, a regiment.
Secessionists were elated. They now believed that Arkansas had to
secede. Unionists at the State Convention had wanted to preserve
the Union with its protection of the Constitution, and because they
feared conflict. But they also abhorred coercion, and Lincoln's call
for troops they saw as coercion and a prelude to conflict. On April 15,

the *Arkansas Gazette*'s editor C. C. Danley urged his longtime political compatriot David Walker to re-call the convention. There was an increasing drumbeat from several sources to re-call the convention, and there was some agitation from persons who usually did not make the press.

Isaac F. Morris (a forty-one-year-old resident of Prairie Township, Newton County) on April 15 asked Richard Johnson (the editor of the *True Democrat*) to stop his subscription "as I am determined not to take it any longer, your secession, tory principles don't suit me,…as I expect to start north this evening….I remain a Union man." Morris received his paper at the Cave Creek post office, and the *True Democrat* congratulated its friends in that county on having rid themselves of a man of low character.[59]

On April 20, Danley published his editorial "The Work of Coercion Commenced—Let the People of Arkansas React to it as One Man," in which this leading conservative Unionist announced his support for secession. The *Van Buren Press* followed by advocating secession since the North had commenced coercion. On April 22, Governor Rector rejected Lincoln's call for troops as an insult. When it became known that Virginia, the last hope of the Border South, had seceded on April 17, there was no more hope for cooperationists.

David Walker re-called the State Convention to meet on May 6 and inquired of his constituents what they wanted him to do: adhere to the position taken before the election (no secession), secede only if the border states seceded, or vote for an unconditional ordinance of secession. Unionist delegates were pushed to learn their constituents' wishes. Only one response to Walker's appeal for instructions has survived. West Fork Township, Washington County, passed resolutions on April 27 to oppose secession under any circumstances, but if secession occurred then to cooperate with other border states, presumably to avoid a conflict. A. W. Bishop, after interviewing other Arkansas Unionists serving with the First Arkansas Cavalry (U.S.), concluded in 1862 that there was not adequate time to instruct the delegates before the convention would re-assemble.

John Campbell, Searcy County's Unionist delegate friend of David Walker and an old Whig, certainly thought so. He wrote an *apologia* to his constituents saying, "The time was so short after I received a notice that we were reconvened, I had, as you were well aware, no opportunity of ascertaining what instruction you would have given me as your representative in this body, and as I have no instruction of any changes in public sentiment whatever in Searcy County, through a sense of Representative duty I felt myself **bound** by the instructions given on the day of the election on the 18th day of February."[60]

Walker formally opened the second session of the State Convention at ten o'clock in the morning on May 6, followed almost immediately by a motion from Phillips County's radical secessionist planter Charles W. Adams for the committee on ordinances and resolutions to prepare an ordinance of secession by two o'clock. William Grace of Jefferson County, the committee chairman, amended the motion to three o'clock to give his committee an extra hour. The convention quickly passed the amended motion. This momentous decision happened so fast that Searcy County delegate John Campbell wrote:

> The Convention of Arkansas was convened again. When we met the news was that everybody had changed from Union to Disunion except Searcy County. The Deligates [*sic*] from Independence County said that out of 2600 votes 2000 were for Secession. The Deligate [*sic*] from Izzard [*sic*] said he would be run over and out of the County if he did not go for Secession. From Newton and Marion [and] Pope in fact all the Counties that had elected union deligates [*sic*] but this; the sentiment had change; or the Deligates [*sic*] lied. Something had changed their mines [*sic*] before they got back for they took the State out on Monday the day of meeting. There was no changes took place at the Rock because they voted before they told each other Howdy.[61]

The Committee on Ordinances presented its efforts on time. Alfred Dinsmore of Benton County made one last effort to avoid

secession by moving that the ordinance be submitted to popular
vote the first Monday in June. It was defeated fifty-five to fifteen.
The fifteen votes came from Conway, Independence, and Pike
counties and the counties along the western border and astride
the Boston Mountains: Benton, Washington, Crawford, Sebastian,
Madison, Newton, and Searcy. The northern tier of Arkansas's
counties voted against Dinsmore's motion, forecasting an evaluation that Confederate captain Joseph M. Bailey would make about
north Arkansas in 1862: "A decided majority of the people of the
Northern tier of counties in Arkansas were Confederates or in
sympathy with the Confederate cause. The mountain counties to
the south were dominated by Union men, mostly deserters from the
Confederate Army."[62]

After Dinsmore's motion was defeated there was a roll call
vote on the original resolution for secession. Only five votes were
cast against it: John Campbell of Searcy, Samuel Kelley of Pike,
Isaac Murphy and H. H. Bolinger of Madison, and Thomas Gunter
of Washington. When the vote was sixty-five to five, Walker was
called to cast his vote. Abandoning his previous Unionist position,
he cast his ballot for secession and addressed the convention saying,
"Enough votes have been cast to take us out of the Union. Now
since we must go let us all go together, let the wires carry the news
to all the world that Arkansas stands as a unit against coercion."

All but Isaac Murphy allowed their votes to be changed.
Samuel Kelley added to his changed vote that he denied the doctrine
of secession but accepted revolution. Campbell, a longtime friend of
Walker's and fellow Whig, who perhaps looked upon Walker as his
mentor, explained his change of vote to an unhappy constituency:

> After the die was cast almost unanimously, and having
> faithfully and honestly discharged my duty, as I thought,
> in casting the vote of my immediate constituency, at the
> earnest appeal and request of the President of the conven-
> tion, and other distinguished gentlemen of the State,
> whose transcendent abilities, patriotism and devotion to
> our common country, claim our respect, I consented that

my vote might be changed so that it might be announced on the telegraphic wire as a unit, in order that it might be known in the Northern States that there was no division in Arkansas. I was the last to consent to this request, the refusal of which would have been unkind in me to men for whom I entertain the highest respect and most kind feelings, and as I did not thereby change or sacrifice any opinion or principle heretofore entertained relative to the grave questions now agitating the country.

In another letter Campbell wrote that there was a protest and that the four protested against the constitutional right to secede and that he did not sign the ordinance.[63]

With the significant vote to take Arkansas out of the Union decided, there were various housekeeping details to make it operable. Remnants of the Unionist county delegates voted against these bills or refused to sign. Isaac Murphy was present but refused to sign the ordinance of secession. Campbell later wrote, "I never signed the devilish instrument." He was absent from the floor, as were anti-secessionists H. W. Williams of Craighead and Poinsett, H. Jackson of Benton, and conservative Joseph Jester of Hot Spring. Campbell stated that even though the ordinance had passed, if it were not signed by a quorum it would have been void. Campbell—joined by Bolinger, Gunter, Murphy, Dinsmore of Washington; William M. Fishback of Sebastian; Jesse Turner of Crawford; and E. T. Walker of Scott—voted to refer the Confederate States' provisional constitution to the people. Thus the measure failed, sixty-three to eight. They wanted the people to have a chance to vote upon ratification. The attempt to refer the ratification of the permanent Confederate Constitution to the people also failed, thirty-seven to twenty-two. The State Convention remained in session for almost another month as they tried to put the state upon a war footing. The proceedings were hampered by efforts of the conservative alliance of old Whigs and The Family to curtail the influence of Governor Rector and Hindman, whom the conservatives considered to be radical and thought would "lead Arkansas to the Devil."[64]

Lincoln's response to Fort Sumter had produced a sea-change upon Southern Unionists. Secessionists immediately had raised a cry to take Arkansas out of the Union, but with more hope for success than previous attempts. Lincoln's action was portrayed as an act to coerce the South, an action that virtually all Southerners had said they would not accept. Unionists had published newspaper columns justifying and explaining their policy change. Little Rock conservatives had published a call to reconvene the State Convention in order to take it out of the Union. Lincoln's call for troops was coercion, the one act that Arkansans saw as unforgivable.

After Arkansas seceded, the Unionists seemed to accept that the world had changed. The federal government had tried to coerce a seceded state and that was not acceptable. Unionists accepted their new role as citizens of a seceded state. Even Isaac Murphy, the lone holdout against secession whose political view was "What is right," remained with the convention and participated in its legislation as did the other Unionists; but he often voted against measures that would enhance Arkansas's wartime potential.

Some immediately embraced Arkansas's Confederate government and assumed offices in the seceded state. Albert Pike had been a Whig, then a member of the American (Know-Nothing) Party, but throughout it all he was a states' rights advocate and a Southerner. Yet he saw secession as a poor choice. In December 1860, he had addressed the legislature on federal-state relations, urging exhaustion of all means of preserving the Union, and he had supported naming a delegation to a Border State Convention. By the end of January, however, Pike, believing that the old Union could not be salvaged, wrote and printed *State or Province? Bond or free?*, a secessionist campaign pamphlet. After secession, the convention sent Pike to the Indian Territory as its commissioner to negotiate treaties with the Five Nations. He was then appointed brigadier general in the Confederate army on August 15, 1861, and in November placed in command of the Department of the Indian Territory. He eventually led an Indian contingent at the Battle of Pea Ridge on March 7–8, 1862.

Although he strongly advised staying in the Union until the very end, Pike had demonstrated that his sympathies were with the cotton South as early as the 1856 Know-Nothing Party Convention. This was not the case with David Walker, a wealthy, slave-owning lawyer from Washington County who was seen as the rock of Unionism when elected to preside at the 1861 State Convention. At the end of the March convention session, Walker seemed to direct the efforts of the Unionists to promote cooperation with the border slaveholding states.

James P. Spring of Fort Smith, H. B. Allis of Pine Bluff, and Mark Bean of Cane Hill reported their efforts and offered ideas to him as they awaited the statewide August referendum. When the convention was re-called, and it was obvious that it had voted to secede, Walker asked for unity and "threw in his fortune with his friends, resolved to sink or swim with them." Why he "joined the revolution he could not say...it was simply impossible for him to embrace the idea of striking down the south in blood." In going with the South, he accepted a commission as colonel and served as judge advocate in General Sterling Price's army.[65]

John Campbell, Searcy County's delegate to the State Convention, voted to refer the secession ordinance back to the people, voted against the secession ordinance, and was the last to change his vote after it had passed. He did not sign the secession ordinance and voted against accepting the provisional Confederate Constitution and various other acts of the convention to put Arkansas on a war footing. Yet, after the convention adjourned on June 1, Campbell was sworn in on August 5 as first lieutenant in Company K, Fourteenth (Powers) Arkansas Infantry. Company K, under Captain James Harrison Love, was the second Confederate company raised in Searcy County. He was discharged in June 1862 and returned to Searcy County to work for the Confederate Nitre and Mining Bureau, then followed them to northeast Texas. In January 1865, he wrote to Governor Harris Flanagin from Texas requesting a recount in an election for Searcy County representative that he had barely lost.[66]

Thomas M. Gunter cast another of the five May 6 votes against secession then allowed his vote to be changed so that Arkansas could be said to be united. Gunter had moved to Fayetteville in 1853 where he entered the law office of his cousin Hugh F. Thomason, studied under him, and was admitted to the bar the following year. He was generally a silent member of the convention, a protégée of David Walker. After the convention adjourned, he accepted a captaincy in J. D. Walker's Fourth Arkansas Infantry, State Troops, where he participated in the Battle of Wilson's Creek on August 10, 1861. He went on to eventually command the Thirty-fourth Arkansas Infantry. Gunter's cousin Hugh F. Thomason had been an elector for the Bell-Everett ticket and a staunch member of the Know-Nothing Party before being elected to represent Crawford County to the 1861 State Convention. He campaigned vigorously before and after the convention's March session for cooperation with the border states and against secession. Once Arkansas was out of the Union, Thomason accepted a seat in the Confederate Congress and ran for reelection later in 1861. However, he was defeated because he had not been an original secessionist. He took no further part in the Civil War.[67]

James P. Spring—former Whig, lawyer, Fort Smith resident, and friend of David Walker—assisted Walker in encouraging cooperation with the border states in Arkansas's north-central mountain counties, where he had once lived. The convention, at the urging of its president, selected Spring to be one of its delegates to the Border State Convention in Frankfort, which was overtaken by the war. His son John Valentine Spring served as captain in John Harrell's Battalion Arkansas Cavalry. Spring himself served as Confederate quartermaster agent as early as October 1861 in Fort Smith, then moved to Huntsville, Texas. In 1864 he was in charge of a clothing factory making Confederate uniforms. Jesse Turner, another Whig Unionist lawyer representing Crawford County in the convention, voted against secession in the March session, but voted with the majority to secede on May 6. After the convention adjourned, he retired to privacy and took no part in the war. Samuel Kelley, prominent planter and minister, Pike County's delegate to the 1861 Convention, was one of the five to vote against secession on May 6, and one of the four to change his vote in response to Walker's plea. He let the Civil War interfere with his efforts to build the Church of Christ, but there is no evidence of what he did during the war.[68]

Senator William K. Sebastian, a Family Democrat, yet also anti-secessionist, opposed Thomas C. Hindman in Arkansas meetings meant to promote secession causes. When Arkansas seceded, he remained for a while in Washington. Yet on June 11, 1861, the Senate expelled him because Arkansas had seceded and he had not repudiated his home state. He returned to Helena, where he remained uncomfortably, as his moderate sentiments were not appreciated by his neighbors. His troubles thickened around him, and by August 1863 he had moved to federal-occupied Memphis. Arkansas Unionists tried to persuade him to reclaim his Senate seat. General S. A. Hurlbut, on Lincoln's orders, approached Sebastian on the matter and was rejected. In Hurlbut's opinion Sebastian did not have the nerve to attempt to re-enter the Senate. Sebastian died two years later in Memphis. Arkansas Unionist leaders of whatever stripe were not inclined to desert the South to save the Union.[69]

William Meade Fishback, Sebastian County's Unionist delegate to the State Convention, campaigned resolutely between the two sessions for the Union. He also advocated vigorous speaking tours by Jesse Turner and Hugh F. Thomason and called for establishing Union Clubs throughout the state to make a show of zeal. Voting with the majority against secession in March and for secession in May, his rationale for the latter vote was a little tortured, claiming Lincoln's coercion policy would collapse when practical men demanded reunion.

In July 1861, a northwest Arkansas writer reported that Fishback was serving as a private in Captain Blakemore's Confederate Arkansas company, having succumbed to local Confederate pressure. Fishback later explained that after the convention he returned home. The military activity in Missouri was increasing and volunteers were called for a company. Every young man in town joined except for Fishback and one other. Because he refused to go, he was insulted on the street and in the parlor by women who taunted him with cowardice or treason to the South. Their insults became intolerable, and he determined to escape to the North. He followed Blakemore's company, as if he intended to overtake and join it, but he was determined to get through the lines if possible.

The Fort Smith papers announced that "Fishback had gone towards the battle-field; it is not known whether to join Lincoln's or the southern army. Look out for a traitor in camp!" Upon over-taking the company, he saw it was impossible to get through the lines, so he joined up. Fishback said that he went to work to undermine Blakemore's company, and in less than three days had broken it up and taken most of the men home with him at the very time they needed them most. Shortly after he returned, and after the battles of Bull Run and Wilson's Creek (August 10, 1861), when the rebels' hopes were highest, it was reported that the convention would be re-called. He immediately resigned his seat and escaped to the North.[70]

Brigadier General Egbert B. Brown, commanding at Springfield, Missouri, reported on June 22, 1862, to Brigadier General John M. Schofield at St. Louis: "Mr. Fishback, a lawyer from Fort Smith on the 17th, left here this morning for Saint Louis and will call on you." Federal cartographer and recruiting officer Lyman Bennett said that Fishback had fled Arkansas with a reward on his head and had gone to St. Louis, where he obtained authority from General Samuel R. Curtis to raise an Arkansas infantry regiment. Traveling with a handful of Unionists in April 1863, Fishback ventured into north-central Arkansas looking for recruits, but he failed to attract enough men for a regiment. His enlistees were incorporated into Colonel Lafayette Gregg's Fourth Arkansas Cavalry (U.S.) while he settled in now federal-occupied Little Rock to publish the *Unconditional Union* newspaper.[71]

A stronger Unionist was Isaac Murphy, Madison County's delegate to the 1861 State Convention, who said his view on secession was "What is right." For him, that meant opposition to secession to the end. He remained with the State Convention until it adjourned on June 3 and participated in all its deliberations. Upon adjournment he returned to Huntsville, where he was occasionally harassed. He was left alone for a while after a public meeting in which he defended his actions. Finally, alerted to an assassination plot, he left home in April 1862 with Dr. James M. Johnson, later colonel of the First Arkansas Infantry (U.S.), and his brother Frank Johnson. They were pursued a short distance, but arrived safely at General Samuel Curtis's army near Keytesville, Missouri. Murphy remained with Curtis until the occupation of Little Rock in September 1863.

Murphy's co-Unionist delegate from Madison County, Dr. Harvey H. Bolinger—one of the five who voted against secession in May (but allowed his vote to be changed)—probably returned home to St. Paul, in Madison County, where he tried to avoid the Confederates and their conscript officers. When he had the chance, he joined fellow doctor J. M. Johnson's First Arkansas Infantry (U.S.) on February 1, 1863, as an assistant surgeon with a date of rank of March 25, 1863. He resigned on April 10, 1864, under pressure. George K. Hubbard, Surgeon U.S. Volunteers, Frontier District Medical Director—with headquarters at Fort Smith— recommended that Bolinger "be discharged from the service at once, as he is notoriously incompetent, and was mustered in on the recommendation of Col. J. M. Johnson who well knew at that time his notorious unfitness for the position."[72]

Of the other twenty-nine Unionists at the convention, ten held company or regimental rank in Arkansas Confederate units. In addition to Unionist activist Hugh F. Thomason, A. H. Garland of Pulaski County and W. W. Watkins of Carroll County went to the Provisional Confederate Congress. Apart from Fishback and Bolinger, no other Unionist delegates appear among the federal Arkansas regiments.[73]

The Unionist leadership (if the Unionist delegates can be so considered) abandoned their anti-secessionist position upon Lincoln's call for troops to adopt the Confederacy. Only three men—Murphy, Fishback, and Bolinger—played roles in a Unionist movement after secession. Other pre-secession Unionists, to the extent they were able, avoided involvement in the strife. For many in Confederate Arkansas, this brought the happy conviction that Unionism was dead.

Throughout the South, Unionists were found among the foreign-born and the Northern-born. In Arkansas there were few of either of these groups. The 1860 Federal census reported 3,741 foreign-born out of a free population of 324,335, or 1.1%. The nativity of the largest groups of these foreign born were 1,143 Germans and 1,319 from Ireland. Both groups far outnumbered the next group of 375 from England. Among the native-born Americans, there were 11,049 born in the free states, 3.8% of Arkansas's population. The largest number were from Illinois (3,899), followed by Indiana (2,554) and Ohio (1,513). These numbers paled before the Tennessee born (66,609) or those from Georgia (18,031) or Mississippi (16,351). Native born Arkansans outdid them all (124,043).[74]

Union sympathizers, or at least anti-secessionists, were initially found among the few Northerners and German and Irish immigrants. Not all Irishmen were as dedicated to the South as Confederate general Patrick R. Cleburne from Helena. Englishman Henry Stanley's experience with the "Dixie Grays," Company E, Sixth Arkansas Infantry, may more reflect the feelings and experience of those Arkansas residents born abroad. Young Stanley, working as a store clerk in Jefferson County, was shamed into enlisting by a gift of chemise and petticoat addressed in a woman's hand. Stanley was captured at the Battle of Shiloh and subsequently enlisted in the Union army. Among the deserters identified by the *Arkansas True Democrat* on March 25, 1863, with a reward for their arrest, were Henry Lazarus, German, private, twenty years old, enlisted at Camden, deserted at Iuka, on September 18, 1862; and Joseph Riley, Irishman, private, twenty-one, enlisted at DeWitt, deserted on April 14, 1862, at Memphis.[75]

Governor Henry Rector revealed that he thought that attitudes of the foreign-born were, or would become, a problem

with Confederate recruiting. In his message to the General
Assembly, on November 6, 1861, when discussing raising troops
for the Confederacy, he said the following:

> It is probable that the troops now in the field and those in
> course of organization from this state, will meet present
> emergencies, whilst it may be safely calculated that a
> much larger number will have to go into service before the
> ensuing spring. In view of which, I beg leave to recommend
> that a law be passed, authorizing the executive authori-
> ties of the state to organize two "class regiments," one of
> Germans, and their immediate descendants; another of
> the Irish and their descendants, choosing their own offi-
> cers from among themselves, the two regiments to form a
> brigade, their general to be appointed by the president.
>
> These people, although brave and patriotic, have been
> deterred from entering the army, mainly because for
> them, there was little chance for promotion, and the indi-
> vidual heroism that might be displayed by one or two in
> a company, establishing no reputation, gratifying to their
> national pride. If I should be mistaken, however, in the
> causes that have deterred them, and it is found to proceed
> from a lack of inclination, then authority ought to be given
> to draft a regiment from each class, to be organized as above
> indicated. It is not a wise or just government, which in a
> war like this, taxes native blood and energy alone, leaving
> the foreign born at home—reaping the fruits of dear bought
> victories.[76]

Rector's message certainly implied a want of enthusiasm
by the Germans and the Irish. This foreign-born opposition to
Confederate military service was prevalent throughout the South,
particularly among the Germans. Such was the opposition to
Confederate military service by Germans in Texas that hundreds
organized to oppose conscription.[77]

After the German 1848 counter-revolution, many liberals
immigrated to America: some to Arkansas and many to Texas. They

almost unanimously opposed the Confederacy. Representing these liberal Germans, the German Hermannsburg colony—Washington County's Dutch Mills—stood at the side of the Union even though surrounded by secessionists. Their experiences and feelings were expressed in a Hermannsburg woman's diary:

> November 12, 1862-We live in constant fear and danger. It is said that all men must join the Southern army. We have been considered sympathizers for the South so far, but if the Northern troops come we will openly declare ourselves.... November 25, 1862-It is now generally known that our men folks are in the Northern camp, and we may as well be prepared to have all our possessions taken by the Southern troops....December 18-Fritz came today with a military escort of 100 men. He says we will leave tomorrow. How gladly I will leave here.[78]

It is unclear when the Snows left Arkansas after Josiah closed the *Pine Bluff News* in late May 1861. Possibly they stayed until 1862, as some report that the Arkansas Confederate government confiscated the telegraph company when Snow refused to swear allegiance to the Confederacy. They undoubtedly did leave, as Unionists in Pine Bluff would have been under severe pressure. Senator Sebastian felt compelled to move from Helena to Memphis in August 1863 because of his moderate opinions. [79]

The Snows, father and son, were active Unionists, both until Arkansas seceded and after the Union army took Little Rock in September 1863. But they were missing for the first two years of the Civil War. As outspoken Unionists, which they demonstrably were, they could hardly have remained openly in Pine Bluff. Nevertheless, they did not provide Unionist leadership during those crucial years. Neither the foreign-born nor transplanted Northerners provided opposition leadership to the Confederacy during its first two years.

Colton's map of Arkansas. (Courtesy of the author)

Chapter 2

Mountain Feds: Origins of the Peace Society May 6–November 17, 1861

During the secession crisis and afterward, secessionist Arkansans most feared a Northern-inspired slave uprising or a federal invasion. They organized vigilance committees to defend their neighborhoods against these contingencies. Mountaineers—the third group of Unionists, in addition to old Whigs and the foreigners and Northerners—were small farmers from the uplands who saw threats to their lives differently: they feared persecution by secessionists. Secessionist civilians who formed vigilance committees sometimes harassed their Unionist neighbors, but they generally did not persecute the Unionists if they kept their heads down. Nevertheless, as their loyalty to the South was questioned and local pressure to join Confederate military units increased, some Unionists deemed it necessary to form their own self-protection committees, sometimes called Peace Societies.

Post-secession Arkansas Unionists were mountaineer yeomen known throughout the South as Mountain Feds (Federals). They stayed in their mountains, and leaders emerged from their own ranks after secession. Coming from the poorest Arkansas counties—Newton, Searcy, Van Buren, Carroll, Marion, Fulton, Pike, and Montgomery—they were subsistence farmers, not slaveholders or large landowners. They owned, or lived on, a small acreage and supported themselves by their own labor. They were predominantly family farmers, only a small minority being paid laborers for others. The archives reveal the names of 338 men who were accused of connection to the Peace Society activity. Most were married (232); seventy-four were single and six widowed, which may have reflected their age: 132 in their twenties; eighty-seven in their thirties; fifty-six in their forties; twenty-four teenagers; twenty-one in their fifties, and fourteen who were older than sixty. No birth years are available for five men. They had emigrated from the southern mountains—Tennessee, North Carolina, Kentucky, northern Alabama, northwestern Georgia, Virginia, and Missouri—and only thirty-six were native Arkansans. Negligible numbers (thirty-three) were from the Deep South (Alabama, Georgia, South Carolina, and Mississippi) or the northeast (three: one each from Massachusetts, New York, and Pennsylvania). A handful (sixteen) came from Illinois and Indiana. Twice as many had only personal property—sometimes only sixty or one hundred dollars for a horse and a cow—as had real estate, reflecting their recent arrival or indecision on where finally to settle.

There was nothing about them to make them appear different from their secessionist neighbors in similar economic circumstances except their adherence to the Union. Because of enhanced Confederate recruiting, 183 saw some Confederate military service, in which forty-one died and more than fifty deserted. Only 119 have been documented with federal military service, including forty-six who had formerly been Confederate soldiers. They were class conscious and resented the wealthy slaveholders. Their two major concerns were to protect their homes and families and to avoid Confederate military service.[80]

The lives of these Mountain Feds were to be sorely tried in the next four years by state and national governments. The State Convention that voted Arkansas out of the Union and into the Confederacy was elected by the people; therefore, it asserted, the convention had the authority to remake state government. This was apropos, as Arkansas now had to be put on a war footing and provide for its own defense, which was complicated by state politics. New officers Governor Henry M. Rector and Representative Thomas C.

Hindman, who had won election in 1860 by defeating The Family nominees, were considered too radical by the anti-secessionists and The Family. Therefore, the old Whigs—who had initially opposed secession—joined with the old Democrat Sevier-Johnson-Conway Dynasty (The Family) in a conservative union to curtail Rector's and Hindman's power. The convention delegates began by electing pre-secession Unionists to the Confederate Congress, denying Hindman a Senate seat, and reducing the governor's term to two years from four. It also virtually divested him of all his military authority, creating on May 15 a three-man Military Board, in which he was the minority member, to administer Arkansas's military.[81]

The Military Board would provide for the defense of the state; it would be responsible for the safety and protection of Arkansas until the authority of the Confederate states could be established over Arkansas. Then it would aid the Confederate government. It was also given control over the county militias and the state volunteer units and responsibility to arm them. It held authority to call them out, to pay for their expenses, and for the remuneration of the militiamen and volunteers. In addition to Governor Rector as president, B. C. Totten from The Family camp, and C. C. Danley— editor of the conservative old Whig *Arkansas Gazette*—were placed on the board to keep the radical governor in check.[82]

After secession, Arkansans' fear of a Union invasion and a Northern-inspired slave uprising made community security more important than protecting the Confederacy or the state. A slave revolt was at least in the back of the minds of Arkansans. An 1838 Arkansas law forbade slaves to hold unlawful assemblies or to make seditious speeches. Any slave found at such an assembly or going from one house to another without permission could be whipped. Efforts were made to keep slaves from congregating off their owner's property, and a white person unlawfully meeting with slaves could be brought to trial. Each county had a board or patrol whose responsibility was to ensure that slaves did not unlawfully assemble. Nonetheless, fears of slave uprisings seemed to grow, especially in the wake of John Brown's raid at Harpers Ferry. The *Searcy Eagle*

on December 17, 1859, reported a slave uprising at Dardanelle insti-
gated by white people; in August 1860 the *Van Buren Press* warned
of an insurrection in north Texas, and an abolitionist was said to
have been captured in Buchanan, Texas, after giving a knife to a
slave and telling him to cut his way to freedom.[83]

As secession and war became ever more real, stories of slave
revolt within the state multiplied. In May 1861, Charles Cavender,
a sixty-year-old Methodist preacher from Oil Trough, Independence
County, was captured in White County with four unidentified
blacks and charged with inciting a slave rebellion. A vigilante group
found them and hanged Cavender and a black compatriot. In June
1861, several blacks were arrested in Monroe County charged with
insurrection. Two men and a girl were hanged. They had planned to
murder white men but spare the women and children.[84]

In addition to fears of a Northern-organized slave revolt,
Arkansans feared an invasion on the western border by abolitionist
Kansans or pro-Union Native Americans, or an invasion on the
northern border by federal forces from St. Louis. Hindman told the
Military Board that a regiment he raised would have gone to protect
the western border if it had been issued blankets and shoes; instead
it would go east across the Mississippi River. In late June or early
July 1861, a squadron of cavalry from Pope County commanded by
Captain John Rice Homer Scott moved to protect the north-central
border and suppress Missouri Unionist raiders. The Pope County
Volunteers held its first court-martial on July 19 in Yellville and
probably remained in Marion County until September. In search of
better forage, Scott moved to Marshall Prairie in southwest Marion
County. By September 17 he was at Camp Culloden, Jefferson
Township, southeast Carroll County (now near Valley Springs,
Boone County), operating there until mid-December.

The squadron, sent to guard the Arkansas-Missouri border
from invasion by Missouri Unionists, accepted Fulton, Marion,
Carroll, Newton, and Searcy counties in Arkansas and Ozark,
Taney, and Douglas counties in Missouri as its turf. The squadron
consisted of Captain Scott's company and that of Captain Thomas

J. Linton, also from Pope County. Later Captain Lafayette Boone's
company from Washington County was added to his command.
On August 18, 1861, Brigadier General William J. Hardee ordered
Hindman—on his way to Fayetteville on Military Board affairs—
to muster Captain Scott's Pope County cavalry squadron into
Confederate service and to station Scott along the northern border
to protect the frontier. Scott was already there, operating out of
Marion and Carroll counties. The week before, on August 10,
Governor Rector (as president of the Military Board) reported to the
secretary of war that an Arkansas regiment (Fourteenth Arkansas
Infantry) was organized and stationed at Yellville for local defense
and should not be moved.[85]

The concern about domestic security was reflected in the
actions of the State Convention. The delegates acknowledged that
Richmond wanted men and munitions from the Ozark saltpeter
mines and that Arkansas needed defending, but their constituents wanted security for their neighborhoods. Their priorities
were obvious, as shown by the various ordinances for community
defense. On May 11, shortly after Arkansas seceded from the Union,
the convention passed an act that authorized counties to levy a tax
for military defense and other purposes. Then, on May 15, it created
the Military Board to provide for the defense of the state.[86]

On May 20, the convention passed an ordinance to organize
an efficient military corps for active service, creating a major
general position and two brigadier general positions. The major
general was to outrank all state military officers (especially militia)
and was empowered to call them to active duty when ordered by
the Military Board. The board could only draft the militia when
the Confederate government did not defend the state, to suppress an
insurrection, or to repel an invasion. Two days later the convention
directed the Military Board to cooperate with Confederate general
Benjamin McCulloch in the defense of Arkansas's western frontier.
On the twenty-third the convention provided that the board would
outrank all state military officers, thus establishing control over all
military operations and expenses.

On May 30, the day before it adjourned, the convention made another attempt to provide for local defense. It authorized county courts to raise home guard minuteman companies of not less than ten men for three months' service in their neighborhoods to see that all slaves were disarmed and kept in subjection. The home guard would be armed and equipped from taxes raised under the act of May 11 that authorized county courts to levy taxes for home defense. Recognizing that these acts would hamper recruitment for national and state regiments and curtail the ability of the administration to raise troops to defend the state, Governor Rector requested the General Assembly to remedy the situation when it met in the fall. He objected to the creation of a Military Board that could and did out-vote him. He held that the state militia was undisciplined because its officers were not paid except when called into active duty, which was infrequent. And he complained that the establishment of a home guard provided by the convention practically superseded the militia, which excused men from the militia and volunteer service.[87]

Some Arkansans, showing a propensity to determine what was in their own best interests for defense of their neighborhoods, created vigilance committees even before Arkansas seceded. New Yorker William G. Stevenson found himself employed in Phillips County in April 1861. On the night of April 17, he was brought before a Phillips County vigilance committee on suspicion of being a Northern man and an abolitionist. The vigilance committee had a constitution and by-laws which stated that, in the present troubled state of the country, the citizens resolved themselves into a court of justice to examine all Northern men and that any man of abolitionist principles should be hanged. Through friends, Stevenson was able to escape and flee to Memphis, only to find a Phillips County vigilante there to meet him at the ferry and report him to the local authorities. To save his life, he joined J. Knox Walker's Second Tennessee Volunteer Infantry (C.S.). Enlistment in the Confederate army was to become an effective way for Arkansas Unionists to save their lives in the short run.[88]

Not all Unionists were so lucky, however. James "Jimmie" (or "Jawbone") Shelton, a Hardshell Baptist preacher who flourished from the early 1840s until 1861, was hanged in Pope County by Confederates for his outspoken Union sentiments. Shelton may have been done in by a vigilance committee that organized on May 25, 1861, at Scotia Mills, Clarke Township, Pope County. The organizational meeting of May 25 preceded the May 30 act of the convention that authorized counties to raise a home guard within its townships, but the organizations were similar in formation, indicating that the convention may have authorized a movement that was already popular in the state.[89]

The *True Democrat* reported that the citizens of Clarke Township had been driven to organize themselves for their mutual safety by the oppressive acts of a Republican president and to appoint Gibson Morrison and others as a committee of vigilance. Its duty was to guard the homes in Clarke Township and to arrest all suspicious persons traveling through the country without any means of support or honorable object in view. The safety of their homes and families demanded the utmost vigilance, and they pledged to sustain the slaveholders in their efforts to expel all suspicious persons and to support the vigilance committee by furnishing arms to those without any. Morrison was elected captain of the home guard and urged to divide his company into squads to serve as patrols throughout Clarke Township.[90]

Lieutenant Colonel Albert W. Bishop wrote that after the State Convention was over, the "ultraist" secessionists stepped up their harassment of Unionists. The secessionists organized "to arouse the people and advance the Confederate cause." Fayetteville attorney William D. Reagan and United States District Attorney for Arkansas's Western District Alfred M. Wilson led an organization to confiscate Unionist property and to pursue those who tried to flee, disarm them, and kill them if they tried to get away. This situation lasted until the beginning of 1863 when federal forces would invest northwest Arkansas. George Gardiner Bosworth, a brick mason born in 1833 in Massachusetts, was one of those Benton and Washington county Unionists who fled before August 1862. By early September 1862, he was onboard the gunboat USS *Mound City*. His September 1862 letter back to Arkansas said that he knew that his arrest could come at any time, and that he wished to be a participant in the coming events instead of being a prisoner. He tried to go to Kansas, but he did not know how to get there—to ask directions would have been a sure way of being arrested as a spy or traitor (or any other charge) if they suspected him of Unionism. So he made the best of his way without aid. When he struck the Neosho road, he realized that it would take him to Kansas. He had many narrow escapes and cross questionings on this road, and finally he had a spirited race to rid himself of a secessionist, which he did by considerable tact and more perseverance. Finally, being obliged to abandon Kansas for a time, he arrived in St. Louis and ultimately found himself a sailor onboard the gunboat.[91]

From before secession, some objected to the highhanded manner in which their neighbors enforced their politics. James B. Lipps, a forty-year-old sawmill master born in Tennessee, was living in the Taylor's Creek neighborhood of Telico Township, St. Francis County, when he was killed on May 4, 1861, by an infuriated crowd of citizens. Lipps had been organizing a company in St. Francis and Poinsett counties to sustain law and order and to put down vigilance committees. A vigilance committee investigated Lipps and determined that he was secretly opposed to Southern interests and was probably in league with the South's enemies. Lipps denied this and promised to join a home guard company to resist federal usurpation, but he failed to appear on the agreed date. A posse of St. Francis County citizens went to his house on May 4, but he was defiant. A fight ensued, and he was killed after a desperate resistance. He left a wife and two children. He had resided in the county for many years, had married respectably, and was well connected. However, he was regarded by some as a dangerous and reckless man with Union sympathies.[92]

Mountain Feds

As aggressive as Southerners were in protecting their homes and families from slave uprisings, abolitionists, and federal invasion, there was another perceived threat that did not attract as much attention at this time. These were the Mountain Feds, the yeomen Unionists in the mountains. Confederate Arkansas acknowledged their existence, and probably saw them as a bother but not a real threat that had to be acted on. Unionists felt bullied, but most did not feel immediately threatened. There were exceptions. On April 15, 1861, before Arkansas seceded but after the bombardment of Fort Sumter began, Tennessee-born, forty-one-year-old Isaac F. Morris of northeastern Newton County canceled his subscription to The Family's *True Democrat* newspaper, explaining:

> I hope when you receive these lines, that you will stop sending the True Democrat to me, as I am determined not to take it any longer, your secession tory principles don't suit me; therefore you will confer a favor on me to stop that worthless sheet; and please let me know when you get your pay for what you have already done for me and I will keep it secret, as I expect to start north this evening. So farewell Dick [Johnson] and secession too; there is two of your papers now in the office at Jasper and if you can't come yourself after them you can send one of your blacks after them. I remain a Union man. Isaac F. Morris.

The *True Democrat* commented that Newton County was fortunate to get rid of such a person and warned those parts Morris would pass through to be on the lookout for such a detestable person.[93]

Saying that native Unionists did not feel threatened is not entirely accurate. They did recognize that vigilance committees could be bothersome. A May 13, 1861, letter from Jesse Weaver in Clark County to his brother Jefferson Weaver in Marion County stated the following:

I have nothing of any great importance to right [sic] to you more than times is hard here and good prospect for no better for there is sitch [sic] a great excitement up here about our president Lincoln that the people is turned upside down[.] [T]here has bin [sic] three companys [sic] of disunion men left here to fight the north. Hura for the union hura for old Lincoln. Arkadelphia is the [worst?] plase [sic] in the united states. [T]hay [sic] say a union man can't go in there and Cheap, but they [sic] union men is just a waiting for them to hurt one union man and then we will blow her asunder. Hura for the union. There is also another company of disunion men made up here on the Caddo going to start in a few days[.] [T]hey meet next sadurday [sic] to drill at point cedar post office [Clark County] and if [I] have the time [I] am going to see them. Jesse Weaver.[94]

Captain Scott and his squadron of Pope County Volunteer Cavalry had been in Marion and Carroll counties since July, and he was getting the feel of pro-Union sentiment in the area. Scott filled out his companies with local recruits which brought him more local intelligence, including a report on September 29, 1861, that John McCoy of White Township—a Democratic elector from Newton County—had said "he wished Jeff Davis and his friends in the whole southern Confederacy were sunk in the middle of hell and that he [John McCoy] could see them there, and he further swore that he would not mind falling in himself if he could fall on Davis and drive him in deeper." When confronted with this information by Scott, McCoy replied that he was pained to hear that evil-hearted men were trying to injure his neighbors and himself by circulating falsehoods, e.g., that they were Black Republicans and enemies of the South. McCoy was accused of making speeches in favor of the North and of cursing Scott's Pope County Volunteers. He denounced these accusations as false and defied the accusers to prove any such charges. He explained, "The most of us voted against the convention believing we were doing right—but now the seperation [sic] is made—and we are hart [sic] and soul for our country—and we hope to God that the North will not be able to make attack on the soil of

Arkansas nor on any of the South." He denied that they were Union men, saying, "Now all we mean by Union is this—we wish we had Union and peace as we once had in the days of our Fathers, but if Union means to support Abe Lincoln or the North—we are not Union men at all for we are for the South first last and all the time." No action was taken against McCoy. Later McCoy recruited for the Union army and on March 10, 1863, was commissioned captain of Company F, First Arkansas Infantry (U.S.).[95]

On November 7, Scott gave General Ben McCulloch an assessment of his situation and local affairs. Operating in Carroll, Marion, Searcy, and Newton counties and across the line in Missouri's Ozark, Taney, and Douglas counties, he found that Unionist Missouri home guard companies were frequently troublesome and often a terror to border citizens. He stated, "In the County of Newton in Arks It is reported that John McCoy once a Democratic Elector and of some Considerable influence there is very clamorous in his Union Sentiments and is Calculated to do Some harm to Southern interests." Scott further declared:

> [I]n this county are situated several Salt Petre Caves and work and machinery are being put up by a Southern Company to manufacture powder and who feel unsafe without government protection distant about 20 miles from my headquarters. There are a few disaffected persons around in this locality but are not noisy or deemed troublesome but are unwilling to dispose of their produce to the government if it can be avoided.[96]

Also on November 7, Scott cautioned Captain Lafayette Boone, whom he was ordering to western Fulton County, to "cultivate a kind & friendly feeling with the Citizens of the Country in which you locate and endeavor by conciliatory efforts to win over those who may hold Union sentiments not in arms against the South." Scott sensed a hostile attitude among the local Unionists beyond an unwillingness to provide their produce to the state government. He ordered Boone to report to him "the disposition of the people in the county and those adjoining across the line in Missouri, and put down and suppress any small organizations of Union men that your force will permit." Scott further ordered Boone to "give protection and respect the rights of all citizens not in arms against us or affording aid and comfort to the enemy." Boone replied on November 12 that he could not learn of any disturbances in Fulton County by Union men, but that there were a great many Unionists who were afraid to make any demonstrations of their faith. He had spared no pains to cultivate amicable relations with the locals, respecting in every instance their feelings and property. Scott had requested augmenting his force, as the demands seemed to be multiplying, and on November 13 he was authorized to increase his companies from 74 men to 114.[97]

While regular troops were protecting the border, local secessionists were organizing to provide local defense In many cases, this meant persecution of Unionists. Thirty-nine-year-old Dr. T. J. Nunnelie of Bennett's Bayou Township, Fulton County, by late summer 1861 had raised two companies of Confederate home guards, one operating in Missouri and one in Fulton County, Arkansas. Peace Society prisoners in testimony before the Military Board in Little Rock said the object of their society was to oppose lawless companies, one in Missouri and one in Arkansas. These were identified as Nunnelie's companies, which had compelled men to join the Confederate army and suppressed Union sentiment. On September 11 Nunnelie's men hanged Jesse B. James and John R. Brown in Ozark County, Missouri, because James—who operated the Dawt Mill on North Fork of White River—had ground corn for some Union men. Brown was hanged because he was found with James when they were cutting timber. A short time after this hanging, Nunnelie and William S. Sapp—a thirty-year-old farmer in Big Springs Township and Bennett's Bayou postmaster—heard that an old man named Rhodes who lived on the bend of Bennett's Bayou in Howell County, Missouri, had openly criticized the James and Brown hangings as murder. Two weeks later about twenty-five men led by Nunnelie and Sapp took Rhodes from his home and killed him.[98]

Silas Turnbo, born in 1844 in Taney County, Missouri, was living in Sugarloaf Township, Marion County, in 1860. He wrote that a majority of the people in Marion County were strict Southerners. However, the citizens who lived on the upper part of Big Creek in adjoining Taney County were nearly all unanimously for the Union. Leaders from that area organized a company that attracted Union men from both sides of the state line and furnished them with new muskets and bayonets. These were some of the Unionists Boone confronted in Missouri. There were also Unionists in the Arkansas mountains, but if they were quiet they were not considered a threat by the establishment and were left alone.[99]

Confederate Recruitment

Unionists were not enthusiastic for the Confederacy, but they were not actively obstructing the war effort. Arkansas was having trouble meeting its troop obligations to the Confederacy and the state, and Unionists were not enlisting. Immediately after secession volunteer companies from the lowland, cotton-growing, slave-owning half of the state flocked to the Confederate colors, and a few devoted regiments went east of the Mississippi River.

In Arkansas in 1861, the primary concern was support for McCulloch and his defense of the Indian Territory and Arkansas's western border. A significant blunder by the Military Board and Brigadier General N. Bartlett Pearce damaged Arkansas's military readiness when the Arkansas troops demobilized and two calls for volunteers by Governor Rector disturbed the state's upland hollows.

On May 13, 1861, McCulloch was assigned three regiments to defend the Indian Territory against an invasion from Kansas. His mission increased to include defense of northwest Arkansas from Union forces in Missouri. Richmond urged Rector and the Arkansas Military Board to furnish troops both for the general war effort and for McCulloch. The board proposed transferring the entire state force to the Confederate government if the men would

be used to protect Arkansas. The secretary of war would accept
the Arkansans but could not promise how they would be used, so
the transfer failed. David Hubbard, Confederate Superintendent of
Indian Affairs, passed through Arkansas to the Indian Territory and
reported to Richmond that "Arkansas had less the appearance of a
military organization than of any people he had ever known." He
recommended that a military leader be appointed for Arkansas who
was not from Arkansas. Consequently, on June 25, Brigadier General
William J. Hardee was given command of eastern Arkansas, and
the regiment under Colonel Hindman—which had not gone east
of the Mississippi River as threatened—was assigned to him. Two
commands in Arkansas, McCulloch's and Hardee's, created competition for troops raised in north-central Arkansas and for military
equipment, but the Military Board agreed that McCulloch's need
was the greater.[100]

Pressured by both Richmond and McCulloch for adequately
armed troops to protect northwest Arkansas, Rector issued a proclamation on July 8 to raise more regiments to defend the state. At
the same time, the Military Board authorized the transfer of the
Arkansas troops to Confederate control if the men agreed to the
transfer. General Hardee sent Colonel Hindman to Fayetteville
to transfer the troops under General Pearce. But before Hindman
arrived, McCulloch with his Arkansas, Missouri, and Louisiana
troops had defeated a Union force under General Nathaniel Lyon
at Wilson's Creek, Missouri, on August 10. (En route Hindman
mustered Scott's squadron.) The victorious Arkansas troops were
encouraged to transfer to Confederate service by Colonel Hindman,
General Pearce, and Colonel Dandridge McRae, who was sent by
the Military Board to assist in the transfer.

All but eighteen or twenty declined to be transferred and went
home. Several took their state-issued weapons with them as surety
for the pay, clothing, and shoes they had not received. Pearce speculated that they would have been willing to be transferred prior to
the Wilson's Creek fight, but they certainly would not serve under
anyone but McCulloch. They also rejected being sent to Pocahontas

in eastern Arkansas under Hardee, as they did not want to leave their homes in northwest Arkansas undefended.[101]

In response to Rector's July 8 call for troops to defend the state, seven regiments were mustered in at Arkadelphia, Benton, Pine Bluff, Springfield, Yellville, and Jacksonport. They were made available to Major General Leonidas Polk to defend and fortify the Mississippi River—except for the Fourteenth (Powers) Arkansas Infantry at Yellville. It was needed for local defense. The Fourteenth was raised under some duress. In Campbell Township, Searcy County, James H. Campbell (the son of Company D's Captain George W. Campbell) later wrote, "My father volunteered under the Governor's call on July 8, 1861....When my father's company was being raised for the Confederate service, I was only 16 years old, but said to the volunteers that when I went to the army I would go to the Union army and fight for our old flag and the Union." Another Searcy County company, K, Fourteenth Arkansas Infantry, was raised in Tomahawk and Richland townships by Captain James Harrison Love, and it relied on persuasion. Private Andrew J. Garner stated, "I had my choice to go with Co. K, Fourteenth Arkansas, or look up a limb to be hanged on." John S. McCarver attempted to raise a regiment in Izard County, but was only able to raise five companies, not the ten required for a full regiment. Nevertheless, a Confederate citizen of Mt. Olive, Izard County, wrote the following on July 27, 1861:

> Although she [Izard County] sent a Union delegate to the convention she has now a regiment of troops ready to be mustered into service; and the Rev. John S. McCarver is now gone to Gen. Ben McCulloch to report the same. On the 4th of July, in Blue Mountain township, we had a barbecue, and Capt. T. W. Edmondson and Capt. Wm. M. Aikin, both had independent cavalry companies. After mustering, they urged the men to form infantry companies, which they did by electing W. L. [sic S.] Lindsey captain;... Then commenced the canvass for the regiment in earnest. All kinds of opposition was thrown in the way, but we now have six companies in Izard county, and one in Fulton.[102]

William M. Aikin, recruiting for McCarver's Regiment, raised the Stars and Bars, but citizens of Harris Township, Izard County, threatened to come in force and pull it down. When the erroneous news first came that Price and McCulloch were beaten at Wilson's Creek, these men threw their hats in the air and hurrahed for the United States of America. These men did not come to hear Aikin speak or to muster. They "swore that they would never muster under the d–d *nigger* flag," but if anyone came with the Stars and Stripes, they would arise at midnight to fight for it.[103]

When Pearce's Arkansas troops went home after the Battle of Wilson's Creek and refused to be integrated into the national Confederate army, their absence decimated McCulloch's army. McCulloch, searching for a solution, informed President Jefferson Davis and General Hardee on August 24 that he only had 3,000 troops because all the Arkansas men had left the service. He urged that a large force be organized at once. McCulloch did not want to lose the arms and artillery left by the departed Arkansans, so urged that they be assigned to his command. He noted that men for twelve months' service could be raised from Arkansas, and he continued to agitate for reinforcements and for control of the arms left in Fayetteville by the Arkansas troops. Responding to McCulloch's plight, on September 5 Secretary of War Leroy Pope Walker told Governor Rector that all the Arkansas troops not with Hardee should be sent to McCulloch and that McCulloch should control the abandoned arms. Walker respectfully suggested that Rector induce by every means in his power to return the Arkansas troops to McCulloch. He also suggested that Rector call for more troops to be enlisted so that McCulloch would have at least ten Arkansas regiments. At the same time, Walker authorized McCulloch to augment his force by calling for five regiments to be raised from Arkansas, Texas, and Louisiana for three years or the war. Two weeks later, he reduced enlistments to twelve months' service.

On September 19 Governor Rector issued a proclamation calling for five regiments to be recruited at five locations in the state—Little Rock, Magnolia, Paraclifta, Batesville, and

Carrollton—and appointing mustering officers. Edmund Burgevin, adjutant general for Arkansas, was assigned to Carrollton, Carroll County, to raise a regiment from north Arkansas. Rector commented that there were portions of the state that had sent but few men while others, applying constant stimulants, had already turned out more than their portion. Prescient to future problems, Rector mentioned that he received letters daily offering to volunteer, but there were problems. It was impossible to raise a company from one county or locality; the men only were procurable in squads of five, ten, or twenty.[104]

Recruiting new regiments from the uplands would not be easy, especially since there was competition from General McCulloch's appeal as well as other governor-appointed mustering officers. Burgevin found this the case in Carrollton. Colonel Frank W. Desha, recruiting at Batesville, was Burgevin's competitor, and he found that he was outbidden on terms of service. The governor had stipulated a twelve-month term plus six more months if the war continued. On October 8, Burgevin wrote the governor from Carrollton that, when he first arrived, despite being assured he would easily recruit a regiment, to that date no volunteer company had reported to him. "There seemed to be great apathy and want of spirit among people of this portion of the Country." Too many men with local influence, each with a few followers, wanted to be captains. Together they would form a company, yet all were pulling in different directions. Some men said they preferred going directly to McCulloch, but not immediately. None wanted to serve for more than twelve months, and the governor's proclamation called for twelve months plus an additional six months if needed. General McCulloch and fellow recruiter Colonel Frank Desha at Batesville, who were only asking for twelve months service, were attracting Burgevin's potential recruits. Therefore, Burgevin informed Rector, he would only recruit for twelve months.[105]

Colonel C. L. Dawson, another of Rector's mustering officers, may have been having trouble as well at Paraclifta, Sevier County, in southwest Arkansas. In a not particularly well-written letter,

William H. Foster informed the governor on October 14, 1861, from Montgomery County that Abe Lincoln had as many friends in Montgomery County as he did in Pike and Polk counties in the Ouachita Mountains. Some Unionist leaders said that they would not have seceded and that in reality they still had not, for they still stuck to the Union. At one gathering, Foster reported that a person in the crowd yelled "Hurrah for Lincoln," and that a committee of Union men had been formed to defy the authorities. These men did not intend to join the Confederate army or fight unless they were drafted. If drafted and then captured, they would tell their captors that they never intended to fight against them. Foster then named ten men involved in the organization and added three others who knew about it. Most of them, he said, lived in Greasy Cove, Pike and Polk counties. As a postscript he mentioned that two men, Jack and Elijah Putnam, had put together a sham company of twenty-five men that was to remain at home, but its secret was discovered. Despite Foster's designating the Putnams' company as a sham, they may have intended to form a home guard unit—authorized by the State Convention on its last full day in session—that exempted them from all other military obligations. Of the twelve men identified as opposed to Confederate military service, six enlisted in November 1863 in the federal Fourth Arkansas Cavalry.[106]

Perhaps in reaction to Burgevin's report, on October 16, Governor Rector wrote Samuel Leslie (Searcy County politician and colonel of Searcy County's Forty-fifth Arkansas Militia) to inquire and berate Leslie about the poor recruiting record for Leslie's home township, Wiley's Cove. Leslie responded on the twenty-first:

> You Say that it has been reported to the Military Board that there are one hundred good fighting men in Cove Township Searcy Co. that has not nor will not volunteer ther [sic] services In behalf of the South. What would prompt anyone to attempt to cast such a stigma upon the people of this township I am not able to comprehend. Were your informant a citizen of Searcy Co I might have some ida [sic] of the cause. This Township, Cove, has not turned out

as many volunteers as she might have done. The County has about 300 men in service of the Confederate States though we are only represented by 2 Captains [George W. Campbell and James H. Love], the rest of our men joined companies in the adjoining counties and those counties is receiving the credit. Cove Township has about 60 able bodied men subject to military duty all told. Only five out of that number single men and eight volunteers which will leave 52 now subject to duty. The great bulk of our men now in service has been furnished by three townships. There is other townships in the County that has don [sic] but little better than Cove, and they pass unnoticed. I will say to you that the citizens of Cove Township is as law abiding a people as lives and the records of our corts [sic] will Bare [sic] me out in the assertion. Which may account in some degree for their not being more ready to volunteer, there is other causes, so many Missourians running off and leaving the State, has had its influence. I know this County has had a bad name. At a distance we have been called Black republicans, abolishionists [sic] etc, but we have never had any of those characters amongst us. It is true, the citizens of this county was Union men as long as there was any hopes of the Union, and perhaps a little longer, but all ida [sic] of the Union as it onst [sic] was is banished. The time has passed for the North and South to live together in peace and harmony and we must be loyal to the Government we live under. This is the feelings of the people of this county as far as I have any knowledge and when you hear men call the people of Searcy Co by hard names, rest assured they are willfully lying or uninformed with the character of our people. I write you this letter Gov.—in order to place the good people of Searcy Co. rite [sic] before you. I feel a duty I have to them to do so. I hope Cove township will yet give a good account of itself that you may have no reason to complain.[107]

It was not just the uplands that had trouble recruiting for the Confederacy. Lieutenant Ira G. Robertson tried for several weeks to raise the Rector Guards, an infantry company from the Little

Rock area, with little success. A November 9 squib in the *Daily State Journal* touted, "A few more recruits are wanted to fill up the 'Rector Guards,' an infantry company just organizing in this City by Lt. Robertson. We cordially recommend the new corps to the favor of those desiring to serve their country. Lieut. Robertson is an old U.S. Soldier, being a graduate of West Point, and has seen many years of service." The paper indicated that the ranks were fast filling up and only a few more men were needed to complete the company, but by mid-December it still lacked more than half of the seventy men needed to complete a company. They would be helped by Peace Society volunteers.[108]

All this Confederate recruiting put pressure on Unionists and small farmers who had to provide for their families. They looked for protection for their families and from Confederate military service. They found it in the Peace Society. A secret Unionist organization known by various names—Peace Organization Society, Peace Society, Peace and Constitutional Society, Pro Bono Publico, and others—had existed since the State Convention in May 1861. But its real growth came with the governor's September 19 proclamation and McCulloch's recruiting efforts. It may have had its origin in the Union Clubs promoted by the old Whigs in late 1860 after Lincoln's election, but its origins are not evident.

The Peace Society (the name used here) was a secret organization of Unionists and those opposed to Confederate military service who agreed to protect each other from any persons who would do them and their families harm. Because the unnamed threatening persons were obviously the Confederate Arkansas government and their secessionist neighbors, the organization had to be secret. Searcy County Peace Society member Benjamin G. Watts described the situation for Unionists in the first months of the war, and the development of the Peace Society:

> When the war came up in 1861 the majority of the people residing in Searcy and contiguous mountain counties were opposed to secession and so declared themselves, but as the war progressed and the excitement increased and feeling

became intensified, the portion of the citizens here who were at heart disloyal to the government of the United States went away and enlisted in the Confederate army and finding it a real hardship and not as much a holiday as they anticipated came back and with others organized the Home Guards or Confederate Militia. The members of this organization were in the main our former neighbors and knew all the Union men in the county.

I was a Union man and was generally known to be such. The Watts family were Union men, without a single exception. Those of us who were known to side with the Union and was organized into a Union League [sic] were by the opposition called "Yaller Rags." They accused us of hanging a yellow piece of fabric out our doors so we could be known by our friends.[109]

Watts also said:

When the war came up Benjamin H. Gary, myself and others in Searcy Co. joined an organization that was reported to have been introduced into the state by a Federal soldier who began in Stone county [then parts of Izard and Searcy counties], and which was organized here by Ab Smith and Thom Harness. We had no place of meeting but pledged ourselves to avoid Confederate Service and to protect the families of those who were forced to quit the country or to go to the service. All who joined were loyal and opposed to secession and to the methods of the Confederates who first took all the guns in the country then began to force men to enlist as early as 1861. I took the pledge at a house raising and several others went in at the same time. We had no list of members and I know of no sign or password except that when a man rode up and threw his right leg across the horse's neck, if he stopped to talk, we knew that he was a member. We never met together as a band and had no officers.[110]

All Peace Society members agreed, when questioned, that it was for home protection, but there was disagreement about from whom. They said that it was "a good thing and for the protection of their homes, property and family against robbers and thieves and that it was a neighborhood society and that the best men and oldest citizens of the County were members." Others said it was "a home protection society and that there was no harm in it but to protect ourselves, our friends and families and property." Van Buren County members said they joined for "home protection against robbers of other states," and "to protect from Robbers and Runaway Negroes." In existing documentation all denied that they had joined an organization that was pro-Lincoln and against the South or that they had joined to avoid volunteering for military service. Many stated that they were ready to volunteer, either then or as soon as they went home to tell their family goodbye. Only Van Buren County's William Gadberry testified that "George Brown sent my son word not to volunteer that there was 300 men willing to help him keep from it."[111]

Although it was a secret society with no written records, several copies of its oath, all similar, were obtained by Confederate authorities. A copy of the Constitution of the Mill Creek [Township] Peace Organization Society, Izard County, indicated that self-preservation was an undisputed natural right, and the right of communities to combine together for the mutual protection of themselves, their families, and their property was the sole purpose for the Mill Creek Peace Organization. They swore that they would protect all the secrets of their society, and that they would on the shortest notice go to the assistance of any other brother. The part of the oath that caused the authorities the most concern was the statement, "any member of this society who shall betray to our enemies the existence of this society he shall forfeit his life and it shall be the duty of each member of this society, having received knowledge of such betrayal to forthwith inform the brethren, each of whose duty it shall be to follow such traitor and take his life at the price of their own."[112]

Confederate authorities believed that the Peace Society was about to lead a rebellion. The most convincing and alarming information was the item in the Peace Society oath that prescribed the death penalty for anyone who betrayed the secrets of the society. When they interrogated Peace Society members, authorities came away with an impression of an organization devoted to something more than simple home protection. Justices of the Peace in southeast Carroll County described it as "tending to insurrection and treason against the State of Arkansas." Despite no existing testimony, Confederate authorities believed they had discovered a Unionist uprising. The Van Buren County men denied knowing that the society was anti-Confederate and pro-Lincoln, which raises the question of why the interrogators thought that it was treasonous. Captain Scott in his December 3, 1861, report refers to "a secret Society under oaths, signs, tokens & passwords with penalty of death if revealed, to aid [&] assist the Federal government in subjugating the South." He thought the organization to be of Northern origin intent on defeating the South. "It breathed treason and insurrection of the most conclusive and positive nature," he said. Colonel Sam Leslie of the Searcy County militia stated that local citizens had learned about an organization hostile to the Confederate government and that he believed the leader intended treachery. Colonel J. J. Kemp of the Izard County militia had called out his militia to repeal an insurrection caused by Union men or men in a secret organization threatening their peace and happiness.[113]

However, the Van Buren County prisoners testified that they had been assured that there was no Northern trick in it, and the Fulton County prisoners "never understood that we were to join the Union army."[114]

The Little Rock newspapers picked up the story and embellished the treason-insurrection angle. The *Daily State Journal* reported that "members of a secret Lincoln organization" had been "furnished with supplies of money from Northern camps." The *True Democrat* said it was "believed that the objects of the society were to co-operate with abolitionists and Lincolnites," and that "there was a great deal of mischievous humbuggery in it, about the rich and poor, and an attempt to array non-slaveholders against slaveholders." The *Gazette* published a letter from Colonel Solon Borland, which referred to a Unionist treasonable society in Izard, Searcy, and other counties that required very decisive measures to suppress.[115]

Many years later, in the 1890s, Peace Society men seeking federal pensions for service in Union regiments insisted that they had been loyal. One man claimed that "the Union men in Searcy Co Ark organized themselves into a Secret organization pledging themselves to not enlist in the Confederate army or otherwise aid the cause of Secession." Another declared, "We perfected an organization composed of Union men for the purpose of mutual protection and to avoid going into the [Confederate] service." "We all taken an oath among ourselves to support the Government of the United States," said another, as did the man who vowed, "We pledged ourselves to avoid Confederate service and to protect the families of those who were forced to quit the country or go to the [Confederate] service." Still another verified that "the object of the society was to oppose the Confederacy and aid the Federal forces." And finally, "It was agreed that as soon as the federals reached this country or its vicinity we would join the federal army."[116]

Unionists were resilient and survived their secessionist neighbors' persecution. A. W. Bishop noted one example:

A few days after the arrival of the federal army at Batesville in the spring of 1862, H. V. Gray, a loyalist from Black River township in Independence county, with about forty of his neighbors, who, with others to the number of one hundred or upwards, had previously banded themselves together to resist, by force if need be, attempts to urge them into the rebel service, made their appearance at the headquarters of General [Samuel] Curtis, and tendered their services to the government.[117]

The Peace Society was not an abolitionist organization, although the secessionists and their press tried to portray it as such. Peace Society members were very aware of this accusation and how it could hurt their recruiting. Bishop in his 1863 Union propaganda book, *Loyalty on the Frontier*, protested:

> Advocates of secession...found no subject so fertile of conversions among hard working farmers, as the absurd notion of Negro equality. It was the burden of discourse, not only, but of conversation, and was well calculated to alienate the poorer classes, who, though owning few slaves themselves, or generally none at all, were yet born on Southern soil, and possessed that aversion to the Negro, which whatever it might concede, could not brook for a moment the thought of his social or political equality.... Men were told that the grand object of the war on the part of the Federal Government was to lift the Negro to a state of equality with the whites, freeing him from bondage, and giving him the right to exercise the elective franchise and hold office; statements whose falsity was only equaled by the lamentable credulity given to them.[118]

Although certainly recognizing that the war was about slavery, Searcy County Peace Society members were ambivalent; but their attitude reflected a decided class consciousness. In Tomahawk Township, opinions about the Confederacy and the war were varied. Several men were for the Union because they believed that in the Confederacy the poor man would be looked on as no better than the black man and that they would be equal. Although supporting the Union, some thought that a man had no more right to take a man's slave than to take his horse. This must have been a common argument concerning property rights at the time because Oliver P. Temple, writing about Unionists in East Tennessee, uses a similar phrase: "No man had either the moral or the legal right to take from another his slaves any more than his horses or his mules." Joshua Reeves said that if blacks had been bought and sent off years earlier, there would have been no war. However, William S. Richardson of

Izard County, born in Missouri, son of a Massachusetts native, was a Peace Society member, and after the war he served as a courier for the Freedmen's Bureau in Izard County for some time.[119]

The Peace Society, in the parlance of the times, was a self-protection association, similar to self-protection committees in other parts of Arkansas. It grew out of the belief that no other organization would provide adequate protection. Where it differed from other Arkansas self-protection committees was in whom it opposed: the state government and secessionist neighbors. This is also why it had to be secret.

There is no documentation of when the Peace Society was first formed in Arkansas, nor from where it came, not even if it was home grown. The similarity of the oaths and the communications across county lines indicate that it was a single movement from Fulton County on the Missouri line to Pope and Yell counties on the Arkansas River. In December 1862, after the Battle of Prairie Grove, Lieutenant John W. Morris, Company H, First Arkansas Cavalry (U.S.), indicated to his lieutenant colonel, Albert W. Bishop, that the Peace Organization Society was in operation in Searcy and surrounding counties at the time of the May 6 convention vote on secession. A variety of affidavits, statements, and memoirs report men joining the secret organization at various times from May to early November. M. M. Brashear early in 1861 organized a secret organization in Searcy County. Colonel J. J. Kemp, Izard County militia, said most of the citizens of Sylamore Township had been engaged in the organization for forty or fifty days as of November 21. Independence County's William Shirley supposed on December 24 that he had joined six or seven weeks before. Searcy County Peace Society member George W. Lee said, "[A]t the outbreak of the Civil War and in 1861 after the war had actually begun, the Union men organized themselves into Companies."[120]

Similarly, there is no definite evidence of the origins for the Peace Society. From Van Buren County, Ananias Stobaugh reported that Jonathan Moody said it came "from headquarters," but he did not know the location of those headquarters. Captain Scott concluded that it was of Northern origin. However, Bishop, in noting that John W. Morris and Paris Strickland both belonged to the Peace Society in Searcy County, did not mention how the organization began. Morris's biography acknowledged that "a peace organization was formed," but did not say how it was formed. In pension files, the origin is often identified as local. "The Union men in Searcy Co. Ark. organized themselves into a secret organization," became a typical declaration. "We perfected an organization composed of Union men," verified another man. Benjamin G. Watts's statement, "[A]n organization that was reported to have been introduced to the State by a Federal soldier who began in Stone County, and which was organized here by Ab Smith and Thom Harness," does not stand up because there were no federal soldiers in Searcy or Izard counties, Stone County's parent counties, in the summer of 1861. Peter Tyler in his December 1861 testimony said, "I heard somewhere after the noise commenced about it that it came from Washington City, but [Lorenzo Dow] Jameson [who initiated Tyler] did not tell me if I recollect right; he said to me it was for protection when invaded by robbers." This is not reliable evidence of its origins either.[121]

A survey of other Unionist secret societies throughout the South does not reveal that they were imported. In fact, "Unionist secret societies operating in East Tennessee and Kentucky" were found to be the roots of the Union League in the Midwest. Indeed, the Peace Society was usually called the Union League in later narratives. In 1863, a Minnesota newspaper urged its readers to join the Union League, which it described as a non-political organization founded in East Tennessee: "The Union League, first organized in East Tennessee by a little band of hunted and prosecuted patriots for their own individual protection, has spread until its councils meet in every state in the Union, and, especially in the Northern States, are agents of mighty power in and of the Government."[122]

Robert P. Matthews of Greene County, Missouri—who served as a lieutenant in John S. Phelps's six-month Volunteer Missouri Infantry—formed a League of over fifty men in the spring of 1861. Under his direction, they swore with uplifted hand to defend the

Stars and Stripes with every drop of their blood. Things drifted along in southwest Missouri until about June, by which time almost everyone had decided what side they would support. Union Leagues and Union societies had been formed as well as secessionist organizations. Both sides' organizations were mainly secret, with covert meetings at night behind guarded doors, a system of passwords, and ceremonies known only to the initiated. These secret organizations were necessary on the border because one did not know who was friend or foe.[123]

Newspapers, however, inflamed the public by depicting the Peace Society as "in communication with persons of the North." It had "been introduced into Arkansas by a Yankee, who some months since died in eastern Arkansas of a disease of the trachea, superinduced by the application of a hempen tourniquet," insisted one observer. Others revealed that they "were furnished with supplies of money from Northern camps," or "with arms and ammunition from tories in Missouri." By many it was supposed to be a league for rapine and plunder.

Silas Turnbo wrote: "The citizens who lived on the upper part of Big Creek in Taney county, Missouri, were nearly all unanimous for the Union....These with others who lived on Little North Fork that espoused the Union cause organized a company and [were] furnished with new muskets and bayonets." Could this be the origin of the comments that the Peace Society was furnished arms?[124]

An opposing view was expressed by Arkansas Unionist J. William Demby in 1863, decrying the lack of federal support, especially arms, for Arkansas Unionists. He wrote: "If loyal citizens of Arkansas had been furnished with the means of defence [sic], as they were in Missouri, there is no doubt but they would have rid themselves of the rebel dynasty about the time the conscript law was being put into force."[125]

Peace Society members said they were sworn in by local men. In Van Buren County, J. W. Curl (Union Township) was initiated by John Gilbreath (Union Township), who was sworn in by John Smith (Griggs Township), who got it from Jonathan Moody (Big

Flat Township, Searcy County—he had lived in Union Township in 1850). In Fulton County, testifiers said they had been initiated by J. J. Ware (Big Creek Township), James Baker (Bennett's Bayou Township), and H. W. Davis (Union Township). In Searcy County, Peter A. Tyler—who lived at Tyler Bend on the Buffalo River (Tomahawk Township)—said that George Long (Crooked Creek Township, Carroll County) and Lorenzo Dow Jameson (Calf Creek Township) initiated him. After Tyler was sworn in, he swore in at least thirty-two other men. Peace Society men used every opportunity to enlist more members. Benjamin G. Watts remembered that he took the pledge at a house raising, and several others went in at the same time. In all the documentation about the Arkansas Peace Society, the only people identified (or reliably mentioned) who initiated members were local residents.[126]

Copies of the Peace Society oath are the only documents that have survived to tell us something definite about this secret organization. Members have stated that there were no membership rosters, no minutes, no paperwork of any kind. Testimony and pension affidavits indicate that the society was divided into companies or camps and that it was a layered organization, with increasing involvement requiring more specific oaths. Some testified that the oath they were questioned about was not the oath that they took, that there were higher levels that were more involved in supporting the federal government or joining the Union army. They met only in small groups in out-of-the-way places. The only way to recognize other members or to communicate was through secret signs, passwords, and tokens.[127]

There were numerous ways to identify one's self and be acknowledged as a society member. In northern Searcy, Carroll, and Marion counties, if a member heard "Secession," he would reply "In the Southern Confederacy." "Hoot like an owl" was answered with "Howl like a wolf." When approaching a house at night, to determine if another party was safe, "Dark night" was uttered; the answer was, "It will be darker before day," if all were clear. If a secessionist was in the house or in the group, the reply was, "Perhaps it will be darker in the morning." One signal was to place the right forefinger on the nose twice, then let it fall to the side. The answer was to place two fingers of the right hand on the throat and draw them down to the breast, then drop to the side. A second sign was to pull the shirt collar with two fingers of the right hand twice, to be answered with placing the opened right hand on the breast. Another sign was placing three fingers of the left hand across the nose. The answer was carelessly feeling under the chin with either hand. The next sign was to place one finger of the left hand in the shirt collar and the answer was to put the right hand on the left breast. Yet another was to lift the hat and replace it to be answered by turning the back to the hat raiser. When leaving home, a member was to suspend from his door or window a piece of "*Yellow ribbon, calico* or *paper*" to distinguish them as members and as a token "that if a friend or Northern Army came along that his property & family would not be molested by seeing and finding *this sign* at his door."[128]

For a secret organization with confidential signs to recognize each other, some members seemed either very dense or very deceptive when interrogated by Confederates. All members said the Peace Society token was yellow except Peter Tyler, who said it was red. Tyler's answers were flimsy, but Tyler's inductee Isaiah Ezell remembered less. He did not know the wording of the oath; he recalled one sign was to place a hand around the nose and the reply was to put a hand under the chin. A sign was to put a piece of cloth around the house, but he did not remember the color, and he did not know what it meant. There was something about an owl, but he did not remember what it meant or how it was to protect their homes or families against robbers. They either had bad memories or were purposely deceptive.

Fulton County prisoners were reticent about the secret signs. Shadrach H. Wren did not know anything about a yellow rag until sometime after he had joined. Other witnesses gave no recorded testimony about secret signs. Most claimed they had not fully joined the society. Van Buren County prisoners similarly had little information about secret signs. Henry Cook did not understand that the ribbon was a sign to the Union army. Edmond Stobaugh thought the ribbon was a sign to ensure the home's protection if they went to fight. G. W. Smith did not understand what the ribbon was for.[129]

Captain Scott discovered a more nefarious signal to be used by subversive Unionists who had joined the Southern army. He wrote, "There was another to be used in camp which some termed a Camp Signal and by which it appears some members (to blind the South) were to volunteer & go into the army of the South and there work our destruction, this signal, word, noise or token was to 'Hoot like an owl' which was to be answered by the 'Howl of a wolf.'"[130]

Confederate colonel John M. Harrell could remember the signs somewhat. In 1894 he wrote, "I had to pass frequently through Limestone Valley [Newton County] and in the vicinity of Marshall [Searcy County] during the war, and so doing I often heard the strange sounds of owls hooting before sundown from the cliffs along my route. Those 'owls' had more cause to hoot then than they do now in the bright light of subsequent events." Was he referring to a Peace Society secret signal to "Hoot like an owl"?[131]

During the Civil War, secret societies were not unique to the South. In the North, some Peace Democrats—dubbed Copperheads for the pennies they wore as identifying badges—aided the secret Sons of Liberty and Knights of the Golden Circle. These organizations supported the Confederacy and planned subversive activities in the North, including helping escaped prisoners, passing intelligence, and blowing up arsenals. Besides the Arkansas Peace Society, similar secret pro-Union organizations existed in Alabama, North Carolina, Georgia, Florida, Mississippi, and Virginia. They went under the names Peace Society and Heroes of America, or Red Strings, the latter named for the red thread they wore in their lapel. These groups appeared in 1862, although there is a hint of a group in December 1861 in Virginia. The Peace Society of Alabama expanded into East Tennessee, Mississippi, Georgia, and possibly Florida. The Confederate authorities believed it originated within the Union lines, but they did not take the organization seriously until August 1863, when it had an impact on elections. The Heroes of America were active in North Carolina, southwestern Virginia, and eastern Tennessee in protecting Confederate deserters and aiding spies and escaped prisoners. An investigation in 1864 into its activities concluded that it had been formed at the suggestion of federal authorities. Both the Alabama Peace Society and the Heroes of America had secret signs and passwords. Conscription invited defiance and banding together for self-protection. The danger of arrest by Confederate authorities caused them to operate clandestinely with secret oaths, handshakes, and passwords. As with the Arkansas Peace Society, the origin of the Alabama Peace Society and Heroes of America, and when they were organized, is uncertain; as in Arkansas, they were dominated in their early days by Unionists.[132]

The Arkansas Peace Society and the North Carolina Heroes of America shared many similarities, both in their organization and the public perception of them. Authors William T. Auman and David D. Scarboro's Heroes of America description allow certain parallels to be noted with the Arkansas Peace Society.

Secrecy was a significant similarity. Auman and Scarboro point out that the secret ritual was based on the Freemasonry ritual, as were the secret rituals of other Civil War secret societies: the Peace Society of Alabama, the Union Leagues, and even the pro-Confederate Knights of the Golden Circle in the North. For the Heroes of America and the Arkansas Peace Society, the rituals included (besides an oath of secrecy) support for fellow members and a death penalty for those who betrayed the society. North Carolina's secret passwords and signs were not like those in Arkansas. Both societies placed ribbons or pieces of cloth on their houses' doors or windows to identify themselves as friendly to invading Union armies to assure their safety and protection. The Heroes of America's color was red, while the Peace Society's was yellow. The Heroes of America had three degrees, or levels, in its organization, so that novices were admitted by stages into its goals. This enlisted men into the society before they learned that joining could lead to involvement in the peace movement in North Carolina or possible enlistment in the Union army. The Arkansas Peace Society had a tiered organization as well, but there is no indication of how many levels it contained.[133]

The Heroes offered mutual protection for lower-class whites, i.e., yeomen, against actions by the Confederate government, including conscription. The group also promised support for the families when the men fled to avoid conscription. Similar goals were expressed for the Peace Society in the poorer Arkansas counties. The members of both organizations showed an antipathy to the economic elites who ruled the state and the Confederacy. Despite descriptions of the Heroes as a cultural movement that included upper-class Unionists, these descriptions did not "distort the picture of the HOA as a mainly white, lower-class movement"[134]

Just as the origins of the Peace Society are obscure, the origins of the Heroes of America are similarly mysterious. Contemporary writers said that the Union army introduced it into the South, just as Arkansas newspapers said the Peace Society was brought to north-central Arkansas by a Union soldier. Others said that the Heroes of America "arose independently in North Carolina." Auman and Scarboro suggest that it did originate in North Carolina, particularly in the "Quaker Belt" in the heart of the state. Despite speculation that the Peace Society came from an unidentified headquarters or from Washington, there is no evidence that anyone outside north-central Arkansas was involved. Therefore, we must presume that both organizations originated locally and independently, despite their similarities.[135]

Perceptions of these secret societies were almost identical among the press and the public in Raleigh and Little Rock. Estimates of the numbers involved were large: 10,000 Heroes of America and as many as 2,200 in the Peace Society. Suspicion existed in both states that these two organizations were introduced by the Union army and were treasonous. However, the local press believed that men in both states had been tricked into joining and that many innocent men had been deceived and deluded into this organization. And there was the belief that "there is a Union league in the South not only among civilians, but among the soldiers of the Rebel army," and that it was particularly prevalent among the conscripts.

This North Carolina evaluation jibes with Captain Scott's report of Peace Society members joining the Confederate army "to blind the South," and General Frederick Steele's finding that rebel conscripts would admit his spies into their camps.[136]

Resentment of slave owners, who were the social elite, also existed in the Heroes of America and the Peace Society and meshed very well with their Unionism, as members felt no affinity for those fighting for slavery. This may have led to the formation of vigilance organizations among secessionists in both Arkansas and North Carolina, indicating a lack of confidence that the state could defend them or their property; North Carolinians organized Home Guards to protect against Lincolnites and abolitionists just as Arkansans went after abolitionists and Northerners. The similarity between secret Unionist organizations in the two states indicates that the Freemasonry ritual was probably the template for the secret Unionists' signs and passwords. The response of the secessionist public, particularly the press, in both states may be cultural, indicating amazement that Southerners could join such a treasonous society if they had known its true goals.

In the summer of 1861, despite vigilance committee activity, Unionist sentiment in Arkansas was not considered a threat to the government. Sometime in the summer of 1861, John A. Harvick, Monroe County clerk, caused the arrest and examination of members of a secret society called Pro Bono Publico. The evidence proved nothing treasonable, and the parties were released. It was said to extend through Van Buren, Searcy, and Randolph counties. They had a constitution that revealed nothing treasonable, but the public believed that the objects of the society were to cooperate with abolitionists and Lincolnites. The *True Democrat* linked the Pro Bono Publico to the Van Buren County Peace Society when the Van Buren group was discovered, but it did not explain why it thought they were the same organization. The press did not connect the Pro Bono Publico with the June 12, 1861, attempted slave insurrection and subsequent hanging of the insurgents in Monroe County. In the summer of 1861 it was possible to be accused of Unionist sympathies, even to belong to a secret pro-Union organization, and be released because no overt act could be proved.[137]

Events outside Arkansas would affect the perception of a secret Unionist organization, however. On the night of November 8, small bands of Unionists burned five strategic railroad bridges between Bristol and Chattanooga in eastern Tennessee and tried to destroy four others. They were captured and hanged alongside the railroad as an example. Reports of this outrage were published in the Little Rock press on November 13, adding that five men had been arrested. Authors John C. Inscoe and Robert C. Kinzer wrote that Confederate lenience ended with the bridge burnings and "prompted immediate repression by Confederate authorities." Tennessee bridge burners also affected Arkansas Confederate authorities' attitudes toward hitherto overlooked Unionist sympathizers. This change came at a particularly inopportune time for the Peace Society; it ended Confederate leniency in Arkansas. Expressions of Unionist sentiment vanished. Unionists were now suspected saboteurs and too dangerous to be ignored.[138]

SEARCY COUNTY.

NO. 8---KNOB OF SEARCY COUNTY, TAKEN FROM THE DAWSON FARM, ON FORREST CREEK.

Eli Dawson's farm, where citizens met before attempting to free Peace Society prisoners in Burrowville. (From David Dale Owen, First Report of a Geological Reconnaissance of the Northern Counties of Arkansas, Made During the Years 1857 and 1858, Little Rock: Johnson & Yerkes, 1858)

Chapter 3

Discovery and Arrest:
November 17–December 31, 1861

By the fall of 1861, Governor Henry M. Rector and Arkansas were hard pressed to raise the troops needed to defend Arkansas and to support the demands of the Confederate government. On September 5, 1861, Secretary of War L. P. Walker had strongly suggested that Arkansas raise at least ten more regiments to reinforce General Ben McCulloch. Rector had responded by creating five recruiting districts to raise five regiments. Edmund Burgevin, sent to Carrollton to raise a regiment from the north Arkansas district, was having difficulty meeting his quota. Pressure on him to raise a regiment led to pressure at the local level to enlist men who did not want to enlist. They found support in avoiding military service in the Peace Society, which saw a decided surge in its membership in September and October. These two conflicting interests resulted eventually in the disclosure of the Peace Society to the community at large. That disclosure produced vigilante activity from the pro-Confederate citizens and arrests by the authorities, who assumed the investigation of the secret movement. The need to support a military was very evident in the second session of the Thirteenth General Assembly's agenda.[139]

Governor Rector recalled the Thirteenth General Assembly in a second session, called an extraordinary session, which met on November 4 in Little Rock. In its regular session, this General Assembly—after gridlock over secession from November to January

1861—had finally authorized the state referendum that produced the State Convention that took Arkansas out of the Union and into the Confederacy. The November 1861 extraordinary session amended many of the acts of the convention, had new members swear an oath of allegiance to Arkansas and the Confederacy, elected Confederate senators, and performed the mundane tasks normally done by general assemblies.

Perhaps the most significant and revealing acts of this second session had to do with the military and how to pay for it. A bit of populism appeared when the legislature voted to increase enlisted pay to $15 a month from $11 and to reduce officers' pay. The legislature defeated proposals to abolish the Military Board and to give 160 acres to all soldiers' widows, but it did endorse the convention's act to require each county to have a home guard.

Senator Decius McCreary, representing White and Jackson counties and chairman of the Military Affairs Committee, proposed that the Senate organize itself into a military company and proceed at once to Pitman's Ferry in Randolph County to aid in resisting a threatened invasion of Arkansas. He recommended that the president of the Senate serve as captain, the secretary as commissary, and the doorkeeper as orderly sergeant. Some opposed the move, saying the Senate could do more for the defense of the state by taking steps to provide for the needs of the troops. Offered in jest, McCreary's proposal provided impetus to consider troop support.[140]

Financial concerns also focused their attention, especially the question of taxes. The assembly repealed a war tax and lowered the convention's tax rate increase. It made Confederate and Arkansas treasury notes, war bonds, and warrants mandatory tender for county collections and payments. Confederate taxes were to be offset by a Confederate debt to Arkansas, and provisions were made to pay a Confederate war tax.[141]

Additionally, Robert W. Johnson and Charles B. Mitchell from The Family were elected senators to the Confederate Senate. Votes from the House carried both men, but Albert Pike (who came in third) received more votes in the Senate. At the governor's suggestion, the General Assembly then adjourned *sine die* on November 18. In his closing address, President of the Senate Thomas Fletcher—representing lowland Arkansas, Desha, and Jefferson counties—stated, "In my section of the State the question of taxation at this time is an important one, and we have done all in our power to relieve our people in this respect. Our brave soldiers who are battling for the rights we hold dearest have not been forgotten or neglected in our legislative deliberations and enactments. We have elected two able Senators to represent us in the Confederate Congress." That summed up the agenda of the extraordinary session.[142]

In light of subsequent events, Fulton County representative Jehoida J. Ware—who had written to his wife from the General Assembly's first session that he feared for the dissolution of the Union and that most of the leading men were in favor of a dissolution—may have left a bit early to return to his home in Big Creek Township. He rode as far as Clinton, Van Buren County, where he learned that local vigilantes on November 17 had begun arresting men believed to belong to a secret pro-Lincoln organization. He then left immediately for home.[143]

His fellow representative, Jerome B. Lewis, was colonel of the Van Buren County Militia. He found a crisis on his hands when he returned home from the legislature and learned of the vigilante activity.[144]

Assuming his role as colonel, he called out 100 militiamen to take over the investigation and arrests. County clerk J. T. Bradley informed Captain John Rice Homer Scott, commanding the squadron of Arkansas Cavalry Volunteers headquartered at Camp Culloden in southeastern Carroll County, of the situation. On November 20, 1861, Scott notified Brigadier General Ben McCulloch that an organized body of Union men had been discovered and that the citizens of Clinton had arrested six men. One of them confessed that a secret organization sworn to support the North then existed in Searcy and Newton counties. The Clinton citizens had begun searching for and arresting them, and they had 100 men guarding the prisoners in the Clinton jail. Nineteen-year-old John W. Holmes of Hartsugg Township and a man identified as Mr. Garrison were "entitled to this miserable distinction [betrayal of the Peace Society] and should they now be living can lay claim to an amount of misery and destruction altogether beyond their feeble power of atonement."[145]

Confederate recruitment efforts were going strong in November 1861, and Holmes's betrayal of the Peace Society may have been connected, as he tried to avoid military service. He later enlisted on March 1, 1862, in Company D, Thirty-first Arkansas Infantry, and deserted before the end of August. On November 25, Captain Scott informed Captain Lafayette Boone of his squadron stationed in Fulton County that Van Buren County militiamen had arrested and jailed fifty men who had sworn to support the North. One man had confessed that in two weeks the secret society would have begun robbing and murdering secessionists. Van Buren County authorities had requested help in guarding and disposing of the prisoners, but Scott was short-handed at the time and could not help. They then had 100 militiamen guarding the jail, and the prisoners reported that 1,700 throughout north Arkansas had taken the secret oath.[146]

County clerk Bradley also advised General Edmund Burgevin— who was still in Carrollton to raise a regiment from north Arkansas—of the Van Buren County activity. He interrupted his mustering of the Sixteenth Arkansas Infantry to make a quick trip to Clinton, where Colonel Lewis assured him that the report was true and that he had called out 100 men who were making arrests. General Burgevin was "satisfied from his [Lewis's] well-known energy of character and fearless nature, that the matter was in good hands," and left the whole affair with the colonel.[147]

The *Daily State Journal* reported that those already arrested were well supplied with arms and ammunition and implied that those still at large were equally well equipped. General Burgevin reported to the governor that the people in Van Buren and Searcy counties were very disaffected, and he named individuals who were fomenting discontent.[148]

John Rice Homer Scott,
a captain in the Pope
County Volunteers,
was assigned to guard
the north-central
Arkansas border.
(Arkansas State Archives)

Peace Society Counties—north-central Arkansas.
(From "A New Map of Arkansas with its Counties, Towns,
Post Offices, etc.," New Universal Atlas (Philadelphia:
Cowperthwait, DeSilver & Butler, 1855)

Samuel Leslie,
colonel in the Forty-
fifth (Searcy County
Arkansas Militia.
(Courtesy of the author)

Franklin Kuykendall,
chain gang survivor.
(Courtesy of the author)

How to handle the prisoners was a major concern throughout the Peace Society event. It was a strain on local resources. Except for Izard County's first prisoners, who were sent to Colonel Solon Borland as volunteers, most of the prisoners went to Little Rock. Van Buren County's first batch of twenty-seven prisoners must have started out about November 23 to arrive on November 28. This was about the time that Van Buren County clerk Bradley asked Scott for help guarding and disposing of the prisoners. The fifty that had been incarcerated, as Scott had been told on November 24, had been reduced to only twenty-seven. They were jailed in Little Rock, questioned by the Military Board about the society, and held until they could be tried by civil authorities. On November 29 the *Daily State Journal* reported that forty more were on the way.[149]

The twenty-seven Van Buren County prisoners, when further interrogated in Little Rock, maintained that they had joined an organization to protect their homes from robbers and runaway slaves and that they were willing to join the Confederate army, but that they would rather go home to say goodbye to their families first. They claimed to be good Southern men, although they had been for the Union before secession. None admitted to a connection with the North, which makes one wonder what happened to the documentation about joining the Lincoln army. However, William Gadberry's son was assured that 300 men were willing to help him avoid Confederate service. Of the nine men mentioned as swearing others into the society, five were sent to Little Rock: John Smith, Ananias Stobaugh (who was captured with a copy of the oath) John Gilbreath, S. P. Pearce, and A. A. Parsley. Four were able to avoid capture: Chris Denton, Abner Smith, Jonathan Moody, and Henry Bradshaw. Moody and Bradshaw were later captured in Searcy County.[150]

The majority of the twenty-seven Peace Society prisoners were in the northeast part of Van Buren County, next to the Searcy and Izard County line. Smith and Denton and eight of the Clinton prisoners were from Holley Township. Six were from Union Township and one from Turkey Creek Township, all adjoining Searcy County. Two were from Wiley's Cove, Searcy County, on the Van Buren County border. Five were from Griggs Township where Clinton is located.[151]

Fulton and Izard Counties

On November 7, Captain Scott—commanding the cavalry squadron sent to protect the northern border—ordered Captain Lafayette Boone's company of Washington County volunteers to establish his headquarters in Fulton County. He cautioned Boone to cultivate a kind and friendly feeling with the citizens of the county and to endeavor by conciliatory efforts to win over those who might hold Union sentiments but were not in arms against the South. Boone replied on November 12 that he had established his Camp Secession at Talbot's Mill on the North Fork of White River near the Salem road. He commented that he could not learn of any disturbances in Fulton County by Union men, but that a great many of that caste were afraid to make any demonstration of their faith. The citizens seemed pleased that Boone was there and were always kind and disposed to extend favors. Boone spared no pains to cultivate an amicable feeling, respecting their feelings and property.[152]

A week later, the situation had changed. Fulton County representative Jehoida J. Ware, after learning that the Peace Society had been discovered in Clinton, rode home immediately to warn fellow Peace Society men. He then left with forty to fifty men for the Union military post at Rolla, Missouri, where Ware and thirty-nine others were enrolled on December 1 in John S. Phelps's Six-month Missouri Infantry. Ware was made captain, Mark J. Haley of Izard County first lieutenant, and Lorenzo D. Toney, also of Izard County, second lieutenant in Company G. Of the forty men who were enrolled on December 1, eighteen were from Fulton County, seventeen from Izard County, and one from Rapps Barrens, Marion County.[153]

Peace Society men continued throughout December to flee to Rolla and join Ware's company. A December 15 newspaper story reported that several Arkansas citizens had arrived in Rolla during the past week and enlisted in the Arkansas company under

Captain Ware. The recently arrived Arkansans reported that a Union society in Izard, Fulton, Independence, and Searcy counties numbering 2,200 could have made an organized stand in a week's time, but it was betrayed, broken up, and scattered. Many were arrested and taken to Little Rock. Some were hanged, and a large number had gone into the woods trying to escape from the state. Twenty-four men enrolled in Ware's company between December 5 to 14, twelve from Fulton County, six from Izard, four from Marion, and one from Carroll County. There was a reason for these men—and twelve more who enlisted before the end of the year—to go to Rolla.[154]

Such a large number of men leaving at one time drew the community's attention, and news of the Clinton arrests certainly raised suspicions. When Ware left for Rolla, Dr. T. J. Nunnelie's companies went looking for Unionists and accused them of belonging to a secret society opposed to the Confederacy. Their scope was wide ranging, taking a prisoner from Independence County and chasing others twenty-five miles into Missouri before bringing both men back to Fulton County for interrogation. Alexander McBee and his son James McBee, and Gehazi Ball and his son Milford W. Ball, were neighbors in Benton Township in the southwest corner of Howell County on the Arkansas line opposite Fulton County. They were fleeing deeper into Missouri with a hostage, William Strother, when they were captured by Nunnelie's men. According to Strother they had tried to recruit him into the Peace Society, but he had rejected them. The four were afraid they would be betrayed if they turned him loose in Fulton County, so they were taking him along into Missouri, intending to release him when they were far enough into Missouri that Strother could not alert Nunnelie's men.[155]

The Ball and McBee fathers knew of the secret society. Milford Ball lived with his father, Gehazi, in Howell County and both were involved in Fulton County activities. James M. McBee and Milford Ball, traveling with their fathers, claimed ignorance of the Peace Society. Gehazi Ball and Alexander McBee admitted some knowledge of the society but denied joining. As a witness before the Military Board in Little Rock, Strother said he left where he lived (in Franklin Township, Izard County) because his life was in danger and he thought he would go to a more peaceful country. He said he was asked to join a guerrilla band to rob and steal from secessionists, and that he had refused to join. Some of the prisoners claimed that they had never heard of the Peace Society until they were arrested; others said that they had been sworn in only to a lower level. Some were willing to volunteer for Confederate service, but others wanted to go to trial to clear their names. They identified Ware, James A. Ball, Shadrach H. Wren, and H. W. Davis as men who had introduced them to the Peace Society. In addition to the Peace Society members, Nunnelie arrested Benjamin Alsup of Hutton Valley, Howell County, Missouri—a strong Union man— and sent him to Little Rock, where he remained in the penitentiary until Little Rock was captured by the Federals.[156]

Izard County

The Izard County recruits for Ware's company were all from Rocky Bayou (now Lunenburg), Mill Creek, and Union townships in central Izard County. But the documented Peace Society arrests were concentrated in Harris Township on the Searcy County line, where William Aikin had so much opposition recruiting for McCarver's regiment in July, August, and September. Whoever betrayed the Peace Society in Izard County—and the "betrayal" may only have been the departure of several men for Missouri— vigilante activity began on November 18 or 19, within two days after the society was first discovered in Clinton, and shortly after Ware and company fled to Rolla. Izard County's investigative committee report of November 28, 1861, submitted to Governor Rector, included a list of forty-seven names. The report stated, "Some ten days ago it became a matter of publicity in this county that a secret conspiracy against the laws and liberties of the people of this state was on foot, extending from Fulton county this state quite through this and perhaps Searcy & Van Buren counties."[157]

Immediately, citizens formed a vigilance committee, and scouting parties were sent out in every direction to arrest those suspected of connections to the secret conspiracy. They elected an investigative committee to study the organization. It found that the prisoners and others who had not been arrested had formed a secret organization with by-laws and secret signs called the Peace Organization Society. The committee was convinced that the secret society was dangerous and subversive, and probably treasonous. However, the investigative committee knew the persons examined—many of them young boys—and determined that they were led ignorantly into the society. They believed that, since the prisoners had been duped into joining without knowing the Peace Organization Society's real goals, and since the society members were willing to enlist in Confederate service to "wipe out that foul stain," that they should do so. The vigilance committee "accordingly gave them the opportunity of so enlisting, whereupon the whole of them...forty-seven...enrolled their names as volunteers." The enlistees would leave for Colonel Solon Borland's headquarters at Pocahontas as soon as transportation could be arranged. The committee members were concentrated in the western and mountainous half of Izard County where the Peace Society was most pronounced: Daniel Jeffrey, William C. Dixon, and Moses Bishop from White River Township; G. W. Gray and Jesse Hinkle from Rocky Bayou; A. W. Harris from North Fork; Simon E. Rosson from Richwoods; Henry Cole from Sylamore; and T. W. Edmondson and Secretary A. P. Mix from Harris. R. B. Dickson's residence could not be determined. Chairman W. F. B. Treat lived in White River Township, Marion County.[158]

A copy of the Mill Creek Peace Organization Society Constitution from the original furnished by a member of the Society was enclosed with the report.[159]

Rocky Bayou Township (now Lunenburg Township) citizens appointed a committee to investigate men who had been arrested and charged with connections to a treasonable organization. Two of the men—John C. Thompson, age 35, of Rocky Bayou Township, and his brother Pleasant F. Thompson, age 22, of Mill Creek Township—were gathering a herd of cattle to take to Memphis. When the Peace Society was discovered, they began their drive three days early. The *Nashville Union and American* picked up on this story and—in hopes that they might be identified, apprehended, and returned to Arkansas—described John C. Thompson as five feet ten inches tall, with dark complexion and black hair, weighing about 145 or 150 pounds, and P. F. Thompson as about five feet eight inches tall, weighing about 135 or 140 pounds with black hair and whiskers. Later, John C. Thompson joined Captain Lorenzo D. Toney's Company D, First Battalion Six-month Arkansas Infantry (U.S.), on July 1, 1862. Pleasant F. Thompson enrolled July 26, 1862, at Lunenburg in Company C, Twenty-seventh Arkansas Infantry (C.S.) and deserted September 13, 1863. Like the other men who had been arrested and later confessed, the Thompsons stated that they considered the North their friend and the South their enemy, and that they intended to cooperate with the North as soon as an opportunity presented itself. Others revealed that the Peace Society was established in Washington DC and sent to Fremont in Missouri, who spread it to Arkansas. All who had been brought before this committee, and before committees in adjacent counties, were men who had strenuously advocated the doctrines of the North and spoken in terms justifying Lincoln's coercive policy. The newspaper declared that the Peace Society was finished by saying, "Many members of this association have been arrested, but the main props have escaped to Missouri. The whole thing is regarded as a grand fizzle."[160]

Izard County's investigative committee was convinced it had discovered a treasonous plot. Harris Township merchant William M. Aikin served half a day on an investigating committee and helped to examine five men. One of them said that he understood the society to be a movement against secession and that he was joining a secret society in favor of the North and against the South. Aikin said that thirty-four of the prisoners were from Harris Township. In the 1860 Federal Census, twenty-five were in Harris and six in adjoining Sylamore Township. Five were from

Mill Creek, three from White River, and one each from Conway, Richwoods, and Union townships.[161]

On December 3, Governor Rector received the Izard County Investigative Committee's communication that said the Peace Society prisoners had been enlisted in the Confederate army. He then asked Secretary of War Judah P. Benjamin if he or President Davis would sanction their enlistment. Rector said it was the Arkansas authorities' opinion that, if enlisted, they should go south. Benjamin replied on December 5 that due to the distance and lack of the facts, he could not give any advice and told Rector to use his best judgment. Rector decided to enlist the Peace Society men. Sixteen of the forty-seven enlisted in Company H, Eighth Arkansas Infantry. Six more went to Company I.[162]

Colonel Solon Borland, commanding Confederate forces at Pocahontas, learned of the Peace Society arrests in Izard County and elsewhere a few days after their first discovery. On November 27, he advised General Albert Sidney Johnston, commanding the Western Department at Bowling Green, Kentucky, of the situation. Borland promised to send an expedition to aid in suppressing this insurrectionary movement. He wrote Johnston again on December 11 to report that the two infantry companies he had sent to Izard County had returned. The troubles were less serious than he had heard. By the time his expedition had arrived at the troubled area, the loyal citizens of the several neighborhoods had organized themselves into companies of home guards for their own protection, leaving little for Borland's two companies to do other than to collect the fifty-seven prisoners who were taken or had voluntarily surrendered. The divergence in Borland's figures and that of the committee may indicate that the committee had picked up ten more prisoners before Borland's men left.

To prove their Southern loyalty the prisoners volunteered to join the army, and Borland permitted those that were suitable to enlist. They enrolled on December 12 at Pocahontas. Both companies had previously been formed on November 6, so they were placed in already existing companies. The sixteen men that joined

Company H, Eighth Infantry, and another six that joined Company I, all enrolled December 12, the day after they arrived, an indication of how rapidly their wish to serve was fulfilled. Those that would not make good soldiers were made mechanics, teamsters, and other auxiliaries. They were armed by impressing guns from the local community. Borland questioned his prisoners and came away with the impression that none of them had committed any overt acts of disloyalty. He concluded:

> Most of them are ignorant men; and although they have continued to be, ever since the accession of Arkansas to the Southern Confederacy, Union men in their associations at least, if not in their real sentiments and decided connections yet they are not found to have engaged in any act of open disloyalty to our Government. The most of them moreover, declare their innocence of any such intentions, alleging that if they have done wrong at all in this respect, they had been misled by others who have made their escape from the country.[163]

Just as the Fulton County Peace Society investigation immediately implicated Izard County, particularly Harris Township, arrests in Harris Township also involved neighboring Big Flat and Locust Grove townships in Searcy County on the Izard County line.

Searcy County

Colonel Samuel Leslie, Forty-fifth (Searcy County) Arkansas Militia, learned on November 20 that about 100 people in Locust Grove Township, Searcy County, were arresting men and confining them. He was not told why. Leslie immediately sent for Adjutant Major Jesse Cypert. As soon as he arrived, they left for Locust Grove Township, about twenty miles away. They arrived late at night at Henry Bradshaw's home, where they found about fifty citizens of Locust Grove and Big Flat townships and some from adjoining Izard County. The men had learned that there was a

secret organization hostile to the Confederacy and had voluntarily, without legal authority, turned out to arrest those suspected
of being in the organization. The first man arrested, said to be
James Treat, revealed the whole secret of sworn bond, secret signs,
and passwords. This information convinced Leslie that the Peace
Society was the beginning of an insurrection.

Excitement was high, and the vigilantes urged Leslie to take
charge and call out the militia. Leslie did so on November 22,
calling out Company A of Big Flat Township under Lieutenant
A. R. Sisk and Company E of adjoining Locust Grove Township
under Captain John R. Redwine, ordering them to arrest as many
members of the secret organization as possible. Also on November
22 he organized support for the militia, ordering Joseph Stephenson
to act as commissary to furnish the militiamen with provisions,
and breveting Lieutenant Sisk as captain in the absence of Company
A's Captain Gibson B. Alexander. On the twenty-third and twenty-fourth, Companies A and E were making arrests. Militia officers
promised that they "wouldn't harm ary hair on their head," which
induced a great many to come in voluntarily, acknowledging their
association with the Peace Society. Others were pulled away from
whatever they were doing.

Alexander Copeland was putting away cabbages for the winter,
and his daughter Mary J. Copeland was carrying them to him, when
the militiamen walked up with their guns and said, "Copeland, we
have use for you. You belong to the League [*sic* Peace Society]," and
they took him away.[164]

Peace Society member Benjamin G. Watts wrote:

> Along about November 1861 Capt Sam Leslie had head-
> quarters at Marshall [Burrowville], and John Redwine was
> a Captain in the Confederate Home Guards and a man by
> the name of [William G.] Garrison and one by the name
> Harris were also officers in the Confederate Militia. These
> men with squads of men under them scoured the county
> and by force took the Union men from their homes or
> wherever they happened to find them and conducted them

under close guard to Marshall where we were about 15 days kept under close guard and in confinement.[165]

Watts also said:

One James Treat gave the organization away and it was reported that we were organized to murder women and children and a band of citizens under Sam Leslie began to arrest us and put us in the Courthouse at Burrowville. I was arrested by one [Waddy Thorpe] Hunt, but I do not know who arrested Benjamin H. Gary, but I know that they brought him in and that we were kept there two weeks. The Sheriff [Thomas M. Alexander] had nothing to do with this, but Col. Leslie was the leader and it is possible that he held a commission from the Governor and we were compelled to surrender by superior numbers. There was quite a crowd with those that arrested me.

All men mentioned in Watts's narratives belonged to John R. Redwine's Company E (Locust Grove), Forty-fifth Arkansas Militia, which was called up on November 22, 1861.[166]

Local citizens, in addition to alerting Colonel Leslie, also requested help from Captain Scott. On November 24, while en route to see Captain Scott in southeast Carroll County, Second Lieutenant J. L. Wilson, Company H, Fourteenth (Powers) Arkansas Infantry, and John Berry Treat of Big Flat Township, Searcy County met one of Captain Boone's lieutenants. They entrusted a letter and details of the Peace Society turmoil to him and returned to Yellville. The letter informed Scott that they had obtained the plans of insurrectionists in Searcy, Van Buren, and Izard counties, that they had arrested fifty prisoners, and that they had 200 more names of men who had not been captured. About forty men had sent a messenger to know under what terms they could surrender.

About 150 citizens were engaged in arresting the traitors. According to the letter, the Unionist plan was to kill and rob every man who was not a friend of the North, beginning two weeks from that time. The writers wanted Scott's help to take care of prisoners and to give instructions about what the vigilantes should do. They asked him to come to Joseph Wallace's at Big Flat, Searcy County. If none of his command knew the way, he could get a guide in Yellville. The hunt was up in Searcy County, and some hunters wanted help and instructions.[167]

On November 25, Leslie ordered the two companies to Burrowville. They arrived the next day with thirty prisoners who were lodged in the courthouse under guard. A January 1861 visitor to Burrowville had this to say about the town and its courthouse; "Burrowville a very small miserable looking place a few shanties and about 3 small frame houses. The Courthouse is a small inferior looking building." To follow the ever-expanding area to which his investigation led him, the next day Leslie ordered into service Company C of Wiley's Cove Township under Captain Samuel L. Redwine, Company F of Campbell Township under Captain Jesse L. Johnson, Company D of Bear Creek Township under Captain Morgan M. Terry, and Company G of Sulphur Springs and Red River townships under Captain William S. Goodnight. All arrived in Burrowville that same day, except Company G, which arrived the following day, November 27. Also on November 26, Leslie sent a dispatch to the governor advising him of the discovery of the Peace Society, describing what action he had taken, and asking what should be done with the prisoners.[168]

The prisoners were kept in the courthouse, guarded by the militia, for about two weeks, although some prisoners later thought that they had been there for fifteen days or three weeks. Militia service was mandatory for all able-bodied men, so the Searcy County Militia invariably contained Peace Society men. The guards were described as "mixed up of both Union and Confederates who lived there. There were rather more Union than secessionists in the militia." The militia armed themselves with confiscated weapons from the citizenry, but "they didn't have many arms and those were given to the most active for secession. The others were compelled to stay there on duty, doing chores, bringing wood, etc."[169]

News of the arrests in Van Buren and eastern Searcy counties spread rapidly through the country, and Peace Society men believed they had to state their innocence. On November 25, thirty to forty Peace Society men met at David C. Ruff's home in Calf Creek Township, Searcy County, to consider their situation. They passed a series of resolutions proclaiming their innocence of any intention of outlawry but stated that all men who wanted to stay peacefully at home were considered enemies and guilty of treason.

They were ready to take up arms against any body of robbers to maintain peace and their liberties, and they were willing for a full investigation, but they proclaimed their right of self-protection. This statement was their attempt to remain neutral like virtually all the Peace Society members, but it was a hopeless task. There is no evidence that these resolutions were presented to Leslie or that they would have had any effect if they had been.[170]

Leslie's messengers, Richard N. Melton and Robert Dewitt Clinton Griffin, arrived in Little Rock on November 28, the same day the Van Buren County prisoners arrived. That same day Colonel Leslie formally mustered into service the six companies he had ordered out. Leslie had called up all the Searcy County militia companies except for Richland Township (on the western border with Newton County, Calf Creek Township which lay just to the east of Richland), Mount Pleasant Township [Mountain] in the extreme southwest corner of the county, and the three townships north of the Buffalo River: Prairie, Tomahawk, and Buffalo. He would later order out the Richland company. These six townships out of thirteen would each present its own problems.

The news of the Peace Society discovery on November 17 reached Little Rock to be published on November 26. The Little Rock press had already printed stories of the Tennessee bridge burners on November 12, 13, 15, and 21. An editorial in Little Rock's *Daily State Journal* on November 30 considered the Peace Society situation, whether to be charged with robbery and tried in local courts or with high treason and tried before the Confederate court in Little Rock. The editorial made a comparison with the Tennessee activity. It commented:

Our authorities have the example of the East Tennesseans
before them. Clemency was exercised toward them. The
strong arm of the law was withheld by the executive and
now we have our reward in the burning of the bridges, the
interruption of travel along the most important railroad in
the Confederacy, and scattered camps of enemies in nearly
every county in that section. Perhaps our neighbors in Van
Buren and Searcy counties have never intended anything
as formidable as the miscreants of East Tennessee. Their
designs are, however, treasonable, their association cher-
ished no kind feelings toward the constitutional authorities,
and they were in communication with persons at the north.
Justice administered hereafter to those taken will have a
most salutary effect upon any inclined hereafter to engage
in such an enterprise.[171]

Governor Rector, as well as many in Arkansas, was thinking
of the East Tennessee bridge burners. On November 30—two days
after the Van Buren County prisoners arrived and the governor
received Leslie's report—the subject of that traitorous conspiracy
had enlisted the attention of the law-abiding community. "If
the prisoners are charged with treason then they would be held
to account by the Confederate Court at Little Rock." The press
reminded the authorities of the example of the East Tennesseans.
Governor Rector did not intend to withhold the strong arm of the
law, and the East Tennessee example was before the authorities in
Arkansas.[172]

Arkansas's authorities were surprised at the discovery of the
Peace Society. At first Governor Rector seemed unsure of the course
he should follow, but he soon determined what to do. Rector replied
to Leslie immediately, saying, "I regret **extremely** that any of our
citizens should prove disloyal to their government. But if they so
conducted themselves, the powers of those in authority must be
exercised to preserve peace and enforce obedience to the constitution and the laws." He wrote that Arkansas had left the Union and
joined the Confederacy by act of the convention, and although there
might be a minority opposed to this, theirs was a government where

the majority ruled and the minority must submit. Undesirables, one or many rebelling against its laws, must be looked after for the safety of the country; if it were necessary to arrest and imprison them or to execute them for treason that would be done. Therefore, Rector ordered Leslie to arrest all men in Searcy County who professed friendship for the Lincoln government or who harbored or supported those hostile to the Confederacy or Arkansas, and he directed them to march them to Little Rock, where they would be dealt with as enemies of the country. Melton and Griffin returned to Leslie on December 1 with the governor's orders. So much for "not harming ary hair on their head."[173]

Colonel Leslie was shocked that the Peace Society had been discovered in Searcy County. The month before, he had assured the governor that the people of Searcy County had accepted that they had to be loyal to the government they lived under and that those were the feelings of the people of Searcy County as far as he had any knowledge. On November 28, the date the Van Buren County prisoners and Leslie's report arrived, Rector telegraphed Confederate president Davis that "a conspiracy has been discovered in the northern part of this State against the Confederate government. Secret oaths, signs and passwords adopted. Their intention seems to be to join Lincoln's army if it gets into Arkansas. Twenty-seven men have been arrested and brought here today and now in prison. A hundred more will doubtless be brought in a day or so. They say there are 1,700 in the State."[174]

In the meantime, Leslie's scouting parties were arresting everyone who could be tied to the Peace Society. Those that were arrested frequently implicated others, so eventually a lengthy list of possible members was developed. Most readily admitted their involvement and named others. However, some claimed ignorance and were dismissed with charges unproven. Ebenezer B. Jameson, a member of the Peace Society, was arrested by the militia and confined in Burrowville for two days, but they could not prove anything against him, and he was released. The authorities were still suspicious, so he hid out.

On December 21, he was forced into the Confederate service, which he deserted to join the federal Third Arkansas Cavalry. In their naivetés, some men rode into Burrowville to learn what was happening and were immediately arrested. John W. Morris of Calf Creek Township had heard that Union men were being arrested without cause in Burrowville, but he could not believe it. On November 28, Morris and his brother-in-law Beverly Conley rode into Burrowville to see if the rumors of arrests were true. They had scarcely arrived in town, gotten off their horses, hitched them, and walked a few steps before two double-barreled shotguns were thrust in their faces by John Smith and Mark Hogan, who took them prisoner. They were taken before one of Leslie's officers and questioned closely, then taken to the courthouse and imprisoned. Hogan was regimental judge advocate, Smith a private in Bear Creek's militia company. Similarly, Frank Kuykendall, who had only arrived in Searcy County the previous December from Georgia, rode in from Campbell Township to Burrowville to learn the latest war news and attend to some business; on entering town he was arrested. Others, more cautious, fled to the woods.[175]

North of the Buffalo River

The squadron of Pope County Volunteer Cavalry, commanded by Captain John Rice Homer Scott, had moved to Camp Culloden in Jefferson Township, southeast Carroll County, by September 17 in search of forage. J. T. Bradley, the Van Buren County clerk, had notified Captain Scott of the Peace Society discovery and arrests. He continued to keep Scott updated on events in Clinton. On November 23, the Van Buren County clerk reported they had about fifty Peace Society men and asked Scott to aid in guarding and disposing of the prisoners. Scott commented that he was shorthanded and could do nothing definite until Lieutenant M. I. Anderson returned from a scout.[176]

Scott saw his mandate as only to defend the border from Missouri invasion and to send scouts into Missouri to disperse

Unionists or to investigate rumors of Union troop movements. He was aware of the Unionist sentiment in the area, but the region was quiet and he did not do anything to disturb it. On the contrary, he had cautioned Captain Boone to treat the natives kindly in order to win them to the Confederacy. Southern companies mining saltpeter in Newton County for the Confederate government had requested that his squadron provide security to protect them from Newton County Unionists, but there is no evidence that he did. On November 24, when citizens requested help with Peace Society prisoners taken on the Izard–Searcy County line, Scott commented that until Lieutenant Anderson returned, he did not have the men to send to the Searcy-Izard area. Anderson was regularly sent on escort and scout duties, so his absence was routine. Scott's squadron often kept scouts out watching for federal activity near Forsythe, and he did not have the men to assist local vigilantes in arresting their fellow citizens or to protect Confederate contractors from perceived threats by the natives.[177]

Scott continued to forward Van Buren County updates to McCulloch, his superior. Then, on November 26, David Smith and George W. Smith of Jefferson Township, Carroll County, brought Thomas J. Faught and his brother William C. Faught (both of Tomahawk Township, Searcy County) before Kelly Featherston, justice of the peace (JP) for Jefferson Township. The two Smiths may have been vigilantes, since they are not mentioned as belonging to Scott's squadron. The Faught brothers were brought before the JP court on suspicion of being connected to a secret organization for subjugating the Southern states and in joining a company of men to liberate the prisoners in Burrowville and Clinton. The Faughts were questioned about the sentiments of their neighbors and about any attempt to free the prisoners.

They identified Solomon Branum of Whiteville Township, Marion County, and Mike Tinkle of Tomahawk Township as leaders in attempting to release the Peace Society prisoners in Clinton and Burrowville. John Brown, a twenty-one-year-old Tomahawk resident, had been alerting the neighborhood of the arrests of Bear Creek

Township residents William Kimbell and John Reeves and of his desire to release them. Mike Tinkle then took up the cause by trying to raise men to free all the prisoners. They planned to meet at 8:00 p.m. Sunday, November 24, at Peter Reeves's house in Tomahawk Township, go to Eli P. Dawson's on Forest Creek near Burrowville, and, at daylight on November 25, to go to Burrowville and free the prisoners. Mike Tinkle reported there were seventy armed men at Dawson's and 100 armed men accounted for in Burrowville, however. There is no evidence that an attempt was ever made at Burrowville. Whether the Faughts' capture alerted the authorities or the Union men lost heart is not clear. But these activities did alert Captain Scott that he had an active Unionist movement in his neighborhood.

Of the thirty-two men the Faughts profiled, they identified nineteen as Unionists, seven as pro-Confederacy to some extent (they had sons in the army), and six as unknown. Among the nineteen Unionists, class opposition to slaveholders was important; humanitarian feelings toward slaves were nil. Samuel Thompson believed that in the Confederacy the poor man would be looked on as no better than a black man by the Southern rich, and that the rich would make the poor fight the battles. William Brown said that in the Confederacy poor folks would be looked on as no more than blacks. Eight saw equality with slaves in the Confederacy as their principal cause to oppose the Confederacy. Joshua Reeves had said that if the slaves had been bought and sent off years ago in the Liberia movement there would have been no war. He agreed with Peter Reeves Sr. that man had no more right to take a man's slave than to take (or free) his horse. Ten were for the "old Union" and the Constitution. Class struggle was the deciding factor among the Tomahawk Unionists, as it was in other parts of Arkansas. On December 5, 1861, the *True Democrat* reported on Peace Society (Pro Bono Publico) activity more than a month before in Monroe and St. Francis counties, saying "There was a great deal of mischievous humbuggery in it about the rich and poor, and an attempt to array non-slaveholders against slaveholders."[178]

Scott began arresting and questioning those identified by the Faughts. Charles W. Price, age 22, lived at the head of Tomahawk Creek when some men went to the Price home to arrest him for belonging to a secret organization. Finding him hiding in a stone smokehouse (which still stands), they dragged him out. He begged them to leave him with his family. Malinda, his pregnant wife, begged them not to take him, and she cried and prayed, but Scott's men led him away afoot with a rope around his waist and tied to one of their horses. That was the last Malinda ever saw of him—praying to be left alone, dragged behind their horses. On December 3, Scott reported the situation to General McCulloch. He said he had between thirty-five and forty men under arrest and was daily bringing in more, positively proven to belong to a secret society, held together by secret signs, tokens, and passwords, and under the penalty of death should a member reveal their secrets. By their own confessions and implication of others, Scott obtained their oaths, signs, and tokens. He concluded that the organization's object was to subdue the South and was of Northern origin, but he did not know how it was introduced into Arkansas. Scott felt it positively breathed treason and insurrection, and numbered several hundred, extending through Fulton, Izard, Searcy, Newton, Van Buren, parts of Conway, Pope, Marion, and Carroll counties. Nearly 100 had been arrested in Clinton, Van Buren County, and Burrowville in Searcy County. Scott's prisoners were from Marion, Searcy, Newton, and Carroll counties, all around his camp. It seemed almost universal in some localities. He wrote:

> We need not go north to find our enemies, they are all around me bound together by solemn secret oaths &c. Some of the prisoners have stated it was an understanding that if the Northern Army did drive your [McCulloch's at Wilson's Creek] command before them that this Squadron would have been attacked or that they "laid such hints" and if I made or attempted to arrest persons in certain places (after I commenced making them and their plans &c. were detected), that they would "give me a fight."

Scott recommended that he station some of the companies of his command in Wiley's Cove, Searcy County, where there was a Methodist camp meeting ground with some good buildings and a very large arbor, conveniently located in the vicinity of this secret society.[179]

The excitement continued to increase with many rumors—including one that was taken seriously—that a large body of men was assembling in the western part of the county to resist arrest. On December 2, Leslie called out Richland Township's Company B under Captain William A. Wyatt to come to Burrowville for muster. It reported December 4 and was mustered on December 5. En route it lost fifteen men to desertion. They belonged to the Peace Society and feared arrest in Burrowville. By this time Leslie had seventy-two prisoners held in the courthouse in Burrowville, and he was preparing to send them to Little Rock in accordance with the governor's orders. Richard N. Melton, one of Leslie's messengers, was a thirty-nine-year-old farmer living in Wiley's Cove who had some blacksmith skills and a forge. He was told to make rings to go around the prisoners' necks for transportation to Little Rock.[180]

Measles broke out among the prisoners held in the courthouse and spread to some of the militiamen. The virus hung around and infected some of Captain Scott's men when they came to Burrowville in late December. The measles outbreak would complicate moving the prisoners to Little Rock, as only militiamen who were immune to measles could escort the prisoners.[181]

As Leslie was planning to send his prisoners to Little Rock, he sought to coordinate his plans with Captain Scott. On December 3, he wrote Scott that he now had seventy-four prisoners, and more were being brought in daily. To preserve peace and arrest the guilty ones, he had decided to move them to Little Rock immediately. This was necessary because some had become sick and others probably would sicken if kept any longer cooped up in the courthouse. In addition, the militia was in bad condition, exposed to the winter weather, and some were unfit for duty because of sickness and other reasons, making it impossible both to guard the prisoners day and night and to operate outside. Leslie asked Scott to send his prisoners with forty or sixty men with tents and camp equipage immediately to help Leslie get his prisoners to Little Rock. Apparently, none of Scott's men arrived at Burrowville in time to aid Leslie.[182]

On December 8, Leslie prepared his prisoners for the march. With the rings made by Melton fastened around their necks, harness trace chains were then used to chain them in pairs, and a log chain—running down the center of the column—fastened all the pairs together in one long coffle. Trying out this chaining method, the authorities learned that fastening the pairs together made the coffle unwieldy, so they removed the log chain, and the prisoners were only chained in pairs. R. D. Clinton Griffin said that the governor had given orders for the prisoners to be safely carried before him, and the militia officers thought it would be safest to take trace chains and chain them by the neck so they could not get away.

Militiaman Joseph Hurley had been ordered to chain the prisoners, but he refused, and thereafter he was a suspect person. Griffin fastened the rings and chain around the prisoners' necks, but he had qualms of conscience. Asa Watts remembered that when it came his turn to be chained, Griffin said, "Ace, I hate to do this." When Griffin came to Asa's brother Benjamin G. Watts, he cried out and refused to chain him. They had been friends from boyhood and had played together. The way the prisoners were chained was humiliating, and their relatives commented that they were chained like slaves.[183]

They remained chained in pairs overnight before they began the trip to Little Rock on December 9. Leslie did not wait for Scott's prisoners. Brevet Lieutenant Colonel Alexander Ham was in charge of a 100-man detail that included Major John Bradshaw and Adjutant Major Jesse Cypert. Leslie sent a list of the names of seventy-eight prisoners, which has not survived. Leslie had no additional testimony beyond that of the prisoners, which is also lost. Leslie commented in his report to the governor that most of the prisoners came in and surrendered, acknowledging their guilt and their willingness to abide by the laws of the country. But there were several men implicated in the secret order who were skulking about in the woods. Leslie wrote that he would do all he could to take them and bring them to justice. He opined that it seemed that the whole country had become engaged in this matter to some extent, and if they had not been discovered when they were, there was no telling what the consequence would have been. Men considered to be among the best citizens acknowledged membership in the secret order, said to be a Home Guard for home protection.[184]

Leslie kept three prisoners that were too sick to travel but promised to send them later. Only seventy-seven made the trip to Little Rock. At the last minute the seventy-eighth man must have been declared too sick to make the trip. Prisoner John W. Morris recalled that the odd-numbered prisoner, fifty-six-year-old Miliken Bratton, carried the other end of the chain thrown over his shoulder. Concerned with the safety of the prisoners, Leslie ordered Alex Ham to "convey the prisoners now in your care safely to Little Rock and there deliver them to the Executive of the State, together with this order and the names of them attached to this order. You will also be careful that they are not mistreated while under your care by anyone." Apparently, the attitude of some of the guards required this special concern to ensure the prisoners were not mistreated. Colonel Leslie claimed that he chained the prisoners for their own protection, as there was much bad feeling and some of the guards wanted a chance to shoot the prisoners. Years later when members of the chain gang were making depositions for federal pensions, they could remember their chained partners.[185]

The chain gang's first night was spent near the Middle Fork of the Little Red River, just across the Van Buren County line, where Thomas Archer (who lived nearby) said that the prisoners chained in pairs with a ring around their necks were marched past his house. They camped nearby, and he went to visit them and talked with them until bedtime. Just as some of the guards may have been looking for an excuse to shoot the prisoners, others were more kindly disposed.

Seventeen-year-old James H. Campbell of Company F (Campbell Township) said his sympathy was with the prisoners. He helped them with rations and prepared poles to help make tents for protection against the cold rain. His help won their sympathy and regard ever afterward, and that of their families. Among the prisoners were his future brother-in-law, Ananias J. Sutterfield, his uncles by marriage Anderson Blasingame and Nathaniel J. Sutterfield, and his uncle John Campbell's son-in-law John W. Morris. William J. Kelley, First Sergeant, Company F (Campbell Township), said that the Confederates carried the prisoners chained together to Little Rock, where the governor told the prisoners that they could go in the rebel army or be cast into prison. It was generally believed that the chained men would be killed if they did not join the rebel army. He had friends and relatives in the chained bunch who wanted him to go along to see what became of them. He accompanied them to Little Rock and saw the prisoners in the State House under guard who were still chained when he left.[186]

Among the guards were Peace Society men who had not been identified. This raised the hope that the chained men might escape. They did not, and John F. Treadwell, a prisoner, explained why:

> There were a great many members of the Union League [sic] who were forced into the militia....I had two brothers-in-law both members of the League [sic]. I was chained to one of them, William Thompson, and the other one, who they did not know was a member, was one of the League [sic] was one of the militia and helped guard us with a gun all the way to Little Rock. We had numerous conferences with those in the militia who were loyal men and with them we were about equal to the secessionists. They were ready to make an attack to set us free when we thought best, but as we were chained together, we gave it up as hopeless. We had a conference about escaping every night when our friends were on guard."[187]

The prisoners arrived in Little Rock on December 14 and were taken directly to the State House. They were placed upstairs in the

House Chamber, where they were confronted by Governor Rector. He read them the part of the Confederate Constitution that dealt with treason and pronounced them guilty of that crime. Then he gave them a choice of joining the Confederate army or going to prison. The recollections of the details of this choice differ from person to person. Some thought he promised at least six months in prison before being brought to trial and sentenced to death. Others anticipated a more immediate execution. Some thought he said that the Searcy County officers had urged the choice of enlistment over prison and trial. B. G. Watts said the governor asked why they were chained and to strike the chains off immediately. Whatever the details, all but two of the chain gang men volunteered for service and were sworn in. The exceptions were two Baptist preachers, William Morris and William Hays, who were thrown into prison and not given the opportunity to enlist. However, they were released after a few weeks. The seventy-five men could select the non-commissioned officers from among themselves, but the commissioned officers came from the militia guard. John Jasper Dawson was made captain, Morgan M. Terry first lieutenant, and John H. Bradshaw second lieutenant, though whether they were elected or appointed is unclear. The men were mustered on December 18 as Company I, Eighteenth (Marmaduke's) Arkansas Infantry. The time between arrival and mustering in was dedicated to interrogation by the Military Board. The December 17 *Daily State Journal* reported that:

> While it was admitted that there was a secret bound orga-
> nization in that region of the country called the "Peace
> and Home Protection" Association, it could not be made
> to appear that its objects contemplated any more criminal
> intent than to ensure against the hostilities of an invading
> army. The leaders of this movement, doubtless contem-
> plated ulterior objects of a much more criminal character,
> but the majority of their followers were doubtless ignorant
> of those purposes, many of them, in fact, being under the
> impression that they were doing credible service to their
> country....Every consideration of patriotism and humanity
> plead in their favor; they were accordingly released, and

forthwith...were sworn into the service of the Confederate States, "for and during the war."[188]

The Memphis press's highly imaginative story downplayed the Peace Society's importance and declared it finished, and the story was picked up throughout the South:

> Memphis, Dec. 17—The peace society recently discovered in Arkansas is a good fizzle. It originated in Washington City, and was sent through Fremont to Arkansas. The members consider the North friendly and the South their enemies. They have signs and passwords, and are to have signs placed over their doors of members to prevent the destruction of their property when the Federals commence the destruction of the Southern people. The members take a horrid oath to assist each other at the peril of life. Many of the members have been arrested and some have escaped. A similar association existed among the Unionists in East Tennessee.

There is no evidence in the existing documentation that the Peace Society originated in Washington DC or that General John C. Fremont (or any other Union soldier) brought it to Arkansas, despite various stories to that effect.[189]

North of the River

Scott persuaded the Carroll County Jefferson Township justices of the peace to set up court at his Camp Culloden headquarters as his investigating board and court for his prisoners, but others besides Scott were searching for Peace Society members. Nathan Woodworth was a thirty-nine-year-old farmer born in Genesee County, New York, who had married Nancy Younger from the extensive Unionist Younger family of Tomahawk Township and had four minor children. He had purchased forty acres just south of the Buffalo River on the Newton–Searcy County line. On December 4, 1861, he was brought before Judge Jacob B. Turney and

Justice of the Peace Kelly Featherston sitting as a court of inquiry, charged with knowledge of the Peace Society.

The citizens of Cave Creek, Newton County, had schemed to arrest Woodworth. Daniel R. Chambers of Scott's command, returning from leave in Pope County, learned of the plans to arrest Woodworth. He thought the Cave Creek people were "pretty exercised" about Woodworth being a Unionist and about some language he had used against President Davis, so he went along to arrest Woodworth and to ensure that he was not harmed. One of the arresting party, Dr. William R. McMahan, rode up to Woodworth's house at night and asked to spend the night; saying he was from Fremont's army.

Woodworth let him stay, but when they went out to put up the doctor's horse, he was arrested by McMahan, Chambers, and Hugh Bonds, a fellow Pope County Volunteer returning from leave. Before the court, Woodworth denied all knowledge of the Peace Society or its signs and passwords. The court found no evidence against Woodworth to show his guilt and ordered his release.[190]

There were others arrested who were released. On a list of eighteen Searcy County men under investigation, all appear on subsequent prisoner lists except five from Tomahawk Township, who apparently were not charged: Peter Reeves, age forty, said the Peace Society was proposed to him but he objected, and he was not sworn; Josiah Lane, age forty-nine, had the oath proposed to him in part, but he objected; Robert Tinkle, age twenty-seven, denied it all; William Caler, age twenty-five, took the oath but objected to it. Later Caler gave a more detailed explanation of his release: "In the fall a squad of Confederates came into my neighborhood and by force took quite a number of us to Valley Springs." (Scott's Camp Culloden was near Valley Springs.)

While he was there, "the motherly kindness of a lady, who, with her husband, stood very high with them (Morrison by name) caused me to be sent home to help take care of my mother and [her] children. The others were taken to Little Rock." Similarly, charges had been brought against Daniel P. Sims, age forty-two, of Jasper,

Newton County. His neighbors on December 6 certified to Scott that he had not been in Burrowville or Searcy County since May 1 and that he was a strong Southern man in word and action. They blamed the charges on the prejudices of the Unionist party, which was numerous on Big Creek, Newton County. Despite the frequent references to Unionist and Peace Society activity in Newton County, there are no Newton County men on any lists of prisoners.[191]

On December 5, 1861, an unidentified witness identified Lorenzo D. Jameson and Wesley Hensley as the persons who administered the oath to him and identified David C. Baker as a member. Justices of the Peace William Owens and Kelly Featherston ordered that the three be arrested and brought before the court. Sergeant G. H. Hickman led a five-man detail to look for them, but the three men had gone into hiding. However, the next day, December 6, David C. Baker accompanied by John Christy, his sons Joseph C. Christy and James F. H. Christy, and Porter M. Hensley and Gilmore Smith appeared voluntarily before the court. They told the court that there was a society represented to them as a Peace Society Organization; that it had been endorsed as a good means of protecting their homes, property, and family against robbers and thieves; and that the best men and oldest citizens of the county were members of it. By this representation, they were induced to join and took the oaths as members.

Immediately this revelation produced a petition signed by thirty Searcy County citizens, four of whom were slaveholders. They insisted that since the testimony of these men was voluntary, and that they had been deceived into joining the society, they should be released, as should all others who voluntarily testified against the Peace Society. Justices of the Peace Featherston and Owens and Captain Scott all endorsed the petition and joined in the application to the governor for the release of the Christys, Hensley, Smith, and Baker, as well as all others who came in voluntarily to testify. Thirty-nine years later, James F. Homer Christy recalled in his pension application: "[We] was caught by the Rebels and taken before one of their officers and tried for treason, as they so called it, and was convicted by the Rebel courts and was sent to Little Rock, Arkansas about one hundred and fifty miles distance."[192]

On December 9, the Carroll County court committed twenty-two prisoners for further trial and ordered that Captain Scott have them taken to Little Rock. The timing was Scott's, but he must have felt that he needed the court's cachet. In addition, the court placed John Christy, Joseph C. Christy, J. F. H. Christy, Porter M. Hensley, Gilmore Smith, Carroll Kilburn, E. L. Dodson, Carlton Keeling, George M. Hays, J. W. Kirkham, John McEntire, and James C. McNair under $500 bond each to appear at once before the governor to testify regarding the Peace Society.[193]

Scott started the twenty-two prisoners to Little Rock on December 9 with Lieutenant M. I. Anderson in charge of a seventy-five-man guard detail. The twenty-two men were chained, but it was expected that those under bond to appear before the governor would accompany Anderson. The prisoners included two from Carroll County, six from Marion County, and fourteen from Searcy County. Four were preachers/farmers, sixteen were farmers, one was a school teacher, and one was a physician. Scott had sent Anderson via Burrowville to pick up Leslie's prisoners, but it appears that he was a day or more late. Leslie's prisoners also started on December 9 and were gone when Anderson arrived. Scott's prisoners arrived in Little Rock on December 16, two days after Leslie's, and seven of the fourteen bonded men were with them: John Christy, Joseph C. Christy, James F. H. Christy, Gilmore Smith, Porter M. Hensley, Carroll Kilburn, and David C. Baker. Three of the bonded men who did not accompany Anderson to Little Rock—George M. Hays, Eli L. Osborn and John W. Kirkham—enlisted in Company H, Fourteenth (Powers) Arkansas Infantry on December 23, 1861.[194]

On that same day Colonel W. C. Mitchell, commanding the Fourteenth Arkansas Infantry, advised the governor that three men enlisted in Captain R. E. Trimble's company, Mitchell's regiment, from Marion and Carroll counties that were bonded to appear at Little Rock. If the governor wished them conveyed to Little Rock, then the governor could make out a requisition for

them. Mitchell assured Rector that they were in safe hands and
would be kept safely, subject to his demand. Bonded men John
McEntire and James C. McNair fled to the woods.[195]

When Scott's twenty-two prisoners and seven bonded men
arrived in Little Rock, they were encouraged to join the Confederate
colors. Ira G. Robertson's Rector Guards had been recruiting in
central Arkansas since sometime before November 9 without much
success.

By December 16, when Anderson arrived with the Camp
Culloden prisoners, they still needed men. Eighteen of Scott's
twenty-two prisoners plus the seven bonded men enlisted in
Robertson's company. The Rector Guards could use still more,
so seventeen of the Van Buren County prisoners, who had been
in jail in Little Rock since November 28, also enlisted. With all
this assistance Captain Ira J. Robertson only mustered seventy,
including officers. They were mustered on December 19 as part of
the First Battalion Arkansas Infantry, which almost immediately
became Company K, Eighteenth (Marmaduke's) Arkansas Infantry.
They were immediately placed on board the steamer *Alamo* with
Dawson's company. The *Daily State Journal* praised the formation
of the two companies: "This is pretty good day's work for one man,
but Capt. Rector has a peculiar way of doing business." The *Alamo*
took the two companies as far as Memphis, where they awaited rail
transportation to Bell Station near Bowling Green, Kentucky.[196]

While the prisoners were being prepared to march to Little
Rock, Scott's men were out looking for additional suspicious men.
Benjamin F. Slay, Thomas J. Slay, and Lewis S. Brewer, residents of
Richland Township, Searcy County, were captured on December 8
in Newton County and taken to Jeremiah Meeks, justice of the peace
in Richland Township, Newton County. All three stated they had
left home because of the troubles or excitement in Searcy County.
The Slays said they were going to the Indian Territory; Brewer said
he was going to Clarksville to work. They claimed that Benjamin
F. Brantly and Paris Strickland had tried to recruit them and had
given them some knowledge of the Peace Society, but they said

that their names appeared on no list, nor had they signed anything. (Their names did appear on lists.) On December 10, the three men were brought before the justice of the peace court under Featherston and Owens at Camp Culloden on suspicion of a connection with, or knowledge of, secrets and oaths of a treasonable and insurrectionary society. After examination, they were considered, for want of sufficient evidence, to be not guilty and so were discharged from custody. They then swore allegiance to the State of Arkansas and to the Confederate States and also swore to support and defend them against the federal government or invasion. The Slays later, in July 1862, joined Company H, First Arkansas Cavalry (U.S.).[197]

Also on December 10, George M. Hays and John W. Kirkham, both of Jefferson Township, Carroll County, and John McEntire and J. C. McNair, both of Tomahawk Township, Searcy County—implicated in a secret treasonable and insurrectionary society—acknowledged themselves to be indebted to the State of Arkansas for $500 each to appear before the governor. This paperwork was apparently necessary because they had not accompanied Scott's prisoners to Little Rock. McEntire and McNair went into hiding until they could escape to Missouri.

Hays and Kirkham enlisted in Company H, Fourteenth Arkansas Infantry (C.S.). Scott had noted on November 7 to General McCulloch that there were a few disaffected persons in his locality, but they were not noisy or troublesome. The Peace Society was not noisy or troublesome, but it had formed a secret conspiracy.[198]

On December 14, Colonel Leslie appealed to Captain Scott for help in handling the Peace Society situation in Searcy County. He had sent a strong guard with the prisoners to Little Rock, which weakened his forces, and he mistrusted the loyalty of some of the militiamen. He could not get horses for scouts, nor get them shod if he had them. Several of his command were sick, and all were undisciplined. Where the militia had been called out there were not enough men to care for the women and children, and the prisoners' families also needed care. There were several men lying out in the woods. Some were in Tomahawk Township, some in

Calf Creek, and some in Mount Pleasant [Mountain] Township: townships where Leslie had not called out the militia. He heard that Peter A. Tyler had been in Tomahawk a few days earlier going toward Buffalo River in Newton County. He requested that Scott send a company of men and station them in Searcy County for a few weeks so that all those engaged in the secret order could be arrested. Leslie could keep a guard and disband the rest of his command, which would be a great savings to the state. He was determined to have his county rid of all men that he could find engaged in this alliance against the peace and harmony of the country. He thought the whole trick led to treason.[199]

Scott could not give an immediate reply because his unit was on the eve of an election for major, and he was a candidate. Scott's squadron of three companies—one commanded by himself, one by Thomas J. Linton of Pope County, and the third by Lafayette Boone—had been augmented on November 29 with the companies of captains William H. Brooks and a man named Davidson to form a battalion. They were directed to have an election for major as soon as they were concentrated. If Scott were elected major, he assured Leslie that he would winter two companies in Searcy County; otherwise he doubted Leslie would get any help.

Brooks was elected major on December 17, and the battalion was consolidated and left state service for Confederate service, although Scott's and Linton's companies had already been mustered into Confederate service by Hindman in August 1861.[200]

While Leslie and Scott were awaiting the decision by the new major, W. H. Brooks, Scott's men were still scouting the countryside for Peace Society men who had not been arrested. They found the elusive Peter A. Tyler, whose home was in Tyler Bend, now part of the Buffalo National River. The Faught brothers had described Tyler as one who held for the Union but was with both parties—as the circumstances required he declared his loyalty to whichever party he was with. Tyler and his neighbor Isaiah Ezell were captured and on December 18 and taken before the court at Camp Culloden. Tyler admitted to being a member of the Peace Society, having been initiated along with Samuel Grinder and Josiah Lane by Solomon Long and Lorenzo D. Jameson about three weeks before. They had been told that the Peace Society was a home protection society. Tyler was given signs and passwords that were similar to ones reported by others, except that a red cloth was to be placed on the door, not a yellow one. After Tyler was sworn into the society, he "rode around among the boys" and swore in thirty-two other men from Tomahawk Township, including at least seventeen who had already been arrested by Scott. The court ordered that Tyler be turned over to Captain Scott and taken to Little Rock. Similarly, Isaiah Ezell appeared before the court on the same date and admitted to being sworn in by Peter Tyler. However, he did not remember any signs or passwords, and it is presumed he was released.[201]

The discovery and arrest of Peace Society members extended south into Pope County, as evinced by a letter found in the ruins left behind in Fayetteville on February 19, 1862, by retreating Confederates. It was given some play in the Northern press, which quoted part of it. The letter was written on December 17, 1861, by James L. Adams, a twenty-nine-year-old physician living in Dover, Pope County. He was applying for a surgeon's post in Confederate General Sterling Price's army. The press quoted:

> Our men over the Boston mountains pen and swing the mountain boys who oppose Southern men; they have in camp [Scott's Camp Culloden] thirty, and in the Burrowville jail seventy-two, in the Clinton jail thirty-five, and have sent twenty-seven to Little Rock. We took up some as low down as Dover. We will kill all we can get, certain; every one is so many less. I hope you [Price] will soon get help enough to clear out the last one in your State [Missouri]. If you know them they ought to be killed, as the older they grow the more stubborn they get.

The information in this letter describes the situation on about December 3, when Scott reported between thirty-five and forty prisoners, Leslie had seventy-two, and Clinton had sent its twenty-seven prisoners to Little Rock. It is interesting that the Van Buren County Militia had arrested another thirty-five, and that Peace Society men were being captured as far south as Dover, Pope County.[202]

Despite Scott's doubt that any help would be given to Leslie, Scott's and Linton's companies were posted in Searcy County on December 20. After first considering using the Methodist campground in Wiley's Cove with its cabins, Scott determined that better quarters could be had in Burrowville, which is where he placed his soldiers. "A list of names belonging to a Secret Order that has not been arrested" had been prepared, probably in November, which Scott began to use as he scoured the countryside for about fifty more men who were lying out in the woods. On December 20, the day that Scott transferred his men to Searcy County, Leslie discharged the Forty-fifth Militia. He was angry with Lieutenant Colonel Alexander Ham, whom he had breveted and placed in command of the escort to Little Rock. Ham had discharged the men in Little Rock and told them to reassemble on December 23 in Burrowville. He did not report to Leslie, who only learned that they had arrived in Little Rock from Major John Bradshaw, who carried a dispatch from the governor.

Leslie's December 27 report to Governor Rector included a bill for repairing the damage the prisoners had done to the courthouse where they had been confined. Leslie thought it only reasonable that the state should pay the account. Existing documentation does not indicate whether Searcy County was reimbursed for courthouse repairs, but paymaster general Ben T. DuVal on February 13, 1862, authorized General Edmund Burgevin—still in Carrollton—to pay off the Searcy County militia called into service by Leslie. DuVal disallowed the claim of Alexander Ham as lieutenant colonel because he was breveted by Leslie, who did not have that authority. Judge Advocate Mark P. Hogan's claim was also disallowed, as it did not appear that his services were necessary. Leslie's voucher for $188.50 was paid.[203]

More Peace Society Prisoners

At least eleven Fulton County Peace Society men were sent to Little Rock to be imprisoned and questioned by the Military Board. They arrived in Little Rock shortly before December 24; they may have started from Fulton County as early as December 14. After being interrogated by the Military Board, the prisoners were held for trial. Captain Boone's company had been in Fulton County in early December before the squadron was reorganized, but his company was not used to escort the Fulton County prisoners to Little Rock. He was occupied with Unionists in Howell and Ozark counties, Missouri, who were harassing and stealing from Confederate sympathizers. Moreover, there were rumored federal forces in Springfield and Forsythe. On November 23, he told Scott, "There has not been the slightest disturbance in this county since I arrived here." The next day the messengers from Company H, Fourteenth (Powers) Arkansas Infantry in Yellville en route to Scott's camp met Boone's lieutenant with news of the Peace Society on the Izard–Searcy County line and a request for help.[204]

After Colonel Lewis had seen off his twenty-seven prisoners, he continued to make arrests and investigations, and by the first week of December he had thirty-five prisoners. He marched them to Little Rock, arriving on December 27. The *Daily State Journal* reported that among the party were some of the most noted ring-leaders of the conspiracy. The paper noted that the Peace Society was now entirely broken up. Only one or two had not been arrested, and they had fled to the North. One of these ringleaders was Christopher Denton, who remained in Van Buren County until the end of the war as a Union guerrilla leader. Unfortunately, there is no known surviving documentation for this second set of prisoners.[205]

J. J. Dawson and John Bradshaw returned to Searcy County after the formation of Company I, Eighteenth (Marmaduke's) Infantry to get supplies for the company; perhaps Morgan M. Terry did as well. If so, all the Searcy County officers were gone, and the men were put under the command of Ira Robertson, Company K.

Leslie's Christmas Day letter to the governor reported that Scott was in Searcy County and that he had discharged the militia on December 20. It went on to say that several of those belonging to the secret order had come in and surrendered. They were willing to volunteer and would return with Captain Dawson to Little Rock. Dawson may have left for Little Rock on December 27 carrying Leslie's longer report to the governor.[206]

Dawson's prisoners were known locally as the Little Chain Gang. They included Peter Tyler, Lindsey Price, and Thomas Thompson, and probably Spencer Adams and James Wiley Wallis. The total number is unknown, but they were sent to Bowling Green to be part of Thomas C. Hindman's Legion. Wallis of Big Flat Township stated the following:

> On the 10th day of Dec 1861 I was taken by force by the Confederate militia and taken to Little Rock Ark. The first squad was taken to Marshall [Burrowville] and the second squad of Union men was taken to Marshall also, but the first squad had departed for Little Rock before we got to Marshall. [Alex Copeland] was taken in the first Squad and when our squad reached there we were all put together... our Squad was taken in chains to Little Rock but before we got to Little Rock they took our chains off.[207]

Continuing pursuit of those who had escaped the November round-up is evidenced by a call-up of the Sylamore Township militia company. Izard County Militia colonel J. J. Kemp reported to the governor that he organized the militia of Sylamore Township on December 21 to repel an insurrection caused by Union men in a secret organization threatening their peace and happiness; he had been ferreting them out ever since. The citizens of Sylamore Township had for forty or fifty days been engaged in arresting the men that went to Pocahontas. Aikin stated that some prisoners were sent to Little Rock in addition to those who volunteered for military service. The Sylamore Militia escorted the Izard County prisoners to Little Rock. The *Daily State Journal* reported on January 4, 1862:

"The last importation of Jayhawkers (who are now confined in the jail here) are to be tried before Judge Ringo, on a charge of treason against the Confederacy—they, having refused to enlist in our army, as those previously did. They are bad eggs—put 'em out of the way!" It later reported: "Sixteen of those Lincolnites arrived here Monday [January 6] and were lodged in jail. Among the number were two of the clerical scoundrels who deluded their poor victims—hypocrites, who stole the 'livery of heaven to serve the devil in.' Another batch of twenty more of these creatures will arrive today."[208]

A side issue involving a local participant illustrates the difficulty in determining the facts about events in north Arkansas, particularly Izard County. It also shows how community relations became very conflicted with the pursuit of the Peace Society. Thomas W. Edmondson, born about 1812 in North Carolina, was living in Harris Township with his family in 1860. He had lived in Izard County since 1847, when he was taxed there and had accumulated considerable acreage between 1851 and 1858. In 1860, he owned nine slaves. He was elected Izard County representative to the Thirteenth General Assembly, which met between November 5, 1860, and January 21, 1861, and in the Special Session from November 4 to 18, 1861. He and William M. Aikin had raised companies of cavalry, and on July 4 they participated in a barbecue to recruit a company for John S. McCarver's infantry, in which he served as quartermaster with the rank of lieutenant.

His service records indicate he was enrolled on September 23, 1861, at Pocahontas and was appointed quartermaster on that date. Edmondson was also prominent in suppression of the Peace Society as one of twelve committeemen who reported on November 28 the discovery and arrest of the Peace Society men. He was one of two members from Harris Township, the most active in the county. His service record shows that he died December 23, 1861, yet in his military file there is a procurement voucher signed by him dated December 25. The *Daily State Journal* of December 31, 1861, reported that on Friday night, December 27, Mr. Edmundson [sic], was murdered by some of the Peace Society.[209]

A week later the newspaper made a correction: "We learn from Mr. William C. Cole, one of the guard which escorted the last importation of the conspirators from that county to Little Rock, that Mr. Edmondson was shot in self defense by one of the truest southern men that lives in Dixie."[210]

However, this correction may not be correct. The *Daily State Journal* said: "We published yesterday a statement to the effect that Mr. Edmondson, of Izard county, had been justifiably killed....We have since heard a counter statement from a highly respectable source, which places this unfortunate affair in a very different light. As the matter will be very soon adjudicated by the proper tribunal, we forbear to make any farther comments."[211]

Still later the *True Democrat* published: "In the case of Mr. Edmondson, those who killed him say it was done in self defense and while he was resisting arrest. His friends say that Edmondson was a true southron; that in the reign of terror he advised certain persons whom he knew to have enemies to escape until the storm blew over, and for this he was accused of being a member of the society; that they sought to arrest him and because he refused to submit, shot him."[212]

Scott and Leslie expected Scott to stay in Searcy County until spring, but that officer was ordered, on January 28, 1862, to march immediately to Pocahontas, Arkansas. General Van Dorn had recently assumed command of the Trans-Mississippi Division and had ordered the concentration of his command. Captain Linton conducted a Board of Survey for all their equipment and supplies on January 28, so they probably left by the end of January. In the six weeks that Scott was in Searcy County, he encouraged several men to join the Fourteenth Arkansas Infantry. In addition to Eli L. Osborn, George M. Hays, and John W. Kirkham—who were under bond and had enlisted in Company H on December 23—there were thirty-four others who enlisted in the Fourteenth Infantry in December and January at Camp Madison.

The regiment had been raised largely in July and August 1861 and mustered in at Yellville, so they were good candidates for Peace

Society men forced into the Fourteenth. Men would naturally gravitate to companies from the same area. Twelve joined Captain James H. Love's Company K, composed of men from Searcy County north of the Buffalo River. Five, including the three bonded men, joined Robert Trimble's Company H from Marion County.[213]

Not everyone stayed at home to be arrested, hid in the woods, or voluntarily gave themselves up. Some saw the danger of remaining at home and fled to Union lines. Paris G. Strickland, Lorenzo D. Jameson, Harmon Hodge, and John H. Jenkins left Searcy County after the November 25 Peace Society meeting at David Ruff's house for Missouri. Arriving at Salem, Dent County, they were arrested as suspicious persons and sent to the federal military post at Rolla. There, Captain Ware of Phelps's Six-month Volunteers vouched for them. Ware had led the Peace Society in Fulton County, and Strickland and Jameson had been instrumental in swearing in members in Searcy County. Strickland, Jenkins, and Jameson were all on the list of those who had not been arrested. Strickland joined the Army of the Southwest at Lebanon, Missouri, as a teamster and courier. Jameson joined Company H, First Arkansas Cavalry (U.S.) in August 1862, then was appointed first lieutenant of Company K, First Arkansas Infantry to aid in recruiting that regiment. Hodge also joined Company H, First Arkansas Cavalry in July 1862 and was appointed sergeant. Both were recruited into the First Arkansas Cavalry (U.S.) by fellow Peace Society member John W. Morris.[214]

Many more on the list withdrew into the woods, only appearing at home occasionally, and sometimes forming a guerrilla group. November and December 1861 shook the foundation of frontier, rural Searcy County. Persons from Searcy County—refugees or Confederate deserters—reported "Bushwhackers & Bad Characters" to the federal provost marshal in Batesville. Calvin Thomas, Jim Shaw, Mark Hogan, Neal McCarn, James Mays, and Bill Garrison were on the list. All played significant roles in arresting those in the Peace Society or later as conscript officers.[215]

An exchange in the *True Democrat* in early 1862 sheds some light on Peace Society issues, especially those in Izard County. The newspaper writers did not know what the true case was for the Peace Society but feared that a great many innocent men and a number of ignorant ones had been shamefully treated. Some charged that the purpose of the society was to aid the enemy, but it was admitted that the majority were ignorant of the ultimate objects of the society. On the other hand, they were assured that there was nothing treasonable in the society, and innocent men were induced to join by being promised protection.

If half of the stories were true "there is a dread state of affairs." Making arrests without a warrant was dangerous and could be done by anybody. So, if anyone had an enemy in north Arkansas, he had only to accuse him of belonging to the society to ensure his death.[216]

The *True Democrat* printed a rebuttal by William M. Aikin, who stated that he had examined five men and one said that he belonged to a secret society that favored the North. Aikin indicated that he had met strong opposition when he tried to recruit a Confederate regiment, and that those who had volunteered in Borland's regiment had returned home. The men who pleaded ignorance of the Peace Society were not as ignorant as they pretended. Aikin had traded with them for six years, and he defied anyone to over-reach them in a trade. Aikin asserted that those who arrested the Peace Society men were the most law-abiding men in the South, and those that were arrested had been investigated and judged to be disloyal.[217]

Twenty-eight years later, writers for Goodspeed's *Biographical and Historical Memoirs of Northeast Arkansas* commented, "At the outbreak of the Civil War nearly all the citizens of Fulton County were in favor of establishing the Southern Confederacy. A very few who remained loyal to the Union departed to the north." Goodspeed also commented about Izard County's Unionists: "At the approach of the Civil War, when the question of secession was first discussed, a majority of the people of Izard County seemed opposed to it, but when actual hostilities commenced, all but a few were naturally in full sympathy with the Southern cause, and soon thereafter favored the secession of the state. Early in the war period, most of the Union men here removed to Rolla, Mo., and were there organized into a company by Capt. L. D. Toney and served in the Federal army."[218]

A generation after the excitement about the Peace Society, all that was remembered was that the Unionists went to Missouri.

Unionists as a Threat

Unionists were perceived as an embarrassment through much of 1861, not as a threat. Abolitionists accused of fomenting slave uprisings—such as White County's Rev. Charles Cavender's slave revolt in May 1861—were hanged. St. Francis County's sawmill master James B. Lipps was killed in an armed confrontation with citizens when they suspected him of raising companies to sustain law and order and to put down pro-secessionist vigilante committees. Lipps's activities sound similar to Fulton County's Peace Society efforts to oppose Dr. Nunnelie's companies. However, the summer 1861 Pro Bono Publico movement in Monroe County, later identified as the Peace Society, was examined, and the parties were dismissed. John A. Harvick, Monroe County clerk, reported— and had arrested—members of Pro Bono Publico or Peace Society, but the evidence proved nothing treasonable, and the issue was dropped. In Searcy County, where the Peace Society was especially strong, it appears that many knew that some men belonged to an organization that would put yellow cloth at their doors for protection. Locally they were known as the "yaller rag boys," and they were left alone.[219]

The *True Democrat*, in a rare evaluation of the Peace Society testimony, stated, "There was a great deal of mischievous humbuggery in it, about the rich and poor, and an attempt to array non-slaveholders against slaveholders." Anti-secessionist sentiment was heaviest in the poorest and non-slaveholding counties. Derogatory comments were made by Unionists in Izard County about Confederate dependence on slaves when McCarver's battalion was being raised; Newton County's Isaac F. Morris wrote a letter to the *True Democrat* when he canceled his subscription and left for the North, telling Richard Johnson to send one of his slaves to pick up the undelivered newspapers if he did not go himself; and references were made to "a rich man's war and a poor man's fight" even in the early days of the secession movement. All three of these examples indicate an existing attitude that encouraged involvement with the Peace Society.[220]

With the attitude toward the Unionists in the state so changed by the Tennessee bridge burners, the Peace Society members did not have a sympathetic environment.

Benjamin Franklin Taylor, Peace Society member and captain, Company M, Third Arkansas Cavalry (U.S.). (Courtesy of the author)

Thomas H. Boles,
captain, Company
E, Third Arkansas
Cavalry (U.S.). Boles
was also a judge of the
fifth Arkansas circuit
and an Arkansas
U.S. representative.
(Arkansas State
Archives)

David C. Ruff,
Peace Society
member and captain,
Company F, 46th
Missouri Infantry
Volunteers. (Courtesy
of the author)

John W. Morris, chain gang member and 1st Lieutenant, Company H,
1st Arkansas Cavalry (U.S.). (Courtesy of the Morris family)

Chapter 4

After the Break-Up: The Captured, January 1862–January 1863

Peace Society prisoners had two options: they could await trial, or they could join the Confederate army. A significant majority opted for military service. Governor Rector's promise of a long imprisonment awaiting a certain conviction (and maybe execution) did not appeal to most of the mountaineers. A stint in the army offered the possibility of desertion and return home—which many of the men did. Very few men stayed with the Confederate colors to the end of the war. Those who waited for the courts either wanted to clear their names, as did Shadrach H. Wren of Fulton County, or (for some reason not now apparent) were not permitted to enlist, such as the two Baptist preachers from Searcy County—William Morris and William Hays.[221]

Information about the trials of the Peace Society prisoners is incomplete. Records of the trials are missing, and newspaper reports are sketchy. The only list of prisoners was published by the *True Democrat,* and it is incomplete, containing only fifteen names. For instance, neither of Searcy County's two Baptist preachers was on the list. One reference to the trial refers to seventy-five men appearing before the court. On January 4, 1862, there is another mention of Peace Society arrivals being confined to jail, awaiting trial for treason before Judge Daniel Ringo, because they had not opted for Confederate service. On January 8 sixteen more Lincolnites arrived, including two preachers, all of whom were put in jail, and twenty more were anticipated that day. Still more prisoners were brought in according to the press, but with no mention of their origin or names. On January 12, the *State Journal* reported that sixty jayhawkers who were brought in the week before had been mustered into Confederate service and transferred to John Quillin's battalion for service in Kentucky.[222]

In Governor Rector's first telegram about the Peace Society to President Davis on November 28, 1861, he bemoaned the absence of the district judge, saying, "He ought to be at his post." Ringo was the Confederate district judge for all of Arkansas and may have been holding court in Fort Smith.

He had been the federal district judge for the Eastern and Western Districts of Arkansas since being appointed by Whig president Zachary Taylor in 1849. He resigned his federal position when Arkansas seceded, but, two weeks later, Confederate president Jefferson Davis nominated him to the newly created Confederate Eastern and Western Arkansas districts. He was confirmed the same day. Ringo's Confederate court opened on January 20, 1862, and the press emphasized the Peace Society prisoners that would be on his docket:

> Some interesting cases will be before the court, among which are the trial of certain persons arrested in North Arkansas, on a charge of treason and known as members of a so-called peace society. There are fifteen of these in confinement in this city, vis: Wm. Gadberry, John Smith, Abner H. Smith, W. Barnes, John Gilbreath, J. F. Bailey, Thos. Harris and Wm. C. Wells, of Van Buren County; W. Yeary, Jas. W. Ball, Shadrach H. Wren, Vincent M. Woodson, Jas. A. Baker, Joshua Richardson and James C. Richardson, of Fulton County.[223]

Witnesses from those counties who had come to Little Rock for the trial told the press that the best men in the county were engaged in making these arrests, which had been authorized by the governor. Many of the arresting officers were known to be patriotic and responsible men, especially those in Searcy County, and all seemed to have acted from a sense of duty. The witnesses predicted that the evidence presented in the trial of the prisoners would reveal how treasonable their actions had been and the extent of their conspiracy. The *True Democrat* was at a loss to know, from the contradictory statements made, how far this matter extended or how dangerous its character, but it stated, "The peace society in Arkansas is pretty effectively 'played out.'"[224]

A minority of the Peace Society members brought to Little Rock did not join the army, and they went on trial. The composition of the jury did not favor them. The jurors were prosperous merchants and farmers from central and south Arkansas who had little in common with the prisoners. The sole exception was John Bradshaw, who was a major in the Searcy County Militia and a lieutenant in Company I, Eighteenth Arkansas Infantry. Nonetheless, once before the judge, the case came apart. Judge Ringo and the district attorney for the Eastern District, William M. Randolph, did not believe that a case could be made against the prisoners. Because they had not committed any overt act against the government, the men would probably be discharged or acquitted if brought to trial. Ringo suggested that the prisoners be turned over to the military authorities to assure a conviction.

Congressman Augustus H. Garland, learning of Ringo's opinion, approached the Confederate attorney general who suggested that the War Department act on the matter. Garland then tried on January 25 to see Secretary of War Judah P. Benjamin. Finding his offices closed, he wrote to him saying that everyone believed that the prisoners were guilty and that turning them loose would encourage their friends and dispirit all true and loyal citizens. Garland knew of no law that permitted the civil and military authorities to work together but hoped that Benjamin would give the problem his full and earnest consideration. Benjamin did not reply, and the trial went forward.[225]

The prisoners' testimony before the Military Board was used by the prosecution, especially the oath which called for the death of anyone who betrayed the society, but this was insufficient to obtain a conviction. On February 27, the Confederate Circuit Court adjourned after a session of more than ten days. The jury failed to find the Peace Society men guilty of treason. The evidence against these men was sufficient to show that some of them were dangerous and disaffected men, but their offense consisted more of words and threats than of overt acts. Some of the principal witnesses on the part of the government failed to attend, and it was thought best to release the accused upon their taking the oath of allegiance to the Confederate States. The *True Democrat* proposed, "If these men are really in favor of the South, they have more an opportunity to show their loyalty and defend the State. If they favor the tyrant, let them go to him. It is cheaper to fight them than to feed them."[226]

The men went home, and they may have been encouraged by their release. At least they were still active Unionists. On March 7, Izard County's fifty-year-old John A. Beck reminded the governor of a February 20 federal raid on West Plains, Missouri, that had destroyed the town. Now Captain Ware's company of Fulton and Izard county men was in nearby Missouri threatening the county. Ware had friends who relayed news to him weekly. He commented that the *True Democrat* recommended that he be sent to Little Rock if captured, but everybody in Beck's section seemed to differ; if they could get hold of Ware they would handle his case locally. The local citizens had sent Ware's chief lieutenants to Little Rock as prisoners in the persons of Shadrach Wren and William H. Yeary only to see the court release them. Consequently, the local citizens vowed that if they got hold of Ware, they would deal with him themselves.[227]

After Gehazi R. Ball and his son Milford W. Ball returned to Howell County from Little Rock, Confederate general James H. McBride's troops arrested Gehazi and his sons Milford W. and Robert E. Ball for refusing to enlist in the Confederate army and for professing loyalty to the Union. They were again taken to the prison in Little Rock, secured with ball and chain attached to a shackle around their ankles, and assigned to the blacksmith shop. Most of the prison guards were reassigned due to more pressing needs on the battle front, so surveillance of the prisoners was negligible. The Balls took advantage of this and removed the chains from the shackles with tools from the blacksmith shop and escaped. They made ropes from their blankets, fastened them to a ball and chain, and threw the ball over the wall. Gehazi first climbed to the top of the wall and helped one son up, then both helped the other son up. They all three made their escape from the prison and, with great caution, made their way to the military post at Rolla, where they had their shackles removed. They then enlisted in the federal army.[228]

Those prisoners from Izard County who enlisted at Pocahontas—especially the Searcy County prisoners who enlisted in Companies I and K, Eighteenth Arkansas Infantry—considered the relative freedom of the Confederate army, from which they could desert, preferable to the uncertainty of a lengthy prison stay and the unpredictable results of a trial. Some men never had an opportunity to desert. Peter Tyler died shortly after he wrote on January 17 to his wife Evaline. Others were found to be too old or disabled to serve and were discharged. James Thompson, age fifty-eight, one of the Camp Culloden prisoners, was discharged at Bowling Green for being too old to serve and carried Tyler's letter home. Thomas McInturff, age thirty-five, with an open leg sore, and William Kesner, age thirty-four, with a club foot (both of Leslie's chain gang), were also released at Bowling Green and returned to Searcy County. The measles that first occurred among the prisoners while held at the Burrowville courthouse continued to affect them in the Confederate army. Van Buren County's John B. Null died on January 17, 1862, at Memphis of measles. John W. Harness also had the measles at Memphis and was discharged. Thomas Martin died of measles in February 1862 at Bowling Green. Benjamin H. Gary was sick at Bowling Green but moved to the hospital in Nashville; he was there when the city fell to the Federals about February 17. He was paroled and arrived home on July 7, 1862. Both Gary and Harness later enlisted in the Union army.[229]

Peace Society men who tried to desert had mixed success. Asa Watts simply walked away from Company I until he came upon a detail of men digging graves. Fearing that if captured he might occupy one of those graves, he pretended to be a farmer out looking for his hogs until he had transited the future cemetery and was out of sight. He had returned to Searcy County by April 1862. John W. Morris tried to escape while his company was at Bell Station, Kentucky. One night in January, he was one of the 600 men Marmaduke marched to surprise 1,000 Federals who had crossed the Green River. He and two comrades planned to desert that night by dropping out of line one at a time in the darkness. No one missed Morris as he hurried on a direct line, he thought, toward the federal camp. However, while scrambling through bushes and overhanging branches, he was surprised by two Confederates on guard duty who took him to the officer of the guard, a lieutenant, who accused him of trying to desert. Morris claimed that he could not help falling out and that he took the wrong road in trying to rejoin his company. The lieutenant accused him of being one of those "damned Arkansas jayhawkers" sent out by General Hindman, told him that none of his company should ever return to Arkansas, and asked the guards why they had not shot him. At this point the captain of the guard intervened and returned Morris to his company.[230]

Other men were more successful. Franklin Kuykendall managed to escape at Bowling Green, Kentucky, and subsequently reported to General Samuel Curtis in the first part of June 1862. David Barnett, Peter M. Sutterfield, and Franklin Wortman "drifted from one place to another" with Marmaduke's regiment until they could run away. Benjamin G. Watts was furloughed a few days after the Shiloh battle because he had mumps and was home on May 9, 1862. His brother-in-law and chain gang partner William Potter accompanied him home.

Alexander Copeland, another of Leslie's chain gang, deserted with William J. Thompson on the second day's march from Bell Station to Bowling Green, after they had served one month and twenty days with the Confederates. Copeland and Thompson then went south to Wayne County, Tennessee, where Copeland's mother, sister, and brother-in-law lived on Indian Creek. They arrived in

February, stayed with Copeland's brother-in-law, and helped make a crop that summer for his mother. Brother-in-law Zack T. Johnson remembered that he and Copeland worked the crop together and that they laid out one day on a hill and listened to the cannonading at the battle of Shiloh on April 6.

In early 1862, Copeland, Johnson, and Thompson joined a company of independent federal scouts being raised by William K. M. Breckenridge to provide protection for Union families in Wayne and adjacent counties. Breckenridge had three companies in all, and Copeland served about four months under him until the units were disbanded. Breckenridge's independent companies were a precursor to Colonel Fielding Hurst's Sixth Tennessee Cavalry (U.S.), in which Breckenridge served as lieutenant colonel.

However, in an attempt to get back home in August 1862, Copeland got no farther than Paducah, Kentucky, when he had to turn back. Two months later, in October, he and Thompson made another attempt, going afoot to Pilot Knob, Missouri, where Copeland had an uncle. Falling ill, Copeland remained there through the winter of 1862–1863, but Thompson left to join Company E, Second Arkansas Cavalry (U.S.) on July 12, 1863. Copeland was finally well enough to walk home to Copeland Branch in Searcy County in February 1863. "I raised a crop the Summer of 1863," he recalled, "and late in the fall of 1863 Jim Young and I wooded it through to Little Rock, Ark. and enlisted in Co. M, 3 Ark Cavlry [sic] and were mustered into Service in Jany 1864. The summer of 1863 I did not sleep in my house at night as a rule but slept out in the woods. I was afraid of being captured by the rebels and punished for desertion."[231]

Other success stories included that of James Mack Hollis, a Marion County schoolteacher, Camp Culloden prisoner, and Company K, Eighteenth Arkansas soldier who deserted by January 1862. He went home to Wayne County, Tennessee, where he married before enlisting on December 18, 1863, at Clifton, in Company E, Second Tennessee Infantry (U.S.).[232]

William C. Singletary, physician from Marion County, was another of the Culloden prisoners marched in chains to Little

Rock. He enlisted in Company K, Eighteenth Arkansas Infantry and stayed with the Third Confederate Infantry, the Eighteenth's successor, until May 18, 1862, when he was assigned as a hospital steward. He deserted October 1, 1864, at Carters Station, Carter County, Tennessee; he was taken prisoner by the Thirteenth Tennessee Volunteer Cavalry (U.S.) and released at Knoxville on the recommendations of loyal citizens after taking the oath of allegiance. Singletary had many friends in the Thirteenth Cavalry from Carter County, so he joined them. He was granted a furlough to visit his ailing mother in Elizabethton, where he had been raised and had begun his medical practice. When his furlough expired, he scouted in the mountains with Union men and doctored those who were sick.

When federal troops occupied Elizabethton, Singletary returned to care for his invalid mother. But when the Confederates re-occupied the town, he escaped, dressed as a woman, to Knoxville. He returned to Arkansas, where he died May 1, 1894, at Elixir, Boone County. Singletary's Peace Society experience was included in the Thirteenth's unit history: "Although in a strongly rebellious country, he was a Union man. He was conscripted and taken into the Confederate army." And, "He moved to Arkansas in 1859. The rebel sentiment was strong in the locality where he lived, but the Union men there, Dr. Singletary among others, held secret meetings to discuss plans for their safety. They were arrested, chained together and taken to Georgia [sic] and forced to join the army."[233]

On January 31, 1862, Marmaduke's Eighteenth Arkansas was designated the Third Confederate Infantry after the addition of two Tennessee companies. At that time, the second of the two Peace Society companies was reorganized, and the officers were replaced. As the Confederates retreated from Bowling Green after General Grant's capture of Fort Henry on February 6, they fell back to Murfreesboro. Hindman had hurried the retreat, and they had to walk in the soupy, muddy road. The soldiers' feet blistered; when the blisters broke, their shoes were full of blood and water. John W. Morris contracted pneumonia and was sick at Murfreesboro two or three days before he was sent to the hospital in Atlanta, Georgia. There, he joined fellow chain gang member Henry Bradshaw, who had been sent to the Atlanta hospital, where he died of exposure. Morris recovered. In late March, a lieutenant was sent to the Atlanta hospital from Hindman's brigade to get every man able to walk a mile and return them to their commands at Corinth, Mississippi.[234]

When Morris arrived at Corinth, he learned that the brigade's original officers had resigned, and they had a new captain, Thomas W. Newton. He did not care much for the Searcy County soldiers. On the morning of April 6, all knew that a battle was impending. Chain gang member Bowman Turney pressed Morris to accept his piece of meat, sensing that he would not need it. After breakfast in line of battle, Captain Newton addressed his troops: "Boys, we are going to have a hell of a fight, and I have no confidence in these men sent out from Arkansas. If they try to get to the Federals, shoot them; if they fall back, shoot them; if they try to run, shoot them down."[235]

About 9 a.m. on April 6, the Third Confederate Infantry— now numbering about 500 men—attacked the Hornets' Nest at Shiloh but drew back after one assault. They probably participated in subsequent bloody attacks, but on April 7 the regiment was in reserve to support a cannon battery and was not again engaged until the close of the battle. Bowman Turney and William Treece were killed, and five members of old Company I were wounded. Morris was wounded in the foot by a spent cannon ball. When the doctor said it was not necessary to amputate his foot, Morris—who had not even considered that possibility—was greatly relieved.

After Shiloh, the Confederates retreated to Corinth, and Morris was among the walking wounded. At Corinth, the army remained for two or three days, and the two Peace Society companies were absorbed into Companies A and G on April 23, 1862. A new captain was put over them. Captain Newton had gone to Arkansas without leave and never returned. George Moore, the new captain of Company A, gave Morris and Morris's friend William McDaniel a furlough to visit home. When Robert Johnson and William Harris (fellow chain gang men) were also given furloughs, the four men went from Corinth to Memphis by train. At Memphis, they took deck fare across the Mississippi to Arkansas, and then waded flooded lands at Grand Glaize in water up to their chins. Upon reaching higher ground, they were fed and boarded at a series of sympathetic households until they reached Searcy County. Morris almost immediately dropped by the roadside from exhaustion and was picked up by James Lawrence, who gave him a ride to the home of Wade Campbell (his wife's cousin), where he spent the night. The following day, walking toward Burrowville, he came to the farm of John Wilson, who recognized the fellow chain gang member. Wilson had come home earlier. Wilson's son-in-law, John F. Fendley, took Morris to Burrowville, where he met old friends and fellow Peace Society members Allen McLane and Carroll Arter. McLane had been in the chain gang and Arter's name was on the list of Peace Society members who had not been arrested. At Burrowville another friend took Morris home by horseback. His family was cheered to see him, but he had sad news for his two sisters: their husbands, Beverly L. Conley and John Castleberry, were dead.[236]

Six Peace Society men deserted at Shiloh and were sent to St Louis by the Federals: John Morris Sr., William Bartlett, and W. R. Chambers of Company I, and James F. Christy, Joseph C. Christy, and Porter M. Hensley of Company K. James Christy recalled: "I with others deserted and made our escape to the Union Army. When we made our escape we went to General [Don Carlos] Buel [sic] headquarters. He sent us back to Springfield, Missouri [sic] to the Ark. Troops where we joined the Union Forces." Bartlett, James Christy, and Hensley later served in the Union army.

At the battle of Stones River (Murfreesboro)—from December 31, 1862, to January 3, 1863—three more Peace Society men deserted and went to the federal lines: Washington G. Lynn, Benjamin Treece, and Carroll Kilburn. They were sent to Gratiot Street Prison in St. Louis, where Lynn and Treece renounced the Confederacy, swore allegiance to the United States, and agreed to stay north of the Ohio River. Treece settled in Wright County, Missouri, for the remainder of the war and was joined by his family, which fled Searcy County.

Kilburn had been left sick at Chattanooga in August, and, although he rejoined his command, was still gravely ill. He died January 24, 1863, in the federal hospital at St. Louis. By the end of the war, only Presley B. R. Turney, Samuel Watts, and J. J. Whitmire—all of Company I—were still with the Confederates.[237]

Of the fourteen Peace Society men who enrolled in Captain Robert E. Trimble's Company H or Captain James H. Love's Company K, Fourteenth (Powers) Arkansas Infantry in December 1861 and January 1862, six died before the end of July 1862, three deserted, one was discharged in April, and another left sick in Arkansas in April 1862 when the regiment was transferred east of the Mississippi. Of the three held under $500 bond—Eli L. Osborn, George M. Hays, and John W. Kirkham—Kirkham died at home in Carroll County in April, Hays was furloughed home sick in December 1862, and Osborn lived until 1886 in Jefferson Township, Boone County. (There is no additional record about Osborn.)[238]

The Uncaptured

After Colonel Leslie discharged the Searcy County militia in December 1861, and Scott's men had been transferred at the end of January 1862, there seemed to be no motivation to go after the remaining Peace Society men. When Morris returned to Searcy County in April 1862, he saw fellow chain gang member John Wilson cultivating his farm. In Burrowville he met known Peace Society men Allen McLane and Carroll Arter, who were openly moving about the community. There were no active efforts being made to recruit more soldiers in the new year, and things were quiet in the north-central Arkansas mountains. Without a strong official Confederate presence, Peace Society men were left alone by their neighbors.

Many of the Peace Society leaders had fled north. Jehoida J. Ware, the leader for Fulton and Izard counties—after learning that its activity had just been discovered in Clinton—rushed home, alerted his men, and fled with them to Missouri to form the nucleus of a federal company. Other Peace Society men stayed in place and kept a low profile. After Shadrach H. Wren was acquitted by the Confederate jury in March 1862, Izard County's John Beck thought Wren and William H. Yeary had gone north. But Wren remained in Fulton County until General Curtis arrived in Batesville on May 3, 1862, then he went to Rolla. Wren later returned to Batesville as a sutler, selling goods to the Union soldiers.[239]

Other society men sensed danger and fled. In Searcy County, Paris Strickland realized that he was in danger when Colonel Leslie called out the militia. Fleeing with Lorenzo D. Jameson, Harmon Hodge, and John H. Jenkins to Missouri, Strickland attached himself to the Army of the Southwest at Lebanon, first as a teamster, then as a courier. In March 1862, he returned home to recuperate from an illness. Arriving at the home of his step-father, John Wortman, on April 2, Strickland was told he was in no immediate danger. That proved not to be the case. On April 6, the Ninth Texas Cavalry of Colonel Thomas J. Churchill's Brigade, en route from Forsythe, Missouri, to Des Arc, camped on the Buffalo River near Burrowville. One officer, Captain James Bates, did not think much of Burrowville. He described it as "a very sorry place about 100 greasy dirty looking individuals—all out to see us pass by. Houses nearly all log huts. Ladies waved their gingham hand-kerchiefs at us as we passed." Taking advantage of the strong Confederate presence, local Confederate civilians James Shaw, Miles Thornton, and Wade Griffin led a nine-man detachment from the Ninth Texas Cavalry to Wortman's two-pen dogtrot house in search of Strickland.

After killing Wortman when he tried to pass a gun to Strickland, they took Strickland and two other men captured en route to Burrowville, where they were put on trial by the leading Confederates in town, including William H. Jones, Strickland's father-in-law. The men were taken from the court to Cooper's Tavern, where they remained until about 9 p.m. Strickland was then taken to a hollow about a mile from town, where Captain R. H. Black of Company E (who had led the detail) put a noose around his neck, snapped his pistol at the prisoner's head, jumped on his stomach, put a knife at his throat, but eventually released Strickland along with the other two captives, John W. McDaniel and Martin Gilliam.[240]

The Ninth Texas left the next day to camp on Searcy County's Cove Creek, where Bates believed that three-fourths of the men were Unionists. Strickland remained at home another five or six weeks, lying in the woods by day and cautiously venturing forth at night, before rejoining the First Arkansas Cavalry (U.S.). The fact that Searcy County Confederates waited until regular Confederate troops entered the county before acting against known Unionists could mean one of two things: either they felt too weak to act alone, or they were inclined to leave their neighbors and relatives alone, even if they were Peace Society men.[241]

Without outside Confederate presence, the locals' somewhat lackadaisical attitude toward the Peace Society men and other Unionists living among them changed drastically with the passage of the conscription act on April 16, 1862. It began to be enforced in north Arkansas in late May and early June. Men who had felt relatively safe avoiding military service now felt threatened, and with good cause. In January 1862, prior to the conscription act, General Earl Van Dorn had tried to raise "The Arkansas Legion." Governor Rector, as president of the Military Board, called for 8,200 men to be raised throughout Arkansas to fill Van Dorn's requisition and designated five recruiting stations in Arkansas. One was Wiley's Cove in Searcy County, but any efforts to recruit were half-hearted at best. It was only in response to pressure from the Military Board that Colonel Leslie—late of the Forty-fifth Arkansas Militia—using the newly created conscription act, began raising a company at the Wiley's Cove recruiting station in May. His recruits were not enthusiastic. At least two, John W. Harness and William Potter, he had marched to Little Rock in the chain gang. He did raise 125 men and was elected captain of Company F, Thirty-second Arkansas Infantry, which was organized on June 16, 1862. Sickness and desertion were rampant. After the Battle of Prairie Grove, on December 7, 1862, so many men deserted that his company lost one-third of its strength by Christmas Day.

The Twenty-seventh Arkansas Infantry had also been recruiting in Searcy County since May 1862. Searcy County militiaman Captain Waddy T. Hunt of Locust Grove Township raised Company F in the eastern part of the county, while Captain Beal Gaither of Company D was recruiting in its western region.[242]

After returning home in late April, John W. Morris was soon approached about re-enlisting in the Confederate army. "Neither reason nor justice demanded that he again imperil his life for men who did not regard his life," declared his biographer, but, "he soon learned that he was in danger, so he sought the protection of the woods until he was well enough to shoulder arms." In July Morris and twenty-one other men decided to go to Springfield. After going to Richland Valley to get a horse for himself, Morris and his fellows traveled by night to the head of Clear Creek, Tomahawk Township, where fellow traveler Hard Trammell's cousin Jarrett Trammell fed them breakfast. The men then gave Jarrett three dollars to lead them through Rolling Prairie to Searcy County's Wayne Hensley, who fed them supper and piloted them on a further seven miles. With luck and caution, the bedraggled men with their long hair and beards made it through Confederate-infested country to Springfield. After identifying themselves to Frederick Bodenhammer, the provost marshal, they received passes and were told that Luther Phillips (a Culloden chain gang member) was farming in the area. He and Morris had become fast friends in Marmaduke's regiment (being fellow Masons), so Morris went to his farm and spent the next twenty-four hours renewing their friendship. The next day, Morris and his companions met Captain John I. Worthington on a street in Springfield. He asked, "Boys, have you enlisted?" He offered Morris a first lieutenancy if he would help raise a company for the First Arkansas Cavalry. In five days, Morris had raised forty men, who were mustered in on August 7 as Company H, First Arkansas Cavalry. Fifteen of them had been Peace Society members, including Harmon Hodge and Lorenzo D. Jameson, who had fled Searcy County with Strickland.[243]

There was opposition to conscription, particularly in the more remote townships such as Mountain in Searcy County's south-western corner, so men like fifty-seven-year-old James Dwyer Shaw were needed to enforce it. A farmer in Bear Creek Township, Shaw had served as Searcy County treasurer for two different terms and as state senator during the Seventh General Assembly (November 1848–January 1849). He was also a staunch Confederate, having reported Paris Strickland to Captain Black in April.

After the Strickland episode, in 1862 Shaw became provost marshal for Searcy County and senior officer of the home guard, whose duty was to capture men to be conscripted into Confederate service. James Ervin Shipman, one of Shaw's home guardsmen, recalled that he went out to Witts Springs during the summer the Conscription Act went into effect and brought in two of the Drewry boys, Wes Roberts, and others. He took them to Burrowville and turned them over to Provost Marshal Jim Shaw. These men had refused to come and volunteer, and Shipman's instructions were to bring all men subject to the conscription act. The home guard took so many different men, both day and night, that Shipman did not remember individual captures; therefore he did not remember whether they took the Drewry boys at night or in daytime.[244]

The men of Mountain Township did not go willingly with the home guard. At the beginning of the rebellion, Benjamin F. Snow lived at Witts Springs, Searcy County. When the conscription act was passed, he and twenty-four other young men of the township were subject to it, but they did not volunteer. Later, home guards were organized in each voting precinct to enforce conscription. The older men in his township refused to organize into home guards, so when Snow and his friends refused to enlist, home guard companies from other townships were sent in to arrest them. The young men hid out in the forest, one of their refuges being a hollow south of Witts Springs called Camp Lincoln Spring (an expression of their sympathies). When home guards managed to capture some of the men, ten of their comrades followed the arresting party and freed them that same night. Soon 125 soldiers were sent to occupy the region. They lived off the community, a devastating experience for the citizens. The twenty-four draft dodgers and some of the old men left for Springfield, Missouri. But when they were within forty miles of their destination, they stumbled into a rebel camp. Held prisoners for a week, they were taken back to Arkansas and released after taking the oath of allegiance to the Confederacy. All was well until a company of rebel soldiers heard they were back and came after them again. The Witts Springs men again went to the mountain.[245]

Finally, in October 1862, Snow and others felt the situation was so bad that they could do no better than to join a Confederate company being raised in Newton County by Hamilton C. Dickey, himself a good Union man. Dickey's company of desperate Unionists, which became part of Samuel W. Peel's Confederate regiment, became so popular among Newton and Searcy counties' Unionists that some men who joined it had to be transferred to other companies because it was oversubscribed. Under the conscript law, the authorities could assign a man to any regiment. Volunteers could choose where to serve and were able to vote for their officers.[246]

Not all the Peace Society men fled to Missouri, joined the Union army, or hid in the woods until federal recruiters penetrated their hills. Others formed resistance groups and remained near their homes for the entire war. Such a man was Christopher Denton, born in 1810 in Jackson County, Tennessee. He was a farmer living in Holley Township, Van Buren County, in 1860. He had been an active agent for the Peace Society, initiating several men in both Van Buren and Searcy counties. After the breakup of the society, he hid in the woods and established his own "home guard." Refugees from Van Buren County reported him to the provost marshal at Batesville as a bad character, someone who "robs women whose husbands have been driven off." A somewhat contentious character, Confederate sympathizers called him a jayhawker, while to Unionists he was a man who protected their homes from Confederate guerrillas and outlaws. According to his grandson, Absalom S. (Jo Absie) Morrison,

Denton's men rode with the Third Arkansas Cavalry when the regiment came to the area on scout.[247]

On June 10, 1865, as Confederate troops were negotiating their surrender, Colonel A. R. Witt of the Tenth Arkansas Cavalry informed General Joseph J. Reynolds, commander of the Department of Arkansas, that he was ready to surrender his regiment at Jacksonport. He added that he could not prevail upon some of his soldiers to lay down their arms until they had some assurance from the U.S. authorities that independent companies and squads had also disarmed. Witt pointed particularly to "illegal" companies of jayhawkers and marauders led by Denton, Thomas Klampton, and Dick or Nathan Williams, who had been committing atrocities on the citizens. No doubt these bands were committing atrocities, but the companies themselves were not illegal.

Denton was commissioned a captain on March 27, 1865, in Van Buren County's federal Arkansas militia. Nathan Williams, son of Captain Thomas Williams of Company B, Six-month Arkansas Infantry, was commissioned on February 22, 1865, as a federal militia captain for Conway County.

Chris Denton's company was very similar to the Williams clan, led at first by Thomas Jefferson Williams, then by his sons, Nathan and Richard, from the Conway-Van Buren County border. It was reasonable to suspect that the Williams men belonged to a Peace Society unit, as they had close connections with Edmond Stobaugh, a member of the Van Buren County Peace Society. Moreover, both Williams and Stobaugh were Disciples of Christ preachers.[248]

Chris Denton may have been an exception as a Peace Society member who led an independent company throughout the war. Nevertheless, there were other men that formed transitory bands, usually until they joined a regular Union regiment. Searcy County's John Franklin Treadwell, who had been taken up in the arrests of the Peace Society, joined Company I, Eighteenth Arkansas, and intended to desert at the first opportunity, which he did. For a year and a half, he hid near his home and commanded a company of

Union men in the Boston Mountains. Treadwell then enrolled on September 15, 1863, at Cassville in Company E, Second Arkansas Cavalry. His neighbor, John Treece, a brother of the three Treece men in the chain gang, had enlisted in the same company on July 12, 1863, along with chain gang member William J. Thompson, Treadwell's brother-in-law.[249]

Chain gang member Benjamin G. Watts deserted Company I after the battle of Shiloh and arrived home on May 9. He lay out with other Confederate deserters until he had the chance to join Peace Society member Benjamin F. Taylor's Company M, Third Arkansas Cavalry in January 1864. Ben Watts's brother Asa also returned to Searcy County after deserting, and hid in the woods, near a spring, where his eight-year-old son, Benjamin Arthur, left food for him. He did not enlist in the Third Arkansas Cavalry with his brother but did ride with them as a "refugee citizen." Asa Watts stated: "I served with Co. M, 3rd Ark Cav from about Oct. 1863, until Apr 1865, but if I was ever enrolled I do not remember when, but my name was called and I did regular duty, and I was considered a soldier, but was never paid, or discharged. I drew ammunition but no clothing. I think that they refused me on account of a sore leg."[250]

Benjamin F. Taylor's name was the first on the list of men belonging to a secret order that had not been arrested. Sometime in December 1862 or earlier, he drilled at the Witts Springs picnic ground with other men who lived as far as seven miles away. They armed themselves with guns impressed from those who had them and bought or confiscated gunpowder.

On January 2, 1863, the same day they organized as a company and elected Taylor as captain, the men fired on Major Ben Elliott's scouts of Colonel J. O. Shelby's regiment, part of General Marmaduke's brigade. Paton Drewry, who had left with Ben Snow in August 1862 to join Dickey's company, recalled: "I came back home in Nov. or Dec. 1862, and participated in a fight with Marmaduke right on this town site (Witts Springs) on the 2nd day of Jany 1863. We were organizing a federal Co. and thought we were opposing Capt. Love's Co. of Confederate army. Love lived over near St. Joe this county and we thought we were able to cope with him, but we could not make a long stand against Marmaduke."[251]

Several of Taylor's men were captured, and some were tried for desertion. Others, who were civilians, were tried for treason. Claiborne Smith was captured, and witnesses identified him as a Peace Society man whose name was on the list but who had avoided capture by the militia. John Rambo, age forty-five, tried to hide but was the first man caught. He said he was captured because he was old and could not run. They did not have a list of their company and had arms for only thirty men, but there were fifty men in all. Colonel John Campbell and other Confederates in the area had observed the company while it was drilling; they were witnesses at the courts-martial held on January 3, 1863, at camp on the Buffalo River. Some of the prisoners said that they had attended Taylor's drill because there was excitement on the mountain. Jeptha McGinnis (deserted from Head's Battalion, Company A), Charles C. Kilgore (deserted from Titsworth's Company K, Carroll's regiment), and William Blair (deserted from Love's Company K, Fourteenth Infantry) were convicted by court-martial and executed on January 4, 1863, by Captain Blackwell, Company G, Shelby's regiment. Blair and McGinnis were Searcy County residents; Kilgore from Franklin County sought refuge there among fellow Unionists after deserting from the rebel army.[252]

With the breakup of Taylor's incipient company, Taylor and David C. Ruff—whose name had followed Taylor's on the list of men not arrested—left for the Union army at Fayetteville. On February 27, 1863, they enrolled in Company K, First Arkansas Infantry (U.S.), recruited by fellow Searcy County Peace Society member Lieutenant Lorenzo Dow Jameson. Jameson had been assigned in January 1863 from Company H, First Arkansas Cavalry to recruit for the First Arkansas Infantry.[253]

As it happened, the other wing of Marmaduke's expedition, Missouri Cavalry Brigade, led by Colonel Emmett MacDonald, had also taken prisoners as it passed through Clinton, Wiley's Cove, and Burrowville. Their haul included Henry H. Thompson, a deserter from Captain Samuel Leslie's Company F, Thirty-second Arkansas Infantry and a brother of Peace Society and Leslie's chain gang member William J. Thompson. After a court-martial, Thompson was found not guilty and sent back to his command. On January 4, they marched to Yellville from the Buffalo River and kept their camp guards regularly mounted because they were in the land of jayhawkers. The Peace Society's reputation lingered, despite the newspapers' reports that it was a "fizzle."[254]

Federal Recruitment

When General Samuel R. Curtis with the Army of the Southwest arrived in Batesville on May 3, 1862, he raised expectations and opened a new world of possibilities for Unionists and the Peace Society in north Arkansas. Unfortunately, many of those expectations were not met. The army did not provide a permanent presence or adequate protection, and it did not control the countryside. Rebels were a constant threat outside the town's defense perimeter. It did provide a military organization for Unionists to join, and they did. After the war, Curtis, reflecting on his time at Batesville in 1862, wrote the following:

> [I]t was evident that very many of the citizens of Arkansas were still loyal to the Constitution and the old Union. They had been juggled out of the union by the tricks of a convention which they had elected to oppose secession. Hitherto their state had escaped the devastation of war. The most bitter rebels had generally found their way into the rebel army. The Union citizens, unable to escape, had remained at home. The rebel law of conscription had not then been put into force, and these men had escaped the rebel army. Under the protection of Union arms, hundreds voluntarily came forward on our allegiance....These were generally the poorer and illiterate classes of the people, small farmers and others, the so styled "poor white trash" of the South, but the yeomanry of Arkansas. They...more frequently lived at distant and exposed points where loyalty to the Union was certain to be visited with outrage and persecution.[255]

So many men wanted to join the Union army that permission was finally granted to raise a six-month infantry unit, and several hundred loyal citizens enlisted at Batesville. A few days after Curtis's arrival, Hiram V. Gray—a loyalist from Black River Township, Independence County—and about forty of his neighbors tendered their services to the government. They had banded together with more than a hundred others to resist by force attempts to enlist them into the Confederate army. Captain Gray requested permission to recruit for a regiment of six-month men. A few months previously he nearly lost his life at the hands of a mob in Batesville for saying that if he did any fighting during the contest it would be under the Stars and Stripes. This circumstance and others, showing his and his compatriots determined bravery and persistent loyalty, convinced the commanding general to authorize him to recruit a regiment, notwithstanding that he had not yet received authority from the War Department. Gray's company was enrolled on June 10 as Company A, First Battalion Six-month Arkansas Infantry.[256]

On June 15, 1862, Curtis wrote this of the efforts:

> Union men for three days past have been coming in from Conway County partially armed. They are running away from the Conscription Act which Gen. T. C. Hindman, Conf. is trying to enforce. All between the ages of 18 and 35 are required to enroll themselves immediately. The country is in great state of excitement. I receive and try to arm these men. They should be regularly mustered as volunteers, but no notice seems to be given to my suggestions.[257]

Thomas J. Williams and George Galloway came into the lines from Conway County, each with about thirty men, and were enrolled on June 10, 1862, as Company B, First Battalion Six-month Infantry. Williams was made captain, and Galloway was first lieutenant. Like the Black River men, they had organized sometime previously for self-defense and were compelled to flee to the federal army, be killed, or go into the rebel service. Among the recruits were three Stobaugh men—Ananias, Edmond, and Edmond's son

James (Peace Society members and Unionists from Van Buren County)—who enrolled on June 10 in Captain Williams's Company B. Later, Edmond was a blacksmith attached to Company B, Third Arkansas Cavalry. The Stobaugh men likely were among the thirty recruits Williams brought with him from the Conway–Van Buren County line. Edmond Stobaugh's nephew, Franklin O. Stobaugh, stated that he himself was not a regular Union soldier, but that he was attached to the Third Arkansas Cavalry for about fifteen months before the war ended. He was with Williams's irregular battalion, which operated with that regiment. This further relationship between Peace Society Edmond Stobaugh and Williams strengthens the probability that the Williamses also belonged to the Peace Society.[258]

Afterward, authority was given to Pleasant Turney of Independence County and Lorenzo D. Toney of Izard County to recruit companies for the First Six-month Arkansas Infantry. Peace Society member Toney had been Ware's lieutenant in Company G, Phelps's Six-Months Missouri Volunteers. Captain Pleasant Turney's company was enrolled on June 10 at Batesville as Company C. Toney's Company D was not enrolled until July 1 at Jacksonport.

Men who lived within the federal lines at Batesville and were recruited under the authority to raise a six-month unit remained at home until the last day of June, when General Curtis unexpectedly moved down the White River. The recruits and many other Unionists left with the army so suddenly that men working only a short distance from home had to depart without saying goodbye or getting clothing. All believed that the country was to be held and that they would not to be subject to rebel violence and oppression again. They were disappointed.

When the army arrived at Helena, the recruits for the First Six-month Arkansas Infantry were organized into an infantry battalion led by Lt. Col. J. C. Bundy. The men had brought their horses, as they expected to mount themselves—and also to keep their rebel neighbors from getting them. They were keenly disappointed then to learn they would not be mounted and would not receive government forage. The horses would either have to die or be sold for a pittance. And if frustration with the government's policies dispirited the men, diseases from the river bottoms so depleted their ranks by October that there were not enough healthy men for camp duty. The Six-month Arkansas Infantry was sent to Benton Barracks in St. Louis, where the men remained until they were discharged in December. This experience so disappointed most men they did not attempt to join the regular army again, but, like the Williams clan, formed their own guerrilla units.[259]

A week or so after Williams and Galloway arrived in Batesville with their men, about two dozen men from central and northern Van Buren County arrived in Batesville. Missouri units were looking for soldiers to fill their ranks, and the Peace Society men and others were happy to oblige. On June 18, eleven men—including Peace Society members Abner Smith and William H. Harness and their relatives and neighbors—brought their own horses from Van Buren County's northern townships to enroll in Company D, Bowen's Ninth Missouri Cavalry. The following day eleven more men—including Peace Society members Elijah Dickerson, James F. Bailey, and Michael P. Tinkle and their kin—also enrolled in Company D, Ninth Missouri Cavalry. Seven of them were from Van Buren County and two were from Searcy County. Five days later, four more Van Buren County men from Giles, Turkey Creek, and Union townships enrolled in Company A, Ninth Missouri Cavalry. One month later Christopher C. Pratt of Turkey Creek Township enrolled at Helena in Company A. These enlistments came from heavily Unionist and Peace Society townships and families.[260]

The Ninth Missouri Cavalry was transferred to Tennessee. Not all Peace Society men relished being sent east of the Mississippi River; it violated their principal concern, which was to care for their families. Consequently, on February 9, 1863, Abner and John T. Smith deserted, taking their own horses and the arms issued to them, and returning to Van Buren County. They were potential recruits for Christopher Denton's guerrilla unit. Denton, like Abner, had been a Peace Society organizer.[261]

Another Arkansas unit tried to organize at this same time, taking advantage of Curtis's presence, but it had problems similar to those of the six-month Arkansas battalion. In July 1862, authority was given to Colonel W. James Morgan of Missouri to raise the First Arkansas Mounted Rangers to be organized at Helena.

Nearly 400 recruits were enrolled in Company A under James William Demby, and Company B under Captain Archibald E. Freeburn. At least one of the recruits had already seen service when Searcy County's Andrew J. Garner enlisted August 27, 1862, in Freeburn's Company B. He had been a private in Captain James H. Love's Company K, Fourteenth (Powers) Arkansas Infantry (C.S.) from August 5, 1861—when he was mustered with the company at Yellville—until August 6, 1862, when he deserted at Saltillo, Mississippi. Garner explained his Confederate service by saying that he had been forced to choose between joining Company K or being hanged. He enlisted before the Peace Society was discovered, but his sympathies were definitely pro-Union. Three weeks after he deserted in Mississippi, he volunteered in Arkansas for federal service, and on October 20 he was promoted to lieutenant.[262]

But many of Morgan's men were soon displeased. The location was unhealthy; they were ignorant of soldier's life; age incapacitated many; sickness was rampant; and Colonel Morgan, who had recruited them, was dismissed from the service. Company C still lacked its full complement of men when Morgan was dismissed, and many already enrolled were so disheartened that they deserted. The unit was so disorganized that Arkansas's military governor, John S. Phelps, re-designated the unit as the Second Arkansas Cavalry Volunteers and sent it to St. Louis. Captains Demby and Freeburn were transferred on October 13, 1862, to the Second Arkansas Cavalry. Companies A and B were consolidated, making Demby a supernumerary, so he was mustered out on May 31, 1863, in St Louis. Demby, from Jefferson County, Arkansas, had been active in a secret Unionist organization that he called a Union League. He later published pro-Union pamphlets sympathetic to Arkansas Unionists and the Union League.[263]

A late-blooming unit of the Peace Society was started in Pope and Yell counties in early 1862. Thomas Boles, later a U.S. congressman in the Fortieth Congress, energetically opposed Arkansas's secession. When the rebellion began, he and other Union men were taught to say nothing positive about the federal government. The Union men of the country knew each other, and early in 1862 they secretly organized a Union League. In July 1862, when the conscript law began to be enforced, Boles pled inability and, due to feeble health, was ordered to Little Rock for examination by a surgeon. While there, he had a severe attack of fever, which guaranteed his exemption. Between that time and the summer of 1863, he was arrested three or four times by the rebels but succeeded in keeping out of their service. In the summer of 1863, when federal forces crossed the Arkansas River, he and other men who had belonged to the Union League immediately enlisted in the Union army.[264]

Boles was enrolled October 15, 1863, in Company E, Third Arkansas Cavalry (U.S.) in Yell County as first lieutenant and was told to recruit more men. The company was fully formed on November 14 and mustered in at Little Rock on the nineteenth. Boles was promoted to captain on February 5, 1864. Before they organized as Company E, most of his men had acted as an independent company to defend themselves and the country against rebel scouts. However, when the rebels overpowered them on November 7, 1863, they had little choice but to escape Yell County and retreat toward Little Rock. The company remained in camp until December 8, when it was ordered back to Yell County to recruit. After five days there it pushed on to Scott County, where seventeen more men were recruited. The company returned to Little Rock on December 27, 1863.[265]

Also, the Second Kansas Cavalry recruited for Arkansas regiments in the Pope and Yell county area. The Kansas regiment, based at Fort Smith at the beginning of November 1863, was scattered along the Arkansas River performing various duties, until there was scarcely the shadow of a regiment at headquarters. Among those on detached service in the Pope and Yell county area was Captain Hugh Cameron of Company F, recruiting for the Second Arkansas Cavalry where he would soon become second in command. He had recruited and armed eighty-five Mountain Feds when, in November and December 1863, he found they were surrounded by more than 600 Missouri rebels. He was sustained and reinforced by the local citizens under the direction of local Unionists Burk Johnson and William Stout. Cameron reported that over 500 recruits were added to the federal army at this time without a single incidence of treachery by the citizens. He praised the local Unionists as faithful scouts and reliable guides. Johnson and Stout, who had organized the local support for Cameron and his recruits, joined the Third and Fourth Arkansas Cavalry regiments as privates at this time. In January 1864, Cameron led his recruits from Dardanelle to Cassville, Missouri, with prisoners equal to one-third of his armed force in as orderly and well-executed a march as any performed by old and well-disciplined troops.[266]

All this was made possible when General Frederick Steele captured Little Rock on September 10, 1863. That greatly expanded federal enlistment opportunities for Peace Society men and other Unionists. Among those to seize the opportunity was Peace Society recruiter Thomas Harness of Holley Township, who left the mountains with Chris Denton's son, William A. Denton, to join a company being raised in Conway County by Leander S. Dunscomb. Dunscomb, a thirty-six-year-old New Yorker, had come to Conway County sometime in 1860 and married Elizabeth Whitecotton, a cook for the wealthy merchant John P. Morgan, on March 3, 1861.

The thirty-six men raised by Dunscomb enlisted on October 28, 1863, to form Company G, Third Arkansas Cavalry (U.S.). Dunscomb was given a first lieutenant's commission while he was recruiting, then was made captain on December 22 when the company was complete. Disciplinary problems and misunderstandings among his troops led him to resign his commission on July 12, 1864, but four months later he petitioned General Steele for authorization to raise a battalion of cavalry in Arkansas. He still wanted to serve his country, and he believed that a number of men in north-central Arkansas not yet in the army would cheerfully enlist for three years, if allowed to elect their own officers and with Steele's assurance that they would do scout duty for the protection of their homes and families. Dunscomb's proposal went nowhere with Steele.[267]

Federal military service provided more security than hiding in the woods from bushwhackers and was preferable to Confederate military service. Most Arkansas federal military units patrolled the areas where the soldiers lived, but they did not control those areas. No one controlled the north-central Arkansas mountains, which left a vacuum filled by bands of jayhawkers, bushwhackers, guerrillas, thieves, and deserters from both sides who brought desolation and death to civilians at home. The Third Arkansas Cavalry (U.S.), operating out of Lewisburg, was the most effective unit in disrupting outlaw and guerrilla bands in north-central Arkansas, but it was far from bringing security to Peace Society and Unionist families. They continued to flee to the security of federal military posts. Acting in concert with other Unionists in such bands as those of Chris Denton and the Williams clan, the Peace Society members protected some homes from their Confederate opponents, but they were not strong enough to bring real change in north-central Arkansas.

James Jackson Barnes Sr., chain gang member and Searcy County representative, 15th General Assembly. (Courtesy of the author)

Chapter 5

Aftermath: January 1863 and On

As the war wore on, Peace Society men and the families they tried to protect were pushed around by the exigencies of the conflict. Paramount in their responses to these forces was a concern for home and an underlying loyalty to the Union. A few members took leadership positions in the military and later in civil government during the war, in Reconstruction, and for years afterward. Most were content to rebuild their lives. The situations and opportunities presented to these men and their responses run the gamut from enlisting in the Union army to hiding in the caves and woods near home until they could safely escape with their families behind federal lines.

The federal army's presence in Arkansas provided some relief for Arkansas Unionists and Peace Society members, as it offered protection to their families at military posts. The Union army could only offer protection where it was camped or at a military post; it could not protect the entire countryside. Rural Arkansas was open to Confederate guerrillas and recruiters, bands of raiders called jayhawkers, boomers, or bushwhackers who pillaged the countryside, especially robbing Union families. The occasional Union guerrilla group, such as Chris Denton's or the Williams clan, provided limited protection to Union families in their neighborhoods, but they could not protect anything as large as a county. The efforts of these men to provide security to the area forced them to be away from home. This left their families subject to raids by wandering bands. A family's only option was to leave if it could; wives usually sought refuge at the husband's military post. At first this meant Springfield, Missouri, where the First and Second Arkansas Cavalry (U.S.) regiments were stationed off and on; later Lewisburg, on the Arkansas River (now Morrilton) was added, the base for the Third Arkansas Cavalry (U.S.).[268]

David C. Ruff fled to Fayetteville, Arkansas, with fellow Peace Society member Benjamin F. Taylor after the disastrous attack on January 2, 1863, on General Marmaduke's brigade at Witts Springs. Fellow Peace Society member Lorenzo D. Jameson enrolled the two men on February 27, 1863, in Company K, First Arkansas Infantry (U.S.).

On May 20, 1863, Ruff was assigned as a clerk to the provost's office in Springfield, where he had knowledge of Searcy County men living in the Springfield area. In October 1864, Ruff was made captain of Company F, Forty-sixth Missouri Infantry, which he had recruited from Arkansas refugees around Springfield. Several men were from Searcy County, including Peace Society members Alexander Younger and Jarrett Reeves.[269]

Peace Society member John W. Morris became ill after the Prairie Grove battle and could no longer fulfil his military duties. He resigned his commission as first lieutenant in Company H, First Arkansas Cavalry on February 15, 1863, and moved from Fayetteville—where the First Arkansas was encamped—to Springfield, Missouri, for better accommodations. In Springfield he reunited with David Ruff.[270]

Morris boarded for a time in Springfield, but he was concerned about his family, which remained on Calf Creek in Searcy County. Fearing it was not faring too well, he joined with Ruff to hire two women to go to Arkansas and pilot their families to Springfield. Only women could make the journey in safety, although it was dangerous even for them. The Morris and Ruff families were joined by the families of Peace Society members Paris Strickland and John H. Jenkins as they pooled wagons and ox teams for the trip. Jenkins and Strickland had fled Searcy County in late November 1861, as the Peace Society men began to be hunted down. Starting out with two wagons and two yokes of oxen, the refugees were robbed of their clothing and other valuables twice before they reached Bear Creek Spring (five miles north of present-day Harrison), where a Confederate checkpoint took one wagon and a yoke of oxen and much of what remained, including Morris's mother's tobacco.

The Morris family lived in Springfield until after the war, with John supporting his family by farming and selling stock to the army. With some trepidation, they returned to Searcy County in 1868 with the William F. McDaniel family. William had been in the Peace Society, the chain gang, and the Eighteenth Arkansas Infantry with Morris and had returned with Morris from the Confederate army to Searcy County. But McDaniel had remained in Searcy County when Morris went to Missouri and joined the Third Arkansas Cavalry with his son Robert. After they were discharged in June 1865, the McDaniel men joined their refugee family in Springfield. Despite fears that they would not be accepted again in their old home, the Morris family was welcomed back into the community by friends and relatives.[271]

On October 24, 1863, Benjamin F. Taylor was put on detached service to recruit for the Third Arkansas Cavalry. He completed his company by February 1864, taken almost entirely from Searcy County men. From January 26 to February 2, 1864, six companies of the Third Arkansas Cavalry operated in Searcy County, where it garnered several recruits, including almost a complete battalion of Confederates under Major J. W. S. Leslie, a part of General Dandridge McRae's command. While Leslie was away conferring with McRae, the officer who was left in charge surrendered the entire battalion to the federals. The majority enlisted in the Third Arkansas Cavalry (U.S.).[272]

Companies I, K, and M of the Third Arkansas Cavalry were formed primarily from Searcy County men. The soldiers' families sought refuge at the regiment's post at Lewisburg, where they were part of a large refugee community with few options for sustenance or shelter. When Lieutenant Colonel I. W. Fuller moved the Third

Arkansas Cavalry headquarters to Lewisburg from the Little Rock area on April 1, 1864, he found many destitute families, most of them unable to provide for themselves. He assisted them as far as his resources would permit. His command was kept actively employed in scouting the country from sixty to 120 miles north and west.

The country above Little Red River to the Boston Mountains was in a desolate, unsettled state, full of bushwhackers, thieves, and rebel sympathizers. It comprised north Van Buren County and all of Searcy County, the center of Peace Society activity. There were numerous bands of guerrillas in the mountains, detachments from General McRae's command, which—numbering about 600 or 700 men—was stationed near White River. Bands of twenty to fifty rebels were constantly scouring the country and "committing every depredation divisable [sic] by the human mind." Fuller did his utmost to protect loyal citizens in the region and bring to justice every enemy of the government, but he could spare only one squadron to track the rebels. "Being well mounted," he complained, "having a thorough knowledge of the country and very many sympathizers and friends, [they] are almost impossible to reach by any scout from this point of such numbers as I am able to send." Fuller's description addresses the original concern of the Peace Society, the security of home and family, and explains Dunscomb's petition to form a battalion of rangers to defend Union families in north-central Arkansas.[273]

In the spring of 1863, a federal recruiting party—composed of the First Arkansas Infantry's Colonel James M. Johnson, anti-secessionist William M. Fishback, General Curtis's cartographer Lyman G. Bennett, and others—went into mountainous north-central Arkansas to raise another regiment of Mountain Feds. Making their base in Jasper, Newton County, they were relatively secure, as the area was then under the control of Captain James K. Vanderpool, Company C, First Arkansas Infantry (U.S.). Bennett described their mission: "It was judged best not to confine recruiting operations to one neighborhood. Accordingly a portion [of the recruiting party] went about thirty miles east, in Pope County, on the border of Searcy and Conway [sic] Counties." This produced results. "Volunteers came flocking in by the score," he said, "and in ten days a company of ninety-six was formed with [Mortimer M.] Brashear, as Captain." Brashear had contacted the party with some of his followers, and on July 12, they enlisted in a unit that became Company E, Second Arkansas Cavalry (U.S.).[274]

Bennett described Mortimer Brashear in this way:

> Another recruiter was Brashears [sic], a resident of Pope County, a tall stalwart and gray haired mountaineer of sixty years. He had three sons then in the federal service, and the fourth, a stripling of seventeen, was one of our first recruits. Brashears had in a short period raised a company of men who had been driven from their homes, hunted like wild beasts from mountain to mountain and from cave to cave. They were like deer that have been incessantly pursued by hounds and hunters, timid and distrustful and wanting in courage to attempt their escape to our lines without aid. Mr. Brashears returned to Springfield alone, hoping that a scouting expedition might be sent down to aid his men in making their escape.

Brashear then accompanied Johnson's recruiting party back into Arkansas from Springfield.[275]

Brashear had some previous Peace Society involvement, as evidenced by the testimony of his son, Lafayette Brashear. Although a bit confused, Lafayette recalled his father's Civil War activities this way in 1897: "M. M. Brashear, early in 1861, organized the Loyal League of America [sic] in Searcy County. Early in 1862 the Confederate conscript law was passed and the rolls of the Loyal League fell into the hands of the enemy. Eighty of the Loyal League were forthwith arrested, and balled and chained and sent to Bowling Green, Ky., and all others ordered to join the service at once on peril of their lives." Mortimer Brashear avoided the conscription officers. But, seeing the danger to his sons, he advised the eldest, Walter, and other young men to enter Confederate service but then desert and go to the Union army. Walter and several other members of the Loyal League joined, or were conscripted into, G. W. Lemoyne's Seventeenth Arkansas Infantry.[276]

Walter W. Brashear was mustered in on December 21, 1861, at Dardanelle in Company E, Lemoyne's Seventeenth Arkansas Infantry (C.S.). In addition to Brashear, there were seven more men from Searcy County who joined Company E at the same time. Four of them (Joseph F. Arter, Ebenezer B. Jameson, Nicholas Seaton, and Hezekiah Taylor) were documented Peace Society members. After deserting the Confederates in June 1862, Walter Brashear returned to Searcy County. Then, with his brothers Alva S. and John W. Brashear, he went to Cassville, Missouri, where they all enlisted on September 11, 1862, in Company L, First Arkansas Cavalry (U.S.). Paton Drewry (Drury) of Witts Springs, a Confederate conscript, had already enlisted on August 27 in Company L.[277]

A pattern can be observed, wherein men from Witts Springs Mountain (Pope, Newton, and Searcy counties) deserted the Confederacy within a year and enlisted in Arkansas Union regiments. The recruiting efforts of Mortimer Brashear and Colonel Johnson made enlistment easier. Brashear's recruits included Peace Society member Nicholas Seaton, and Edmond Aday and his sons John W. and Francis M. Aday. (One of B. F. Taylor's guerrillas, Edmond had been captured by Colonel Shelby at Witts Springs.) Brashear was later killed on August 5, 1863, in southern Searcy County by Confederates sent from Dover to disrupt his recruiting efforts. Killed before he and his men were mustered into service, Brashear was replaced as captain by Jesse Millsaps of Hartsugg Township, Van Buren County, when the men were mustered on December 21, 1863, as Company E, Second Arkansas Cavalry (U.S.). Later recruits included John F. Treadwell, a Peace Society member from Searcy County, and Levi J. Hodges. Treadwell had led a Union guerrilla unit and Hodges was one of his men.[278]

In January 1864, federal brigadier general John B. Sanborn, commanding southwest Missouri, heard that Confederates were gathering in north-central Arkansas for a raid into Missouri. To counter this plan, he ordered 600 men from the First and Second Arkansas Cavalry regiments and the Eighth Missouri State Militia Cavalry into Newton and Searcy counties. They operated there and in Van Buren County, tracking down Confederate guerrillas, from January 23 to 29. This being the heart of Peace Society country, some men came out of hiding to join Company M of the Second Arkansas Cavalry. Forty-three men enlisted between January 17 and January 28 in Searcy County, including Peace Society member William Caler and his brothers Benjamin F. and Thomas J. Caler, Henry Treece—younger brother of three Treece men in Leslie's chain gang—and Peace Society member Andrew N. Kimbrell, John F. Treadwell's brother-in-law, who had guarded the chain gang to Little Rock.[279]

The Second Arkansas Cavalry escorted 100 wagons to Berryville with Unionist families from the area seeking homes in the North. From Berryville, they went to temporary homes in Missouri. Military escorts were necessary to protect all wagon trains against Confederate guerrillas and their check points, such as at Bear Creek Spring. Among the refugees was chain gang member Benjamin Treece's extended family, which met him in Wright County, Missouri, where they remained for the duration of the war. James Claiborn McNair and his family were also among the evacuees. He was under $500 bond from the Camp Culloden justice of the peace's court to appear before the governor, but he avoided the prisoner march to Little Rock and went home to his 120-acre farm at the foot of Tomahawk Creek's Pilot Mountain. Some said McNair was a Southern man, but others (including himself) said he was a Unionist. He had, in mid-1861, run as a Southern man in an election to elect a captain of a volunteer company and said that he would take the company directly to General Ben McCulloch. He was not elected. Four of his brothers served in the Confederate army, but McNair seems to have had no inclination to do military service unless he could be captain. His main objective was to support and protect his family. He hid from conscription officers and jayhawkers in the Pilot Mountain caves near his home in Searcy County's

Tomahawk Township, where he smoked the date "1862" on the wall of one cave.

Pressure from raiders and conscription officers made the federal escort past the Bear Creek Spring seem like a godsend as McNair fled with his family and their possessions. Once arrived at Springfield, his daughter Martha Delilah helped support the family by doing washing for Union soldiers. She eventually married one of her clients from the regiment that escorted her from the dangers in Searcy County: Benjamin F. Henley, Company M, Second Arkansas Cavalry. J. C. McNair and his extended family returned on May 1, 1866, to his farm in northern Searcy County.[280]

The federal army by late 1863 had re-established a presence in Batesville, which became a hub of Unionist activity. William Monks, a contractor providing scouting services to the federal army in north Arkansas (particularly around Batesville), employed Fulton County Peace Society members and others of the Fulton County diaspora in Batesville. Jehoida Ware, after he left Phelps's six-month Infantry Volunteers, served with Monks. Although personnel and dates for his contracts varied, one of them began on December 11, 1863, at Batesville. Ware's service began on February 10, 1864.[281]

The Fulton County Unionists in Batesville were organizing politically for the future. On February 24, 1864, the Unconditional Union men of Fulton County met at Batesville to draft resolutions and to nominate candidates for Fulton County offices. Governor Isaac Murphy was trying to form a state government and get recognition from, and representation in, the U.S. Congress. They never succeeded, but in early 1864 local Unionists were encouraged to dream, and Fulton County Unionists did dream. Peace Society leader Ware called the meeting to order and appointed his Peace Society accomplice Shadrach Wren to preside. Simpson Mason was appointed secretary and Ware, James A. Baker, John H. Baker, and Hiram Turner were appointed to draft resolutions for the meeting. Wren and James Baker had been among the 1861 prisoners taken to Little Rock. James and John Baker and Mason were fellow scouts for William Monks.[282]

Their resolutions opposed allowing former Confederates to vote in the reorganization of the state government until they had fully proven their allegiance to the United States. They also resolved that the military should be more aggressive in ridding the countryside of the bushwhackers, who daily shot soldiers and Union men all over the country. They gave their hearty cooperation and support to the president in putting down the rebellion and endorsed the Emancipation Proclamation, as well as all congressional actions to get rid of slavery. However, they believed that the actions of the January 1864 State Convention were premature, although they embraced the first opportunity to reorganize the state government and resume Arkansas's position in the Union.

The public meeting made the following nominations: W. H. Padgett for prosecuting attorney, J. J. Ware for state senate, Simpson Mason for representative, Hiram Turner for county judge, Shadrach H. Wren for sheriff, William P. Wyatt—Ware's neighbor—for clerk, and James Baker for assessor and collector. None of the county offices were filled by these nominees, but Ware and Mason did serve in the Fifteenth General Assembly (1864–1865). Wyatt had been another of Monks's scouts, and Mason and Wyatt were made federal militia captains for Fulton County on April 24, 1865.[283]

When secession reared its head, Joshua Richardson of Fulton County and three of his sons joined J. J. Ware's Peace Society. When Ware fled to Missouri in November 1861, Joshua's sons William S. and Thomas F. Richardson went with him and joined his Company G, Phelps's Six-month Volunteer Infantry. They fought at Pea Ridge, where Thomas was mortally wounded. Joshua and his twenty-three-year-old son James Calvin Richardson were swept up by Dr. Nunnelie's vigilantes, taken to Little Rock, and questioned by the Military Board. James won the opprobrium "character bad as a boy can be," when he was identified as a "son of Joshua Richardson." In his testimony, he stated "[I] was a member of a secret organization, sworn in at my father's house. The object of the society was for keeping down mobs [like Nunnelie's vigilantes], and protecting our property from being destroyed.—Bad health or he would have volunteered." When the Richardsons were released by the January 1862 court, they went to Crawford County, Missouri.[284]

William Richardson joined his father in Crawford County upon his discharge from Phelps's Six-month Volunteers. On April 18, 1864, he joined W. H. Ferguson's Crawford County Provisional Enrolled Militia. James Richardson—he with the bad character— moved to Springfield and enrolled in May 1864 in Company A, Seventy-fourth Enrolled Missouri Militia. At the end of the war, William returned to Izard County, where he saw some service with the Arkansas militia and as a courier with the Freedmen's Bureau. He became a Republican in politics, as did many Peace Society men, but he held no public office, returning home only to rebuild a ruined farming operation.[285]

Except for strongly Unionist Searcy County, where Union influence lasted for some time after Reconstruction, Peace Society men played only a minor part in local Reconstruction politics. Benjamin F. Brantley, the Peace Society recruiter active in western Izard and northern Searcy County, served as Izard County treasurer from 1868 to 1872. The Fifteenth General Assembly contained Fulton County's Jehoida Ware as senator for Fulton and Lawrence counties, Simpson Mason as Fulton County representative, and James J. Barnes as Searcy County representative.

Ware moved to Webster County, Missouri, before 1870 to become a stock dealer and farmer. Maybe he moved because Fulton County was unfriendly. In 1878, he became interested in the National Greenback-Labor party and ran as its candidate for the U.S. Congress. He narrowly lost to incumbent Richard P. Bland. Ware said he detested and abhorred the financial policy of the government, which rendered the masses of citizens—especially the industrial workers—tributary to a few money manipulators at home and abroad. For this reason, he had left the Republican Party for the Greenbacks.[286]

Simpson Mason became a county militia captain on April 24, 1865, later served as an official in the Freedmen's Bureau, and eventually became a county official when Governor Powell Clayton appointed him to the Board of Registration in Fulton County. Mason had organized a Union League, a post-war arm of the Republican Party with Peace Society connections. His political activities as registrar aroused the fury of disenfranchised ex-Confederates. On September 19, 1868, several gunmen ambushed and killed Mason near Bennett's Bayou, Fulton County. Unionists immediately suspected a group of ex-Confederates that included Colonel Jesse H. Tracy and his brother Nathaniel H. Tracy. Jesse Tracy had been first lieutenant, Company H, Eighth Arkansas Cavalry, along with his son J. H. Tracy Jr. and brother N. H. Tracy, who all enlisted in the latter half of 1862. All three deserted in August and September 1863. Jesse Tracy succeeded Mason as state representative for Fulton County in Isaac Murphy's Sixteenth General Assembly (1866–1867).[287]

Searcy County's representative to the Fifteenth General Assembly, James Jackson Barnes, had been in Leslie's chain gang and in Company I, Marmaduke's Eighteenth Arkansas Infantry. He was sent to the Confederate hospital in Tupelo, Mississippi, on July 20, 1862, and somehow made his way back to Searcy County. He enlisted in Archibald Napier's Company I, Third Arkansas Cavalry (U.S.) in January 1864 and was elected Searcy County representative to the Fifteenth General Assembly that first met on April 11, 1864. Sometime during the first session, the legislature considered creating a regiment of Arkansas Rangers. On June 16, Barnes advised some Searcy County recruits in the Third Arkansas to withhold being mustered so they could join the new regiment. As a recruit, the forty-nine-year-old Barnes was arrested, charged with exciting mutiny, and sentenced on July 29 by court-martial to reduction in rank—he was a corporal—forfeiture of all payments, and confinement at hard labor for one year at the military prison in Little Rock.

On August 11, Governor Murphy asked Major General Frederick Steele that Barnes be pardoned. The request, which was co-signed by Arkansas's secretary of state, state auditor, state treasurer, attorney general, and members of the judiciary, pointed out that Barnes was a tried patriot who—because of his Union sentiments—had been conducted 150 miles into Little Rock with an iron chain about his neck to the very prison where he was now confined. The petition worked, and on August 27, Barnes's sentence was remitted. He was restored to duty and attended the second session of the legislature but received a medical discharge on May 29, 1865. Governor Murphy then appointed him county judge for Searcy County, though a stable government could not be established in the county until sometime after the Confederate surrender.[288]

Captain Benjamin Franklin Taylor, Company M, Third Arkansas Cavalry (U.S.), was discharged with his regiment on June 30, 1865, at Lewisburg. His was the first name on the list of men belonging to a secret organization but not arrested in 1861. He succeeded Barnes as Searcy County's representative, was elected to the Sixteenth General Assembly (1866–1867), and subsequently served in the Eighteenth General Assembly in 1871, the Twenty-third in 1881, and the Twenty-fourth in 1883. He was a farmer and entrepreneur in Calf Creek valley, owning a cotton gin, sawmill, grist mill, and store. In June 1897, Taylor was appointed deputy marshal for the federal court's Batesville division, dedicated to the suppression of illegal distilleries. On Sunday August 24, Taylor led a posse into northern Pope County to capture an illegal still operated by Harve Bruce, an ex-Confederate soldier from western North Carolina. The posse was ambushed about nine in the morning, with Taylor and Joe Dodson (another deputy marshal) killed.[289]

Others of Searcy County's Peace Society who later served as public officials included Josiah Lane, who succeeded J. J. Barnes as county judge for the 1866–1874 term. Lane had been sworn into the Peace Society by Peter Tyler. John W. Morris, a chain gang member and Eighteenth Arkansas Infantry soldier, held several county posts: county clerk 1876–1878, treasurer 1874–1876 and 1888–1892, and coroner 1868–1872. Benjamin White Hensley, on the list of Peace Society men not arrested, was postmaster for Burrowville from May 31, 1866, assessor 1868–1872 and sheriff 1872–1874. James F. Homer Christy, a Culloden prisoner and in Marmaduke's Infantry, was appointed postmaster at Point Peter, Searcy County, on July 13, 1885.

The cachet of being a Peace Society member continued to carry some weight for the next few years. W. H. Huffines, Company K, Third Arkansas Cavalry (U.S.), came to Searcy County about 1861 from Wayne County, Tennessee. By the 1872 elections, he was irate over the crooked election machinations he observed in Locust Grove Township. He complained of names being stricken from the rolls without cause. (At the Big Flat precinct thirty-three names were erased including two who belonged to the Union League.) His own name had been scratched, despite his being a U.S. soldier with an honorable discharge who had held office and voted at the civil polls for the ratification of the state constitution.[290]

Benjamin Treece, chain gang survivor. (Courtesy of the author)

Chapter 6

Other Arkansas Mountain Federals and Secret Unionists: 1862–1868

North-central Arkansas Unionists and their secret organizations were the largest and most active secret Unionist groups in the state, but they were certainly not the only Unionists who remained in Arkansas; and the Peace Society in these north-central Arkansas counties was not the only secret Unionist society. James William Demby, captain of Company A, Second Arkansas Cavalry (U.S.), was a forty-three-year-old watchmaker living in Jefferson County, Arkansas, in 1860. In 1864, as editor of a Little Rock Unionist paper, he wrote the "Secret Union League," for the *Home Aegis and Monthly Review*. In it he quoted a piece from the May 22, 1864, *Louisville Journal*: "It is announced on good authority that there is a secret Union league extending through all the Southern States, the existence of which is unknown to the rebel authorities. Only men of northern interests, and those who are known to be tried Unionists, are admitted to the 'order.'" Demby agreed with that statement, saying that from personal knowledge he could confirm that the league existed. He had been an active league member and recruited men to its ranks. Only well-known, firm Unionists were invited to join. The Union League kept no record of any kind and held no large gatherings of members. Fear of discovery and persecution kept them from expressing their sentiments openly, so a secret society—which allowed them to reveal their opinions freely—was a source of protection and sympathy. However, Demby believed that when men could express their views without fear, secret political societies were dangerous; and he did not favor a secret Union League for Arkansas once a federal government was established.[291]

Since there is little mention of secret Unionist organizations in Arkansas apart from those in north-central Arkansas, the extent and location of Demby's secret Union League is unclear. Since his residence and property were in Jefferson County, his Union League activities were likely in that neighborhood, maybe extending as far as Little Rock. However, there was additional Unionist activity in Arkansas. Elijah Harbour of Caswell Township and John H. Haslow of Locust Bayou Township, Calhoun County, in south-central Arkansas made depositions for the Southern Claims Commission that stated the Union men of Calhoun County had formed secret Union Leagues before April 1862, promising to support each other and avoid Confederate military service. In February 1861, they had voted against holding a convention and had voted for Unionist candidates. Several of the members were hanged for their Unionist sentiments, and others fled.[292]

There are only hints of secret Union League activity elsewhere. The upland of southwest Arkansas most closely resembled the ambiance of the Boston Mountain region, and men there were opposed to Confederate military service. When conscription officers appeared, men in the Ouachita Mountains did as those in the Ozark Mountains did: they hid in the hills. The major difference is that federal troops in 1862 were closer to the Ozarks than they were to the Ouachitas, so Unionists from Montgomery, Pike, Polk, Sebastian, and neighboring counties had to wait until there was a Union presence in Fort Smith or Little Rock to have a refuge or to join the Union army. Unionists did band together for self-protection and to avoid Confederate conscription, and they later joined the federal army. They were particularly prevalent in the southwestern uplands of Arkansas. However, there is no record of them forming secret societies.

When Montgomery County's William H. Foster advised Governor Rector in October 1861 of Union sentiment in the area and an aversion to Confederate military service, he named ten men who vocally refused to serve the Confederacy and two more—brothers Jack (Jacob) Putnam and Elijah C. Putnam—as instigators who were raising a sham company that would remain at home. This may have been an attempt to organize a home guard, as established by the State Convention, to supplant service in the state or Confederate military. The majority of those named lived in Greasy Cove, in Pike and Polk counties. Greasy Cove, a mountain pass at the head of the Little Missouri River, later became a base for Captain Greer, a Unionist guerrilla. Of the sixteen men Foster named as Unionists or witnesses, eleven lived in Mountain Township in the northwest corner of Pike County and one in adjoining White Township. In November 1861, Thomas Ellison, Scott Forrester, and William Houston C. Walker—also on Foster's list (Ellison and Walker were witnesses)—enlisted in a company of the Fourth Arkansas Infantry (C.S.) from Pike County raised by William J. Kelley, the county circuit clerk.

Scott Forrester later said that he involuntarily enlisted for one year on November 10, 1861, in Captain Kelley's Murfreesboro or Pike County Riflemen. Kelley's men were assigned as Company H on December 4, 1861, to the Sixteenth Arkansas Infantry, the one regiment recruited by Burgevin at Carrollton. Forrester was medically discharged on November 21, 1862, at Port Hudson, Louisiana. He had enlisted in Kelley's company to relieve Confederate pressure on his father-in-law, Dr. Jacob Putnam, a large land owner with two slaves.

Forrester and his father-in-law's family (which included two teenage sons) were all noted uncompromising Union sympathizers—so much so that they became obnoxious and repugnant to the dominant rebel element of Pike County, who threatened their lives. This threat could be relieved if someone from the family enlisted in the Confederate army or in some other way quieted the fury against them. Therefore, Forrester enlisted in the rebel service to appease their wrath and save the family from their secessionist neighbors' vengeance. They could not seek refuge behind federal lines because there were no Union troops nearer than Springfield, Missouri, three hundred miles away.[293]

Not surprisingly, eight men on Foster's list of Unionists joined the federal Fourth Arkansas Cavalry, accompanied by several more Pike County men. On November 9, 1863, Jacob Putnam and William H. Walker enlisted in Company A; on November 19 Elijah C. Putnam, W. Houston C. Walker, David White Jr., Henry L. White, and William V. White enlisted in Companies D and H, Fourth Arkansas Cavalry (U.S.) at Benton, Arkansas. Scott Forrester enrolled December 29 at Little Rock in Company D. All lived in Mountain Township, Pike County.[294]

Lorenzo Dow Jameson, Searcy County Peace Society member, was recruited on August 5, 1862, in Company H, First Arkansas Cavalry (U.S.) by fellow Peace Society man John W. Morris. In January 1863, he was detailed to recruit for the First Arkansas Infantry, and his first recruits were fellow Searcy County Peace Society men David C. Ruff and Benjamin F. Taylor, who enlisted on February 27, 1863, in Company K. Jameson was made second lieutenant in Company K, but—believing himself incompetent—resigned his commission in May 1863. The bulk of Company K was enlisted in March 1863 in Fayetteville, but the company continued to receive recruits from Van Buren, Crawford, and Scott counties.[295]

The Second Kansas Cavalry, stationed at Fort Smith in late 1863, received authorization to recruit a company of Arkansans whose knowledge of the area could greatly help in scouting and tracking down rebel guerrillas operating in western Arkansas. Recruiting began on December 1, 1863, at Waldron, where Colonel J. M. Johnson of the First Arkansas Infantry (U.S.) commanded the post. The organization of Company L, Second Kansas was completed on March 2 by the promotion of First Lieutenant Pat Cosgrove to captain. Men from Polk, Scott, and Sebastian counties were attracted to the new company. Several had prior service in the Confederate army.[296]

On January 13, 1863, William H. Pierre—chief of scouts for the Army of the Frontier—reported to General Curtis that Union men in Clark and Sebastian counties had armed themselves from Confederate supplies and were only awaiting federal occupation of Little Rock to cooperate with the Union forces. When Union forces occupied the Arkansas River valley, these men came flocking to enlist.[297]

John Powell of Middle Township, Franklin County, Arkansas, enlisted on September 1, 1863, in Company D, First Arkansas Infantry (U.S.) at Fort Smith, and mustered on February 26, 1864. Thirty-three men enlisted with him; most of them lived in the adjoining counties of Crawford, Franklin, Scott, Sebastian, Montgomery, and Hot Spring in the western Ouachita Mountains. Powell related that his company was made up of Union men who had been hiding out in the mountains south of the Arkansas River since the early months of the war to avoid Confederate conscription officers. After the occupation of the area by Union forces, these Union men—known as Mountain Feds—came to federal army posts to enlist. In dodging the Confederate conscription officers, their lives were constantly in peril, so much so that they could not safely stay at home a single night. They were obliged to hide out in the hills and mountains and have their families clandestinely supply them with food and clothing.[298]

Living as they did in dens and caves in the Ouachita Mountains, these Mountain Feds had come to have the appearance of wild men. Their hair and beards had grown out and were unkempt. Their clothing, which was homemade, was patched all over, with many of the patches themselves being patched, all of which gave them a most uninviting appearance when they came into the federal lines. After these men enlisted in the Union army and put on the blue uniform, each recruit was sent to a barber to be shaved and have his hair cut and his beard trimmed.

When one recruit refused to have his hair cut and started to leave, a sergeant ordered Powell and another recruit to seize the rebellious recruit and take him to the barber. Powell refused to help in arresting his neighbor and so he was himself arrested and put in the guard house. This was his first taste of military discipline.[299]

The First Arkansas Infantry, as with most Arkansas Union regiments, was interested in protecting Unionists. Detachments of the regiment stationed at Fort Smith were frequently sent out to provide succor to Union men—a duty which, because of their familiarity with the country, they were particularity well qualified to perform. In September 1863, Union officers at Fort Smith learned that several hundred Unionists had sought safety near Mount Magazine. Though generally having arms of their own, they desperately needed ammunition.

Colonel Johnson ordered Captain William C. Parker, with sixty men of the First Arkansas Infantry, to relieve the Mountain Feds at their rendezvous. As early as the summer of 1862, bands of Union men similar to those relieved by Captain Parker had consorted together in various posts of western Arkansas. Though compelled by oppression and violence to leave their homes, they were accustomed to taking refuge among the hills and in the woods. No extent of persecution succeeded in driving them from the state. They remained true to the Union under the most discouraging circumstances. From time to time they gave valuable assistance to the organized forces operating in the state. To those in command in Fayetteville, Fort Smith, Van Buren, Clarksville, and Dardanelle, they were especially useful for their knowledge of the country and people. They were never entirely driven from Newton County in north Arkansas, for example. Through their efforts, which were organized and directed by Captain James R. Vanderpool, First Arkansas Infantry, rebel conscription was suppressed there.

In Yell County, William J. Heffington (well known in western Arkansas as "Wild Bill") maintained himself with a band of these men for months when the surrounding country was held by the rebels and despite repeated efforts to capture him. Finally offering his service to Colonel Johnson, First Arkansas Infantry, he and his men were organized into Company I on March 20, 1863, with himself as captain. He almost immediately, on April 15, moved south of the Boston Mountains from his regiment's base at Fayetteville, Arkansas, on detached recruiting service. Crossing the Arkansas River, he was

preparing to conduct other citizens to the federal lines when he
heard that Union forces were abandoning Fayetteville for Cassville,
Missouri. He determined to remain in the state, which he did. On
August 15, 1863, he was killed by guerrillas in Crawford County
near the Arkansas River while on his way to rejoin his regiment at
Cassville. He was going north to procure relief for a large number of
Union men who had banded together in the vicinity of Magazine,
Short, and Petit Jean mountains, and who were successfully resisting
Confederate efforts to capture them. After his death, these men still
held together. On the occupation of Fort Smith and Little Rock by
Union forces in September 1863, most of them enlisted in various
Arkansas regiments. John Whiteford, a refugee from Texas, replaced
Heffington as captain of Company I and was immediately placed on
detached service recruiting in Sebastian County. By early 1864, the
company had mustered eighty-two men.[300]

Colonel William F. Cloud, Second Kansas Cavalry, also
found those Mountain Feds useful. Following the battle of Devil's
Backbone Mountain on September 1 in Sebastian County, Cloud's
regiment took prisoners and received deserters who came flocking
to him. As his unit returned to Little Rock, he was gratified to be
joined by six companies of Union men, about 300, with the Stars and
Stripes flying and cheers for the Union. These men had assembled
at a day's notice and joined him in attacking Dardanelle on
September 12. In addition, three officers and about 100 men who
had fought against Cloud at Backbone Mountain joined him at
Dardanelle. He thought it novel to see men in Confederate gray
fighting side by side with the blue of the federal army. Cloud was
told that hundreds of men on both sides of the Arkansas River were
ready to fight for the Union. He was convinced that thousands of
men stood ready "to take arms" as soon as they could be furnished.
"This is the case also with Northern Texas," he insisted. "The
people come to me by the hundreds, and beg of me to stand by them
and keep them from being taken by the conscript officers or from
being taken back to the rebel army, from which they have deserted,
and to show their earnestness they came in with their old guns and

joined us." He put these men to work hunting guerrillas and hoped to make good soldiers out of some of them.[301]

Most of Arkansas was in such a state of chaos that the only venue to form a civilian government and have elections was among the Arkansas regiments and in occupied towns. On October 24, 1863, while the First Arkansas Infantry was on duty at Fort Smith, a mass meeting of Union men was held there to inaugurate measures that should lead to the restoration of civil government in the state and recognition by the U.S. Congress. Colonel J. M. Johnson of Madison County was unanimously nominated representative for western Arkansas to Congress, but the U.S. government refused to recognize the Murphy government and Johnson was never seated.[302]

The countryside was controlled by Confederate home guards and conscription officers, leaving no other option for Unionists but to flee to the woods. Major Jeremiah Hackett, Second Arkansas Cavalry (U.S.), residing in Cole Township, Sebastian County, on the Indian Territory border, recalled avoiding Confederate conscription officers. He lay in the mountains with Benjamin F. Henley (future husband of Peace Society daughter Delilah McNair) for a little while in 1862 and for much of 1863. Whenever a Confederate scout came near, the men went to the brush. Henley and his father William were outspoken loyalists from the beginning of the war. Old man Henley provided food, information, and assistance to the men hiding in the mountains.

Henley's cousin, Jim Bethel, and Mark Callahan had been killed early in the war at Fort Smith by Confederates for their Union sympathies. Hackett had been captain of Company H, Second Cavalry, and recruited Henley on December 3, 1863. Henley had previously been caught by conscription officer Major James Ousley but escaped. Ousley led a home guard unit out of Massard Prairie, south of Fort Smith, to enforce the Confederate Conscription Act. Hackett had known the Henley family and lived about fifteen miles from them. The Henley home was in Tomlinson Township, Scott County, at the foot of Poteau Mountain. Hackett and Henley and other Mountain Feds hid and fought in and around the mountain for some time. In the fall of 1862, Hackett's son lay out with Ben Henley in the mountains to avoid conscription.[303]

There was disenchantment with the war in southwest Arkansas by 1863. In the spring of that year, violence broke out in that part of the state. Soldiers deserted, Unionist organizations appeared, and armed clashes took place between Confederates and anti-Confederates. Notably, however, all this occurred in the lowlands—not the mountainous upland where the war had always been unpopular. Concern for family welfare, opposition to conscription, and class prejudice caused this new wave of anti-war sentiment in the cotton-growing area. But while the Unionist mountains had exhibited such feelings from the beginning of the war, the lowlands' response came two years later.[304]

Unionist resistance to Confederate conscription in southwest Arkansas also exhibited a strong class element. A resident of Camden insisted that many who attacked conscription were "poor men whose families are unprovided at home." A Clark County resident told Governor Flanagin that "the cry of poor men obliged to fight for the rich may be heard on all sides." As a consequence, bands of deserters and those avoiding conscription hid in the hills and plundered the countryside.[305]

Just as the Peace Society in the northern counties responded to the yeomen's animosity to affluent slave owners and thus their opposition to the Confederacy and its imposition on sustenance and security, so small farmers in the southwestern counties secretly organized to oppose conscription.

Antagonism between the social classes was heightened by the exemption from the military draft of one man per twenty slaves on a plantation. Military service took food and the security-provider away from home: this was their major concern. The response from the southwest counties was similar to that in 1861 in the uplands. This was particularly prevalent in the adjoining mountains of Unionist Pike and Polk counties. Unionists in those counties, as well as lowland Calhoun County, organized secret societies that, by February 1863, were calling for an end to the war. The Calhoun

County Union League company, formed before April 1862, took an oath to be true to one another (resembling the Peace Society oath's "that I will on the shortest notice go to the assistance of any brother at the peril of my life") and to avoid Confederate military service. The men had voted in February 1861 against a state convention and for Union candidates.

Persecuted by secessionist neighbors and local officials, some were hanged, especially if they opposed conscription. The secret Union League organization that appeared in Calhoun County in early 1862 spread into neighboring Ouachita County. It was composed of men who voted against secession. For example, Elijah Harbor of Caswell Township, Calhoun County, voted against the convention and for Unionist candidates in February 1861. He was told that he would have to leave the country. Many other men were afraid to vote at all with men at the polls watching and threatening to hang them if they voted the Unionist ticket. Harbor ran away in April 1862 to save his life and was chased to the Mississippi River by 300 men with dogs. He said that this happened because he was a Union man and a member of the Union League.[306]

Such secret organizations as the Peace Society and Union League were only useful when their members continued to live in a hostile environment. Once their opposition to conscription was evident and their members had fled to the woods and mountains, secrecy was no longer relevant. Occasionally, a leader would emerge, such as Chris Denton, Thomas Jefferson Williams, a Greer, or William J. "Wild Bill" Heffington. Their bands sometimes operated with regular federal troops or as home guards, but they just as often became guerrillas, harassing the Confederate government and its citizens. In early 1863, about 300 followers of Captain Greer were in the mountains of Pike and Clark countries committing outrages on local Confederates. One report of their action stated the following:

> Mr. Henderson, of Hot Spring, while on his way to Sevier county was attacked by these villains, his mules and wagon stolen, himself tied, shot in the back of the head

and left for dead. The perpetrators of this bloody deed were pursued and a number of them caught.

Their captain, Greer...and the lieutenant of the company were recognized by Mr. Henderson. They attempted to escape and were killed in the attempt. Others of the band are on their way here [Little Rock].[307]

Federal expeditions into the Ouachita Mountains rounded up many of the Unionists hiding there. Rigorous enforcement of the conscription law had forced Unionists into the open. Whatever secret associations they once had now became useless. On an expedition by the Third Iowa Cavalry in November 1863, Lieutenant Colonel Henry C. Caldwell reported from near Murfreesboro, Pike County: "At this point I sent out all the loyal men of that region then with me to notify the loyal men who were in the mountains to meet me at Caddo Gap, which point I determined to take possession of and hold till these people would join me. Accordingly, on the 12th instant, I marched up to the gap, where I left part of my command to hold that position." Caldwell then went in search of a small Confederate force at Mount Ida, but they were gone. Still, while scouring the countryside around Mount Ida, he was able to capture "several leading guerrillas of that country, who had been prominent in robbing, persecuting, imprisoning and hanging Union men." Caldwell collected their names and those of witnesses to their crimes and forwarded them to the provost marshal. He asked that these men not be treated as prisoners of war subject to exchange, but as criminals—to be tried by commissions and executed (if found guilty) for their many inhuman and horrid crimes.[308]

On November 14, those of Caldwell's men whom he had left at Caddo Gap joined him, bringing nearly 300 more men from the surrounding mountains who wanted to join the Union army. Not all were viable recruits. Some were old, gray-haired men who fled their homes to save themselves from being hanged by the rebels. Caldwell was impressed by the quality of the young men. They were hardy, vigorous, and resolute, and they represented every trade and profession. As soon as they arrived in his camp, Caldwell furnished them with arms brought along for that purpose and put them under the command of Colonel Shelton Arnold, a twenty-eight-year-old farmer from Sulphur Springs Township, Polk County. On April 28, 1862, he had enlisted in Company K, Twenty-fourth Arkansas Infantry (C.S.) in Pike County with J. R. Arnold as his captain and himself as second lieutenant.

Neither Shelton nor J. R. Arnold was re-elected, and both were discharged on August 26, 1862. His Confederate company suffered twenty-one desertions before the end of 1862, and fourteen more men were discharged. Showing his Unionist sympathies, Shelton Arnold was then commissioned to raise a federal regiment from the area's Unionists. Arnold apparently never completed his regiment, and there is no documentation of his efforts. The Third Iowa marched through the Ouachita Mountains' Hot Spring, Clark, Pike, Polk, and Montgomery counties before returning to Benton, and Caldwell's scouts under Arnold went on to Hempstead and Sevier counties. Caldwell commented:

> The great majority of the inhabitants of the district of country through which I marched are soundly loyal. They occupy the mountainous districts in the counties named, and from commencement of the rebellion they have never faltered in their devotion to the old flag. Every conceivable means has been used to force these loyal men into the rebel service; they have been hung by scores; they have been hunted down with bloodhounds by the slaveholding rebels of Red River Valley; they have been robbed of their property, chained and imprisoned, yet amidst all this persecution and suffering these people stood out, and everywhere I went through their country they greeted my column with shouts of joy. There are several hundred more loyal men in the same region of country, but farther south who are anxiously waiting for an opportunity to get out of the rebel lines and enlist in our service. I cheerfully acknowledge my indebtedness to Colonel Arnold. His perfect knowledge of the country, intimate acquaintance with the people, energy

and courage, enabled him, with the assistance of the men, to keep me constantly advised of the movements and position of the enemy.[309]

Documentation for Unionist secret self-protection organizations outside north-central Arkansas is scarce. However, reports by federal scouts into the Ouachita Mountains of hundreds of Mountain Feds awaiting the opportunity to join the Union army indicate strong Unionist sentiment there. Even more elusive, as they were meant to be, are the secret Union Leagues from south Arkansas. Affidavits from the Southern Claims Commission files mention that a secret Union League existed in Calhoun County before Arkansas seceded. As in north Arkansas, men farming only small acreages could not provide for their families if they were away in the Confederate army protecting the rights of slaveholders, and they had an inherent loyalty to the old flag.

Before the Confederate Conscription Act was passed in April 1862, only social and community pressure existed to encourage men to enlist in Confederate service. Afterward, there are references to men banding together, both secretly and openly, to avoid Confederate military service. Certainly Demby's 1864 article on the secret Union League implies that it was active and widespread, and the depositions in Southern Claims Commission files mention the secret Union League in Calhoun County. Other commission documents reveal the presence of Union Leagues in Clark County and Hempstead County, the latter in Moscow, on the Ouachita County line. Unionists in those places were harried by Confederate military courts because they dodged Confederate military service, committed thefts while banded together in the hills, or simply expressed Unionist sentiments. However, the documents are missing for these proceedings. This lack of documentation is the problem in assessing the prevalence of Unionist organizations in Civil War Arkansas. As secret organizations they created no paperwork; only in north Arkansas does documentation exist to show the persecution of the Peace Society. It is also very likely that

Union sentiment, and therefore Unionist organizations, was much stronger in north-central Arkansas.[310]

The morphing of the name Peace Society into the Union League occurred sometime during the war, but it is impossible to say when or why it occurred. Was Thomas Boles's secret Unionist organization in Yell County called a Union League or a Peace Society when it originated? In 1868, Boles called it a Union League, but that was the accepted name for Unionist organizations by that time. When the Calhoun County secret Union League was formed, was it originally called a Union League? There is no mention of Peace Society in any documentation after January 1862, nor in any reference outside north-central Arkansas, even though rumors of secret Unionist organizations were widespread throughout the South.

Documents and newspaper articles in 1861 and early 1862 referring to the Arkansas secret organization always used "Peace Society" or "Peace Organization Society." A. W. Bishop, in 1863, in articles about John W. Morris and Paris Strickland, used "Peace Organization Society." However, on January 22, 1862, when the trial for the Peace Society men was beginning in Little Rock, the *Daily State Journal* declared the presence of "A Union League in the South" in quoting a letter to the *Cincinnati Gazette*. The article posed the question, "If there can be any truth in the following extract from a Washington letter to the *Cincinnati Gazette*, why is it that the Yankees are always whipped so outrageously whenever they come in contact with the Union men and Northern sympathizers in the Southern army?" The article went on to quote the letter:

> I have information of an unquestionable character, that there is a Union league now extending throughout every State in the southern Confederacy, numbering nearly or quite seven hundred thousand members.—Singular as it may seem, many of these are at present in the rebel army, but will be prepared to strike for freedom and their country—to rally again under the old stars and stripes the moment an opportunity is afforded for doing so.

Even earlier references to "secret meetings of Unionists" came from Charleston, South Carolina, where a "Union league... numbering nearly 500 members" was reported in February 1861. On September 5, 1861, North Carolinians read in the local press clippings from the *New York Herald*: "There is a Union League throughout the state, which embraces many thousands of loyal men."[311]

The questions remain: at what time and how did the Union League penetrate Arkansas; and what was its role? There certainly was Union sentiment among Arkansas's Confederate troops. On December 3, 1861, Captain John R. Homer Scott informed General McCulloch that intelligence he had gathered from prisoners had led him to believe, "There was another [signal] to be used in Camp which some termed a Camp Signal and by which it appears some members (blind to the South) were to volunteer & go into the army of the South and there work out our destruction, this signal word, noise or token was to 'Hoot like an owl.' Which was to be answered by the 'Howl of a wolf.'" Nonetheless, Unionist sentiments in the army were most often expressed through desertion.[312]

A report to Lincoln, dated December 25, 1862, reveals another reference to Unionists in the Confederate army. President Lincoln had sent old Whig William M. McPherson of St. Louis, who had written David Walker at the beginning of the secession crisis to see if elections were possible in north Arkansas. When he consulted with General Frederick Steele at Helena, the general told McPherson that his spies had been taken into Confederate camps and fortifications by conscript soldiers. By these means he had been well posted on the strength and condition of the enemy. This confirmed McPherson's observations that "the conscripts of Northern Arkansas had no heart in the unholy cause into which they had been dragged by Hindman's bands of guerrillas."[313]

Union Leagues after the war are often seen as an adjunct to the Freedmen's Bureau and an arm of the Republican Party. However, the Union League in Missouri was active as early as March 1863, vouching for the Unionism of men who were moving to another

town or exposing anyone with Confederate sympathies employed
by the U.S. government. William J. Hammond, a "galvanized
Yankee," stated that he joined a Union League after he returned to
Hempstead County from the Union army in 1865, but it may not
have existed until the end of the war.[314]

The dearth of documentation about secret Unionist organizations in Arkansas outside north-central Arkansas may reflect
the lack of Unionists outside that region. There were Unionists in
the Ouachita Mountains who flocked to the federal army when it
came close, but the scarce mention of secret Unionist organizations
outside north-central Arkansas (except for an occasional mention
in Southern Claims Commission files) makes the pursuit of secret
Unionists outside the Ozarks difficult. One only surmises that the
documentation is strongest where secret Unionist organizations
were strongest—in the counties around Searcy County, which
became Republican in 1868 and have remained so ever since, just as
Luther Warren said in 1941.

Unionist counties—Southwest Arkansas. (From "A New Map of Arkansas with its Counties, Towns, Post Offices, etc.," *New Universal Atlas* (Philadelphia: Cowperthwait, DeSilver & Butler, 1855).

1861 State Convention Members

This table shows the names of members of the State Convention, the county in which each resided, along with their post office, profession, age, years of residence in the state, place of birth, political affiliation, and marital status. The table is from the *Arkansas True Democrat*, April 18, 1861, 1:3/5. The information listed in parentheses is from a chart by Ralph Wooster in his article "Arkansas Secession Convention," *Arkansas Historical Quarterly* 13 (Summer 1954), and is not listed in the *True Democrat* table. The race in the Fulton County election ended in a tie and forced a new election. The convention would not seat Cochran until after it had voted to secede.

Name	Counties	Post Office	Profession	Age	Residence in State	Birth Place	Politics	Marital Status
R. K. GARLAND	Hempstead	Moscow	Farmer	30	27	Tenn.	Union	Married
A. W. HOBSON	Ouachita	Camden	Physician	35	12	Ga.	Conservative	Single
A. H. GARLAND	Pulaski	Little Rock	Lawyer	28	27	Tenn.	Union	Married
H. H. BOLINGER	Madison	St. Paul	Physician	36	10	Tenn.	Union	Married
S. J. STALLINGS	Conway	Lewisburg	Physician	35	10	Ky.	Union	Married
E. T. WALKER	Scott	Black Jack	Physician	42	14	Ill.	Conservative	Married
SAM KELLEY	Pike	Murfreesboro	Planter	44	44	Ark.	Union	Married
T. F. AUSTIN	Marion	Yellville	Lawyer	42	20	Tenn.	Union	Married
JOHN CAMPBELL	Searcy	Witt's Springs	Farmer	54	25	Tenn.	Union	Married
ISAAC MURPHY	Madison	Huntsville	Lawyer	60	27	Pa.	What is right	Widower
JAS. H. STIRMAN	Washington	Fayetteville	Merchant	51	21	Ky.	Union	Married
J. P. A. PARKS	Washington	Billingsly	Farmer	53	7	Tenn.	Union	Married
WILEY P. CRYER	Lafayette	Lewisville	Farmer	35	35	Ark.	Secessionist	Married
THOS. M. GUNTER	Washington	Fayetteville	Lawyer	35	9	Tenn.	Union	Married

Name	County	Town	Occupation	Age	No.	State	Party	Status
A. H. CARRIGAN	Hempstead	Washington	Farmer	33	9	N. C.	Union	Married
W. W. WATKINS	Carroll	Carrollton	Lawyer	34	6	Tenn.	Conservative	Married
B. H. HOBBS	Carroll	Berryville	Physician	34	11	Ky.	Cooperationist	Married
WM. M. MAYO	Monroe	Indian Bay	Farmer	36	4	N. C.	Democrat	Married
G. W. LAUGHINGHOUSE	St. Francis	Madison	Farmer	45	3	Ala.	Secessionist	Married
J. GOULD	Bradley	Warren	Lawyer & Planter	49	27	Mass.	Secessionist	Married
W. F. SLEMONS	Drew	Monticello	Lawyer	31	10	Tenn.	Secessionist	Married
ROBERT T. FULLER	Dallas	Princeton	Lawyer	39	13	N. C.	Secessionist	Married
WM. V. TATUM	Union	El Dorado	Farmer	45	16	Ga.	Secessionist	Married
H. FLANAGIN	Clark	Arkadelphia	Lawyer	43	22	N. J.	Secessionist	Married
THOMAS B. HANLY	Phillips	Helena	Lawyer	46	27	Ky.	Secessionist	Married
HEZ BUSSEY	Union	El Dorado	Farmer	43	8	Ala.	Secessionist	Widower
ALEXANDER M. CLINGMAN	Montgomery	Mt. Ida	Physician	30	25	Tenn.	Secessionist	Single
JAS. YELL	Jefferson	Pine Bluff	Lawyer	50	23	Tenn.	Secessionist	Married
JAS. S. DOLLARHIDE	Sevier	Neltaboc	Farmer	42	37	Ky.	Secessionist	Married
BENJ. F. HAWKINS	Sevier	Rocky Comfort	Planter	48	27	N. C.	Secessionist	Married
J. A. RHODES	Drew	Monticello	Farmer	45	10	N. C.	Secessionist	Married
J. P. JOHNSON	Desha	Lacot Is.	Planter	39	16	Ky.	Secessionist	Married
H. HILLIARD	Chicot	Grand Lake	Planter	49	17	N. C.	Secessionist	Single
C. W. WALLACE	Columbia	Shangalo, La.	Planter	53	1	Ga.	Secessionist	Married
A. RAY	Polk	Dallas	Hunter	57	3	N. C.	Secessionist	Married
J. R. LANIER	Mississippi	Osceola	Planter	31	23	Tenn.	Secessionist	Married

1861 State Convention Members (continued)

Name	Counties	Post Office	Profession	Age	Residence in State	Birth Place	Politics	Marital Status
MARCUS L. HAWKINS	Ashley	Hamburg	Lawyer	28	5	Ala.	Secessionist	Married
W. W. FLOYD	Johnson	Clarksville	Lawyer	51	20	Tenn.	Democrat	Married
J. N. SHELTON	St. Francis	Cotton Plant	Farmer	58	7	N. C.	Secessionist	Married
B. C. TOTTEN	Prairie	Brownsville	Farmer	55	14	Tenn.	States' rights	Married
WILLIAM STOUT	Pope	Dover	Farmer	55	18	Tenn.	Union	Married
M. SHELBY KENNARD	Independence	Batesville	Editor & Lawyer	28	7	Ala.	Cooperationist	Married
SAML. L. GRIFFITH	Sebastian	Fort Smith	Merchant	44	22	Md.	Anti-secessionist	Married
J. N. CYPERT	White	Searcy	Lawyer	37	11	Tenn.	Anti-secessionist	Single
JAS. W. BUSH	Greene	Greensboro	Medicine	31	6	Ky.	Anti-secessionist	Single
W. M. FISHBACK	Sebastian	Greenwood	Lawyer	28	2	Va.	Union	Single
URBAN E. FORT	Independence	Convenience	Farmer	43	20	N. C.	Anti-secessionist	Widower
A. W. DINSMORE	Benton	Bentonville	Merchant	40	12	Penn.	Anti-secessionist	Married
H. JACKSON	Benton	Bentonville	Farmer	50	4	N. C.	Anti-secessionist	Married
H. W. WILLIAMS	Poinsett & Craighead	Jonesboro	Farmer	49	4	Tenn.	Anti-secessionist	Married
FELIX I. BATSON	Johnson	Clarksville	Lawyer	44	21	Tenn.	Southern rights	Married
SAML. ROBINSON	Lawrence	Lauratown	Farm	56	20	Ky.	Southern rights	Widower
WILLIAM W. MANSFIELD	Franklin	Ozark	Lawyer	30	8	Ky.	Anti-secessionist	Married
JOSEPH JESTER	Hot Spring	Hot Spring	Farmer	37	18	Tenn.	Conservative	Married

Name	County	Town	Occupation	Age	Years	Born	Position	Status
MILTON D. BABER	Lawrence	Smithville	Lawyer	25	2 1/2	Ky.	Anti-Imdt-sec	Single
ISAIAH DODSON	Newton	Cave Creek	Farmer	51	21	Tenn.	Cooperationist	Married
ALEX ADAMS	Izard	North Fork	Farmer	36	36	Ark.	Union	Married
JABEZ M. SMITH	Saline	Bentonville	Lawyer	30	9	Ky.	Cooperationist	Single
W. F. GRACE	Jefferson	Pine Bluff	Lawyer	37	14	Ky.	Secessionist	Married
J. H. PATTERSON	Jackson	Augusta	Lawyer	49	21	Ohio	Secessionist	Married
PHIL. H. ECHOLS	Calhoun	Hampton	Physician	28	1 1/2	Ga.	Secessionist	Married
J. STILLWELL	Pulaski	Little Rock	Lawyer	34	34	Ark.	Union	Married
FRANKLIN W. DESHA	Independence	Batesville	Lawyer & Farmer	42	32	D. C.	Anti-secessionist	Married
L. D. HILL	Perry	Perryville	Physician	52	8	Tenn.	Conditional sec.	Married
JESSE TURNER	Crawford	Van Buren	Lawyer	53	29	N. C.	Union	Married
J. HENRY PATTERSON	Van Buren	Clinton	Merchant	40	21	Md.	Union	Married
G. P. SMOOTE	Columbia	Magnolia	Lawyer	31	10	Tenn.	Secessionist	Married
JAS. M. TOTTEN	Arkansas	St. Charles	Farmer	58	6	Tenn.	Secessionist	Married
THOS. H. BRADLEY	Crittenden	Oldham	Planter	52	16	Tenn.	Union	Married
JAMES W. CRENSHAW	Randolph	Pocahontas	Farmer	62	5	N. C.	Secessionist	Married
H. F. THOMASON	Crawford	Van Buren	Lawyer	35	32	Tenn.	Union	Married
JAS. W. ADAMS	Phillips	Helena	Farmer & Lawyer	43	25	Mass.	Secessionist	Married
WM. H. SPIVEY	Yell	Dardanelle	Merchant	31	?	(N. C.)	(Union)	?
(S. W. COCHRAN)	(Fulton)	(Union)	(Farmer)	40	?	(S. C.)	(Secessionist)	(Married)
(S. H. WREN)	(Fulton)	(Union)	(Farmer)	36	?	(Ky.)	Union	(Married)
(DAVID WALKER)	(Washington)	(Fayetteville)	(Lawyer)	54	?	(Ky.)	(Union)	(Widower)
(GEO. C. WATKINS)	(Pulaski)	?	(Lawyer)	44	?	(Ky.)	(Union)	?

Appendix II

Peace Society Members

Name	County	CSA	Enl	Died	Desert
Adams, Greenberry	Searcy	27 Ark Inf, I	62, 07-01	**	62, 07-01
Adams, Joseph	Searcy	**	**	ca 1864	**
Adams, Spencer	Searcy	3 CS Inf	**	**	62, 06-
Addison, Mayfield	Searcy	**	**	**	**
Arter, Carroll	Searcy	**	**	**	**
Arter, Joseph L	Searcy	17 Ark Inf, E	**	**	**
Bailey, James F	Van Buren	**	**	**	**
Baker, David C	Searcy	18 Ark Inf, K	61, 12-19	**	**
Baker, James A	Fulton	**	**	**	**
Baker, Joel	Searcy	**	**	**	**
Ball, Gehuger	Howell, MO	**	**	**	**
Ball, James A	Fulton	**	**	**	**
Ball, Milford W	Howell, MO	**	**	**	**
Barnes, James Jackson	Searcy	18 Ark Inf, I *	61, 12-18	83, 05-14	62, 08
Barnes, William F	Van Buren	**	**	62, 08-25	**
Barnett, David	Searcy	18 Ark Inf, I	61, 12-18	15, 03-03	62, 04
Bartlett, William	Pope	18 Ark Inf, I	61, 12-18	**	62, 06
Becket, Elijah	Izard	**	**	**	**
Becket, Josiah J	Izard	**	**	**	**
Becket, Thomas	Izard	**	**	**	**
Becket, Thomas R	Izard	8 Ark Inf, I	61, 12-12	62, 09-20	**
Bishop, Lindsey	Carroll	**	**	**	**
Black, Simeon B	Carroll	18 Ark Inf, I *	61, 12-18	**	**
Blasingame, Anderson	Searcy	18 Ark Inf, I	61, 12-18	1862?	**
Bohanon, John	Izard	Harrells/Adams	**	**	**
Boles, Thomas	Yell	**	**	1905	**
Bradshaw, Henry	Searcy	18 Ark Inf, I	61, 12-18	1862	**
Bradshaw, William	Searcy	18 Ark Inf, I	61, 12-18	1862	**
Brantley, B. F.	Izard	8 Ark Inf, H	62, 01-13	**	**
Branum, Solomon	Marion	27 Ark Inf, C	62, 02-15	**	**
Brashear, Mortimer M	Searcy	**	**	63, 08-05	**
Bratton, William Milican	Searcy	18 Ark Inf, I	61, 12-18	**	**
Brewer, Aron V B	Izard	18 Ark Inf, K	61, 12-19	**	**
Brewer, Jonas	Izard	18 Ark Inf, K	61, 12-19	**	**
Brewer, Lewis S	Searcy	**	**	79, 12-00	**
Brewer, Wiley J	Izard	**	**	**	**
Brown, George	Van Buren	**	**	**	**
Brown, Jefferson C	Fulton	**	**	**	**
Brown, John	Searcy	**	**	**	**
Brown, John J	Fulton	**	**	**	**
Brown, Solomon I	Searcy	**	**	**	**
Brown, Thomas	Van Buren	18 Ark Inf, K	61, 12-19	**	**
Brown, William	Searcy	18 Ark Inf, K	61, 12-19	**	62, 11-2

Union	Enl	Born	PS Activity	Occupation	POB	M/S	Real	Prop
**	**	1837	J, U	Farm	AR	Wid	**	500
**	**	1831	U	Farm	IL	S	1500	900
**	**	1819	U	Farm	KY	M	1000	1200
**	**	1823	P, Q	Farm	TN	M	**	200
**	**	1816	J	WagonWright	TN	M	**	620
**	**	1831	J	Blacksmith	TN	M	**	765
10 Mo Cav, D	62, 06-19	1843	A1	Lab Farm	TN	S	1200	200
**	**	1836	D, L, N	Lab	AR	S	**	**
**	**	1828	X, A1	Farm	TN	M	665	1550
**	**	1802	J	Farm	NC	Wid	**	600
**	**	1816	X	Blacksmith	NC	M	**	500
**	**	1814	X, A1	Farm	VA	Wid	300	130
**	**	1838	X	Farm	NC	M	120	**
3 Ark Cav, I	64, 01-26	1815	B, C	Farm	TN	M	2000	1000
1 Btn Ark Inf, A	62, 06-10	1842	A1, A2	Carp	TN	M	**	**
3 Ark Cav, M	64, 01-01	1827	B, C, G, U	Farm	TN	M	**	500
3 Ark Cav, I	64, 02-01	1840	B, C	Lab Farm	IL	M	**	**
**	**	1838	I	Farm	TN	S	**	**
**	**	1842	I	Lab Farm	TN	S	**	**
**	**	1809	I	Farm	TN	M	1300	1000
**	**	1835	I	Farm	TN	S	**	**
**	**	1833	U	Farm	TN	M	**	150
**	**	1831	B, C	Farm	NC	M	**	258
*	**	1826	B, C	Farm	TN	M	1200	800
*	**	1800	I	Farm	NC	M	**	100
Ark Cav, E	63, 10-15	1837	Text	Lawyer	AR	S	**	**
*	**	1813	B, C	Farm	TN	M	1500	1200
*	**	1813	B, C	Farm	TN	M	**	250
*	**	1820	O	Farm	NC	M	**	**
*	**	1842	F, G, K, P, Q	Blacksmith	TN	M	**	200
Ark Cav, E	**	1817	Text	Farm	KY	M	**	500
*	**	1805	B, C	Farm	TN	M	**	600
*	**	1804	D	Lab Farm	TN	S	**	**
*	**	1840	D	Farm	NC	M	620	1025
*	**	1833	D, S	Farm	TN	M	2000	1000
*	**	1827	I	Farm	TN	M	500	2000
*	**	1822	A2	Farm	MO	M	1000	1000
are's Co G	61, 12-01	1837	A3	Lab Farm	TN	S	**	**
	**	1842	G, H, J, U	Lab	AR	S	**	**
are's Co G	61, 12-01	1834	A3	Lab	TN	**	**	**
	**	1836	G	Farm	AR	M	**	250
3tn Ark Inf, C	62, 06-10	1834	D	Farm	GA	M	**	250
	**	1834	D, G, H, P, Q, U	Farm	TN	M	**	300

Peace Society Members (continued)

Name	County	CSA	Enl	Died	Desert
Browning Jr, William	Izard	**	**	**	**
Broyles, James F	Van Buren	18 Ark Inf, K	61, 12-19	13, 07-17	**
Bryant, Calvin	Izard	1 Ark Mtd Rifles, D	**	**	**
Bryant, John H	Izard	8 Ark Inf, H	62, 03-01	**	**
Byler, Edward R	Fulton	**	**	**	**
Campbell, Stephen A	Izard	8 Ark Inf, H	61, 12-12	**	62, 10-06
Cantrell, Alexander	Webster, MO	**	**	**	**
Carlton, John D	Izard	**	**	**	**
Carr, Larkin	Izard	8 Ark Inf, I	61, 12-12	**	62, 06-23
Carruthers, John M	Marion	18 Ark Inf, K	61, 12-19	**	**
Cash, Levi C	Searcy	**	**	65, 01-17	**
Castleberry, John R	Searcy	18 Ark Inf, I	61, 12-18	62, 01	**
Castleberry, Washington Cahal	Searcy	18 Ark Inf, I *	61, 12-18	09, 04-24	**
Cates, William A J	Van Buren	18 Ark Inf, I	61, 12-18	**	**
Chambers, William R	Van Buren	18 Ark Inf, I *	61, 12-18	**	62, 06
Christy, James F Homer	Searcy	18 Ark Inf, K *	61, 12-19	06, 12-24	62, 06
Christy, John	Searcy	18 Ark Inf, K	61, 12-19	**	**
Christy, Joseph C	Searcy	18 Ark Inf, K *	61, 12-19	**	62, 06
Clark, Lewis	Searcy	18 Ark Inf, I	61, 12-18	**	**
Clemens, Jeremiah	Izard	8 Ark Inf, H	61, 12-12	62, 04	**
Conley, Beverly L	Searcy	18 Ark Inf, I	61, 12-18	62, 12-10	**
Cook, Henry	Van Buren	18 Ark Inf, K	61, 12-19	**	**
Cooper, Allen	Izard	**	**	**	**
Cooper, Jefferson B	Izard	**	**	**	**
Copeland, Alexander N	Searcy	18 Ark Inf, I	61, 12-18	**	62, 02
Copeland, James B	Searcy	18 Ark Inf, I	61, 12-18	**	**
Copeland, William	Searcy	18 Ark Inf, I	61, 12-18	**	**
Criswell, James	Fulton	**	**	**	**
Cummins, William Joseph	Searcy	14 Ark Inf, K	62, 01-06	62, 07-19	**
Curl, John W	Van Buren	18 Ark Inf, K	61, 12-19	**	**
Curl, Samuel M	Van Buren	18 Ark Inf, K	61, 12-19	**	**
Curry, David Anderson	Searcy	18 Ark Inf, K	61, 12-19	77, 02	**
Curry, James E	Searcy	18 Ark Inf, K	61, 12-19	**	**
Daniel, William W	Izard	1 Ark Inf, E	**	**	**
Davis, Hezekiah W	Fulton	8 Ark Inf, I	61, 11-06	**	62, 10-2
Davis, William	Searcy	18 Ark Inf, I	61, 12-18	**	**
Denton, Christopher	Van Buren	**	**	**	**
Dickerson, Elijah	Van Buren	18 Ark Inf, K	61, 12-19	**	**
Downey, Patrick L	Searcy	18 Ark Inf, K	61, 12-19	**	**
Duck, Timothy Arthur	Searcy	**	**	95, 06-30	**
Duer, James	Fulton	**	**	**	**
Duer, William	Fulton	**	**	**	**
Dugger, Jasper	Marion	18 Ark Inf, K	61, 12-19	**	**
Dugger, Thomas	Marion	18 Ark Inf, K	61, 12-19	**	**

Union	Enl	Born	PS Activity	Occupation	POB	M/S	Real	Prop
Ware's Co G	61, 12-01	1834	A3	Farm	TN	M	**	**
**	**	1837	D, A2	Farm	TN	M	**	**
**	**	1845	I	Lab Farm	TN	S	**	**
**	**	1814	I	Blacksmith	TN	M	**	300
Ware's Co G	61, 12-01	1836	A3	Farm	TN	M	**	**
**	**	1834	I	Farm	AL	M	500	200
Ware's Co G	61, 12-01	1838	A3	Lab Farm	TN	S	**	**
Ware's Co G	61, 12-01	1819	A3	Farm	TN	M	**	200
**	**	1840	I	Farm	MO	M	**	**
**	**	1829	D, P	Clerk	AL	M	300	500
3 Ark Cav, M	64, 01-01	1823	J	Farm	TN	M	250	500
**	**	1817	B, C	Farm	AL	M	800	1215
**	**	1841	B, C	Lab Farm	AR	S	**	**
**	**	1813	B, C	Farm	NC	M	**	**
**	**	1821	B, C	Farm	MS	M	**	40
1 Ark Cav, H	62, 09-10	1839	D, N, P, Q	Lab Farm	AR	S		
**	**	1811	D, N, P, Q	Farm	NC	M	1500	1900
**	**	1831	D, N, P, Q	Farm	TN	M	**	600
**	**	1818	B, C	Farm	TN	M	**	300
**	**	1832	I	Farm	TN	M	**	50
**	**	1821	B, C, J	Farm	TN	M	**	370
**	**	1833	D, A2	Farm	TN	M	**	**
Ware's Co G	61, 12-01	1814	A3	Farm	TN	M	2750	15500
Ware's Co G	61, 12-01	1840	A3	Lab Farm	TN	S	**	**
3 Ark Cav, M/2 TN	64, 01-28	1831	B, C	Farm	TN	M	**	300
**	**	1835	B, C	Farm	MS	**	**	100
**	**	1816	B, C	Miller	TN	M	**	**
Ware's Co G	61, 12-01	1841	A3	Lab	AR	S	**	**
**	**	1835	J, V	Farm	AR	M	**	150
**	**	1836	D, A2	Carpenter	GA	M	**	150
**	**	1837	D, A2	Lab Farm	MO	S	**	**
4 Mo Vol Inf	62, 06-10	1827	D, G, P, Q, U	Farm	TN	Wid	**	150
*	**	1821	D, G, P, Q, U	Farm	TN	M	**	500
*	**	1835	I	Farm	TN	M	300	200
Ark Cav, E	62, 07-03	1816	X	Farm	TN	M	960	220
*	**	1838	B, C	Lab	TN	S	**	**
rk Mil	**	1811	A2	Farm	TN	M	**	1600
Mo Cav, D	62, 06-19	1831	D	Lab	TN	S	**	**
*	**	1801	D, G, H, P, Q, U	Farm	KY	M	**	300
*	**	1817	J	Farm	NC	M	400	250
are's Co G	61, 12-01	1840	A3	Lab Farm	AR	S	**	**
are's Co G	61, 12-01	1817	A3	Farm	PA	M	1200	300
	**	1843	D, P, Q	Lab Farm	TN	S	**	**
	**	1841	B, D, P, Q	Lab Farm	TN	S	**	**

Peace Society Members (continued)

Name	County	CSA	Enl	Died	Desert
Dugger, William M	Marion	18 Ark Inf, K	61, 12-19	**	**
Elliott, John M	Izard	8 Ark Inf, H	61, 12-12	**	63, 09-09
Elms, Henry	Izard	**	**	**	**
Elms, James	Izard	**	**	**	**
Ezell, Isaiah	Searcy	**	**	**	**
Ezell, John	Searcy	**	**	**	**
Faught, Thomas J	Searcy	**	**	**	**
Faught, William C	Searcy	27 Ark Inf, G	62, 06-19	62, 11-03	**
Ferrill, John	Searcy	**	**	**	**
Ferrill, William A C	Izard	8 Ark Inf, H	61, 12-12	**	62, 08-15
Fisher, William Thomas	Searcy	18 Ark Inf, I *	61, 12-18	1885	63, 08-06
Forehand, John	Searcy	**	**	63, 12-25	**
Forehand, Jonathan	Searcy	18 Ark Inf, I	61, 12-18	**	**
Foster, James B	Searcy	18 Ark Inf, I	61, 12-18	**	**
Gadberry, William J	Van Buren	31 Ark Inf, D	62, 01-04	62, 05-22	**
Garner, Parrish, Sr	Searcy	18 Ark Inf, I	61, 12-18	**	**
Gary, Benjamin H	Searcy	18 Ark Inf, I	61, 12-18	91, 03-03	**
Gilbreath, John	Van Buren	**	**	**	**
Goodrich, Charles	Izard	**	**	**	**
Grinder, Robert	Searcy	**	**	1863	**
Grinder, Samuel	Searcy	**	**	70, 03-01	**
Guthrie, Thomas	Searcy	**	**	**	**
Haines, William	Van Buren	18 Ark Inf, K *	61, 12-19	**	65, 05 Par
Haley, Mark J	Izard	**	**	**	**
Haney, Burwell	Izard	**	**	**	**
Haney, Elijah	Izard	8 Ark Inf, H	61, 12-12	**	62, 07-02
Harley, John	Searcy	18 Ark Inf, I	61, 12-18	**	**
Harness, John T	Searcy	18 Ark Inf, K	61, 12-19	**	**
Harness, John W	Searcy	18 Ark Inf, I *	61, 12-18	**	(62, 04)
Harness, William H H	Searcy	18 Ark Inf, I	61, 12-18	**	**
Harris, Henry B	Izard	**	**	**	**
Harris, Thomas	Van Buren	**	**	**	**
Harris, William	Searcy	18 Ark Inf, I	61, 12-18	**	(62, 05)
Harrison, Ransom Horn	Searcy	**	**	**	**
Hatly, James R	Searcy	18 Ark Inf, I *	61, 12-18	1862	**
Hatly, John W	Searcy	18 Ark Inf, I	61, 12-18	**	**
Hays, George M	Carroll	14 Ark Inf, H	61, 12-23	**	**
Hays, William M	Searcy	45 Ark Mil, Comm	61, 11-24	07, 10-29	**
Helton, James T	Izard	**	**	**	**
Helton, William V	Izard	**	**	**	**
Hensley, Benjamin White	Searcy	**	**	21, 09-18	**
Hensley, Fielding H	Van Buren	**	**	**	**
Hensley, Porter M	Searcy	18 Ark Inf, K	61, 12-19	**	62, 06
Hensley, Wesley Green	Searcy	**	**	88, 08-22	**

Union	Enl	Born	PS Activity	Occupation	POB	M/S	Real	Prop
**	**	1819	D, P, Q	Farm	TN	M	1500	1275
**	**	1827	I	Farm	TN	M	**	**
Ware's Co G	61, 12-01	1841	A3	Lab Farm	AR	S	**	**
Ware's Co G	61, 12-01	1811	A3	Farm	KY	M	500	475
**	**	1816	G, J, U	Blacksmith	TN	M	1250	1800
**	**	1841	G, J, U	Lab Farm	AR	S	**	**
1 Ark Inf, C	63, 02-12	1837	F, G	Farm	TN	M	**	50
**	**	1838	F, G	**	TN	**	**	**
**	**	1800	I	Farm	NC	M	**	125
**	**	1832	I	Farm	TN	M	**	100
46 Mo Inf, F	64, 09-05	1827	B, C	Farm	TN	M	500	600
1 Ark Cav, H	62, 07-22	1837	J	Farm	IL	S	**	**
**	**	1802	B, C	Farm	NC	M	300	600
**	**	1830	B, C	Lab	IL	M	**	100
**	**	1843	A1, A2	Lab Farm	TN	S	**	**
**	**	1806	B, C	Farm	TN	M	250	200
4 Ark Cav, E	64, 01-01	1832	B, C	Farm	AL	M	**	**
**	**	1810	A1, A2	Farm	TN	M	**	100
Ware's Co G	61, 12-01	1843	A3	Farm	AR	S	**	**
**	**	1830	G, J, U	Farm	TN	M	**	700
**	**	1819	G, J, U	Farm	TN	M	800	300
**	**	1837	J	Lab	AR	M	**	18
**	**	1834	D, A2	**	TN	M	**	**
Ware's Co G	61, 12-01	1830	A3	**	**	**	**	**
**	**	1827	I	Farm	TN	M	1000	225
**	**	1830	I	Farm	TN	M	**	**
**	**	1838	B, C	**	**	S	**	**
**	**	1837	D, A2	**	TN	M	**	500
3 Ark Cav, M	64, 01-28	1840	B, C	Lab Farm	TN	S	**	**
10 Mo Cav, D	62, 06-18	1839	B, C	Lab Farm	TN	S	**	**
Ware's Co G	61, 12-01	1838	A3	Farm	AR	M	400	150
**	**	**	A1	**	**	**	**	**
3 Ark Cav, M	64, 01-28	1824	B, C	Lab Farm	GA	S	**	**
**	**	1812	J	Farm	KY	M	**	40
**	**	1835	B, C	**	AL	M	**	**
2 TN Cav, D	63, 11-01	1823	B, C	**	AL	M	**	**
**	**	1831	P, Q, R, V, W	Farm-Blacksm	TN	M	**	1100
**	**	1828	B	Teach	KY	M	**	300
*	**	1838	I	Farm	TN	S	**	**
*	**	1815	I	Farm	TN	M	300	230
Ark Cav, H	62, 07-02	1837	J	Lab	TN	S	**	**
*	**	1832	A2	Farm	TN	M	425	200
4 MO EMM	**	1837	D, N, P, Q	Lab	TN	S	**	**
*	**	1829	L	Farm-Blacksm	TN	M	650	600

Peace Society Members (continued)

Name	County	CSA	Enl	Died	Desert
Hodge, Harmon Willis	Searcy	**	**	1885	**
Hogan, William C	Searcy	**	**	**	**
Holley, Absalom	Van Buren	18 Ark Inf, K	61, 12-19	**	**
Holley, Alexander	Van Buren	18 Ark Inf, K	61, 12-19	**	**
Holley, Ruben C	Van Buren	18 Ark Inf, K	61, 12-19	**	**
Hollis, James Mack	Marion	18 Ark Inf, K	61, 12-19	06, -1-28	62, 01
Holmes, John W	Van Buren	31 Ark Inf, D	62, 03-01	**	62, 08-31
Hooten, George	Searcy	18 Ark Inf, K	61, 12-19	**	**
Jackson, John Burgol	Searcy	45 Ark Mil, D	61, 11-26	1863	**
Jameson, Ebenezer B	Pope	21 Ark Inf, I	61, 12-21	00, 01-23	**
Jamison, Lorenzo Dow	Searcy	**	**	15, 04-03	**
Jamison, Maston C	Searcy	14 Ark Inf, K	61, 12-24	62, 02-17	**
Jeffreys, William	Searcy	18 Ark Inf, I	61, 12-18	**	**
Jenkins, John W	Searcy	**	**	**	**
Johnson, Robert	Searcy	18 Ark Inf, I	61, 12-18	63, 03-05	(62, 05)
Jones, George W	Marion	**	**	**	**
Jones, Stephen	Marion	18 Ark Inf, I	61, 12-18		**
Jordan, Isaac L	Izard	**	**	**	**
Jordan, Wyatt G	Izard	**	**	**	**
Kaler, William	Searcy	14 Ark Inf, K	62, 01-22	20, 01--8	**
Keeling, Carlton	Marion	**	**	**	**
Kennemore, Roland W	**	**	**	**	**
Kerley, John W	Izard	**	**	**	**
Kesner, William A	Searcy	18 Ark Inf, I	61, 12-18	1902	(62, 01)
Kilburn, Carroll	Searcy	18 Ark Inf, K *	61, 12-19	63, 01-24	63, 01-01
Kimbell, Basil	Searcy	**	**	**	**
Kimbell, Basil William	Searcy	**	**	**	**
Kimbell, John	Searcy	**	**	14, 08-22	**
Kimbrell, Andrew N	Searcy	45 Ark Mil, C	61, 11-26	13, 03-23	**
Kirkham, John W	Carroll	14 Ark Inf, H	61, 12-23	62, 04-16	**
Kuykendall, Francis	Searcy	18 Ark Inf, I *	61, 12-18	99, 06-10	62, 05
Ladyman, Richard C	Searcy	18 Ark Inf, I *	61, 12-18	**	64, 09-02
Lambert, Henry	Fulton	**	**	**	**
Lambert, John	Fulton	**	**	**	**
Lane, Josiah	Searcy	**	**	**	**
Langston, Samuel	Izard	**	**	**	**
Lee, George W	Searcy	31 Ark Inf, D	62, 01-22	07, 05-25	**
Lee, Robert	Searcy	18 Ark Inf, I	61, 12-18	**	**
Long, George	Carroll	**	**	**	**
Long, Isaac	Izard	32 Ark Inf, G	**	**	**
Long, Solomon	Carroll	**	**	**	**
Love, Andrew J	Searcy	**	**	66, 04-23	**
Luttrell, James	Searcy	18 Ark Inf, K	61, 12-19	**	**
Lynn, Washington G	Searcy	18 Ark Inf, I *	61, 12-18	**	63, 01-0

Union	Enl	Born	PS Activity	Occupation	POB	M/S	Real	Prop
1 Ark Cav, H	62, 07-02	1840	A	Farm	AR	S	**	**
**	**	1835	J	Lab	TN	S	**	80
**	**	1834	D, A2	Farm	TN	M	**	600
**	**	1832	D, A2	Farm	TN	M	**	**
**	**	1826	D, A2	Farm	MS	M	**	50
2 TN Mtd Inf	63, 12-10	1832	D, P, Q	Farm	TN	M	**	**
**	**	1841	A, B	Farm Lab	ab	M	**	**
**	**	1830	D, H, P, Q, U	Lab	TN	S	1000	400
**	**	1842	J	Farm	TN	M	**	**
3 Ark Cav, I	63, 11-21	1831	J	Farm	MO	M	**	725
1 Ark Cav, H	62, 08-05	1835	A, J, L, U	Farm	MO	M	800	300
**	**	1829	Text	Farm	MO	M	1000	500
**	**	1827	B, C	**	**	**	**	**
**	**	1841	A, J	Farm	TN	M	**	1600
**	**	1813	B, C	**	SC	M	**	**
Ware's Co G	61, 12-01	1824	A3	**	TN	M	800	414
1 Ark Cav, H	62, 08-06	1810	B, C	**	TN	M	1000	200
Ware's Co G	61, 12-01	1841	A3	Lab Farm	AR	S	**	**
Ware's Co G	61, 12-01	1810	A3	Farm	NC	M	400	250
2 Ark Cav, M	64, 01-28	1836	H	Lab	KY	S	**	**
**	**	1795	P, Q	Farm	NC	M	**	450
Ware's Co G	61, 12-01	1833	A3	**	GA	**	**	**
**	**	1818	I	Farm	NC	M	200	80
**	**	1828	B, C	Farm	IL	M	**	**
**	**	1814	D, P, Q	Farm	TN	M	2000	1500
ArkCav, C	62, 07-02	1801	J	Farm	NC	M	100	
Ark Cav, C	62, 07-02	1836	J	Lab Farm	TN	M	**	**
Ark Cav, C	62, 07-12	1843	J	Lab Farm	AR	S	**	**
Ark Cav, M	64, 01-28	1824	Text	Farm	TN	M	**	470
**	**	1831	P, Q, R, V, W	Farm	GA	M	400	375
Ark Cav, I	64, 02-01	1826	B, C	Farm	GA	M	**	**
US Vol Inf	65, 04-06	1838	B,C	Farm	TN	M	**	100
Ware's Co G	61, 12-01	1836	A3	Farm	VA	S	300	100
Ware's Co G	61, 12-01	1840	A3	**	VA	**	**	**
**	**	1812	G, H, J, U	Farm	TN	M	1000	800
Ware's Co G	61, 12-01	1830	A3	Farm	AR	M	**	**
**	**	1844	Watts Pension	Lab Farm	TN	S	**	**
**	**	1832	B, C	Lab	IN	M	**	150
**	**	1829	P, U	Farm	TN	M	800	565
Ark Cav, A	63, 10-29	1817	I	**	TN	**	**	**
**	**	**	Q	**	**	**	**	**
o Mil	**	1828	U	Farm	MO	M	400	700
Ark Cav, M	62, 10-16	1823	D, G, H, P, Q	Farm	TN	M	**	300
**	**	1835	B, C	Farm	AR	M	**	100

Peace Society Members (continued)

Name	County	CSA	Enl	Died	Desert
Mackey, Yong (Henderson G)	Searcy	**	**	Bef 1889	**
Manes, Claiborn L	Searcy	**	**	84, 11-21	**
Marshall, James A	Fulton	**	**	**	**
Marshall, William H	Searcy	18 Ark Inf, I	61, 12-18	**	**
Martin, Thomas	Searcy	18 Ark Inf, I	61, 12-18	**	**
McBee, Alexander	Howell, MO	**	**	**	**
McBee, James H	Howell, MO	**	**	**	**
McDaniel, William F	Searcy	18 Ark Inf, I	61, 12-18		(62, 05)
McEntire, John A	Searcy	**	**	93, 10-30	**
McGinnis, Elijah	Izard	**	**	**	**
McGinnis, John	Izard	**	**	**	**
McGinnis, W J	Izard	**	**	**	**
McInturff, Thomas W	Searcy	18 Ark Inf, I	61, 12-18	91, 11-06	(62, 01)
McLane, S Allan	Searcy	18 Ark Inf, I	61, 12-18	**	62, 01
McMillan, E L	Searcy	18 Ark Inf, I	61, 12-18	**	**
McNair, James Claiborn	Searcy	**	**	06, 09-01	**
Moody, Jonathan	Searcy	18 Ark Inf, I	61, 12-18	1864	**
Morris, John Jr	Searcy	18 Ark Inf, I	61, 12-18	**	**
Morris, John Sr	Searcy	18 Ark Inf, I *	61, 12-18	**	62, 06
Morris, John Wortman	Searcy	18 Ark Inf, I *	61, 12-18	19, 08-14	(62, 05)
Morris, William	Searcy	**	**	**	**
Null. John R	Van Buren	18 Ark Inf, K	61, 12-19	1861, 12	**
Osborn, Squire [A] J	Searcy	14 Ark Inf, K	62, 01-06	1862, 06	**
Osburn, Eli L	Carroll	14 Ark Inf, H	61, 12-23	86, 07-20	**
Packet, W J	**	**	**	**	**
Palmer, Benjamin E	Van Buren	18 Ark Inf, I	61, 12-18	**	**
Parks, Daniel J	Searcy	**	**	**	**
Parks, Theophilus (Dink)	Searcy	**	**	**	**
Parsley, Abraham J	Van Buren	18 Ark Inf, K	61, 12-19	1862, 01	**
Parsley, Archibald A.	Van Buren	18 Ark Inf, K	61, 12-19	**	**
Parsley, John B	Van Buren	**	**	**	**
Passmore, Benjamin J	Van Buren	**	**	**	**
Passmore, Joel Henry	Van Buren	18 Ark Inf, I	61, 12-18	**	**
Paton/Peyton, Samuel	Izard	**	**	**	**
Pearce, Stephen P	Van Buren	18 Ark Inf, K	61, 12-19	**	**
Pearce, William	Searcy	**	**	**	**
Phillips, Luther P	Marion	18 Ark Inf, K	61, 12-19	62, 11-15	62, 04
Pierce, Austin	Searcy	**	**	**	**
Potter, William F	Searcy	18 Ark Inf, I	61, 12-18	**	62, 04
Prater, Davis	Izard	8 Ark Inf, H	61, 12-12	**	61, 10-0
Prater, John	Izard	**	**	**	**
Prator, Basil	Izard	**	**	**	**
Prator, Brice	Izard	**	**	1861	**
Presley, Ammon H	Van Buren	**	**	**	**

Union	Enl	Born	PS Activity	Occupation	POB	M/S	Real	Prop
1 Ark Cav, H	62, 07-12	1833	J	Farm	TN	M	120	150
**	**	1814	J, U	Farm	TN	M	1600	156
Ware's Co G	61, 12-01	1840	A3	Farm	TN	M	**	200
**	**	1840	B,C	Lab Farm	AR	S	**	**
**	**	1841	B, C	Lab	AR	M	**	**
**	**	1800	X	Farm	TN	M	**	200
**	**	1834	X	Farm	TN	S	**	100
3 Ark Cav, I	64, 03-01	1816	B, C	Farm	TN	M	**	300
**	**	1818	H, P, Q, R, U	Farm	NC	M	**	400
**	**	**	I	**	**	**	**	**
**	**	1836	I	Farm	TN	M	100	100
**	**	1841	I	Lab Farm	TN	S	**	**
**	**	1827	B, C	Farm	IL	M	**	125
**	**	1827	B, C	Farm	TN	M	**	500
**	**	1833	B, C	Lab	TN	M	**	**
**	**	1822	G, H, P, Q, R, U	Farm	TN	M	1500	100
Ark Mil (Denton)	**	1815	B, C, A2	Farm	TN	M	1500	5230
**	**	1834	B, C	Farm	TN	M	**	**
**	**	1791	B, C	Farm	NC	M	**	**
1 Ark Cav, H	62, 07-23	1834	A, B, C	Farm	TN	M	**	**
**	**	1815	B	Farm	TN	M	**	300
**	**	1832	D, A2	Farm	MO	M	**	15
**	**	1815	V	Farm	TN	M	350	1000
**	**	1830	P, Q, V, W	Farm	AL	M	600	1165
**	**	**	A2	**	**	**	**	**
**	**	1831	B, C	Farm	TN	M	700	500
**	**	1815	J, U	Farm	TN	M	**	**
Ark Cav, I	63, 11-21	1824	J	Farm	TN	M	2000	500
*	**	1838	D, A2	Farm	TN	M	800	130
*	**	1826	D, A2	Farm	TN	M	**	**
*	**	1838	A2	WagonMaker	TN	M	**	**
MO Cav, L	64, 01-27	1847	B	**	AR	M	**	**
*	**	1833	B, C	Lab Farm	AR	S	**	**
*	**	1810	I	Lab	KY	M	**	100
*	**	1813	D, A2	Farm	TN	M	900	857
Ark Cav, M	64, 01-01	1829	J	Farm	TN	M	**	**
Ark Cav, K	62, 07-25	1834	B, D, P, Q	**	**	**	**	**
*	**	1815	G, U	Farm	VA	M	**	500
Ark Cav, M	64, 01-28	1838	B, C	Lab Farm	TN	S	1400	2073
*	**	1845	I	Lab Farm	TN	S	**	**
*	**	1843	I	Lab Farm	TN	S	**	**
	**	1810	I	Farm	KY	M	1200	**
	**	1826	I	Farm	TN	M	**	100
	**	1828	A2	Lab	GA	**	**	**

Peace Society Members (continued)

Name	County	CSA	Enl	Died	Desert
Price, Charles William	Searcy	18 Ark Inf, K	61, 12-18	**	**
Price, Lindsey	Searcy	18 Ark Inf ?	**	**	**
Price, William	Searcy	**	**	1864	**
Pritchard, H J	Izard	8 Ark Inf, H	61, 12-12	**	(62, 07-08)
Pritchard, James W	Izard	8 Ark Inf, H	61, 12-12	**	62, 05-10
Pritchard, John H	Izard	**	**	**	**
Rainbolt, Emanuel B	Izard	8 Ark Inf, H	**	1862	**
Ramsey, Smith	Searcy	18 Ark Inf, I	61, 12-18	62, 00	**
Rand, John T	Fulton	**	**	**	**
Ray, James	Izard	8 Ark Inf, H	61, 12-12	**	62, 04-30
Reeves, Asa	Searcy	**	**	**	**
Reeves, Jarrett	Searcy	14 Ark Inf, K	62, 01-06	**	62, 04-13
Reeves, Joshua	Searcy	**	**	**	**
Reeves, Peter	Searcy	**	**	**	80, 07-10
Rich, Bazel M	Izard	**	**	**	**
Richardson, James C	Fulton	**	**	**	**
Richardson, Joshua	Fulton	**	**	**	**
Richardson, Thomas F	Fulton	**	**	**	**
Richardson, William S	Izard	**	**	**	**
Ridings, James C	Van Buren	18 Ark Inf, K *	61, 12-19	**	**
Ruff, David Crockett	Searcy	**	**	69, 10-18	**
Sanders, John L	Searcy	18 Ark Inf, I	61, 12-18	64, 02-02	**
Scott, James B	Izard	**	**	**	**
Scott, William Franklin	Searcy	**	**	**	**
Seaton, Nicholas	Searcy	17 Ark Inf, E	61, 12-21	**	**
Shelton, William	Izard	**	**	**	**
Shipman, Matthew	Searcy	18 Ark Inf, I	61, 12-18	**	**
Shirley, William	Independence	**	**	**	**
Sims, Daniel P	Newton	**	**	**	**
Singletary, William C	Marion	18 Ark Inf, K *	61, 12-19	94, 05-09	64, 10-01
Slay, Benjamin F	Searcy	**	**	63, 03-01	**
Slay, Cornelius D	Searcy	**	**	63, 04-27	**
Slay, Levi G	Searcy	**	**	63, 02-03	**
Slay, Thomas J	Searcy	**	**	63, 02-03	**
Slay, William Henry	Searcy	**	**	63, 02-23	**
Smith, Abner H	Van Buren	8 Ark Inf, A	61, 07-06	**	**
Smith, Claiborn M	Searcy	Cocke's Inf, G	62, 09-02	01, 08-08	62, 10-2
Smith, Elias	Van Buren	26 Ark Inf, I	**	**	**
Smith, George W	Van Buren	18 Ark Inf, K	61, 12-19	**	**
Smith, Gilmore	Searcy	18 Ark Inf, K	61, 12-19	**	**
Smith, John	Van Buren	18 Ark Inf, F	**	**	**
Snellgrove, Gasaway	Searcy	18 Ark Inf, I	61, 12-18	**	**
Stephens, William S	Izard	8 Ark Inf, H	61, 12-12	62, 06-15	**
Stobaugh, Ananias/Armenias	Van Buren	18 Ark Inf, K	61, 12-19	**	**

Union	Enl	Born	PS Activity	Occupation	POB	M/S	Real	Prop
**	**	1839	D, G, H, P, Q, U, Z	Farm	TN	M	**	100
**	**	1835	G, U, Z	Farm	TN	M	**	400
**	**	1800	G	Farm	NC	M	600	3000
**	**	1826	I	Farm	TN	M	2000	400
**	**	1840	I	Farm	TN	M	**	120
**	**	1844	I	Lab Farm	AR	S	**	**
**	**	1825	I	Farm	AL	M	**	400
**	**	1814	B, C	Farm	VA	M	**	75
Ware's Co G	61, 12-01	1838	A3	Lab Farm	TN	S	1--	100
**	**	1822	I	Farm	TN	M	**	270
**	**	1812	G	Wheelwright	TN	M	**	50
46 Mo Inf, F	64, 09-01	1836	V	Farm	TN	M	**	100
**	**	1820	G, H, P, Q, U	Farm	TN	M	**	1000
**	**	1821	G, H, J, U	Farm	TN	M	1500	1500
Ware's Co G	61, 12-01	1840	A3	Lab Farm	AL	S	**	**
**	**	1839	X, A1	Lab Farm	MO	S	**	**
**	**	1802	X, A1	Farm	MA	M	4000	1000
Ware's Co G	61, 12-01	1837	A3	Lab Farm	MO	M	**	300
Ware's Co G	61, 12-01	1830	A3	Farm	MO	M	1500	300
**	**	1829	D, A2	**	TN	**	**	**
1 Ark Inf, K	63, 02-27	1819	A, J	Brickmason	TN	M	**	400
3 Ark Cav, I	64, 01-04	1817	B, C	Farm	TN	M	**	600
4 Ark Cav, A	64, 05-22	1823	I	**	**	**	2000	200
**	**	1828	J	Farm	TN	M	**	225
2 Ark Cav, E	63, 07-12	1815	J	Farm	NC	M	**	400
**	**	1826	I	Farm	NC	M	260	400
**	**	1830	B, C	Farm	TN	M	**	20
**	**	1826	X	**	TN	**	**	**
**	**	1819	M	Landlord	TN	M	200	150
**	**	1829	D, P, Q	Physician	NC	**	**	**
4 Ark Cav, H	62, 07-23	1843	J, S	Lab Farm	AR	S	**	**
4 Ark Cav, H	62, 07-21	1834	J	Farm	GA	M	**	300
4 Ark Cav, H	62, -7-21	1836	J	Farm	GA	S	**	**
Ark Cav, H	62, 07-04	1831	J, O, S	Farm	GA	M	**	250
Ark Cav, H	62, 07-21	1841	J	Farm	AL	S	**	**
0 Mo Cav, D	62, 06-18	1825	A1, A2	Farm	TN	M	400	375
Ark Cav, H	63, 08-27	1830	J	Farm	AL	M	**	250
*	**	1835	E	Farm	TN	M	200	600
*	**	1836	D, A2	Farm	TN	M	400	260
*	**	1811	D, N, P, Q	Farm	TN	M	**	100
*	**	1815	A2	Farm	TN	M	200	150
*	**	1801	B, C	NoOccupation	SC	M	**	**
*	**	1837	I	Farm	AR	M	800	450
Btn Ark Inf, B	62, 06-10	1824	D, A2	Farm	TN	M	1500	900

Peace Society Members (continued)

Name	County	CSA	Enl	Died	Desert
Stobaugh, Edmond	Van Buren	**	**	**	**
Strickland, John Anderson	Searcy	**	**	**	**
Strickland, Paris	Searcy	**	**	**	**
Strickland, Samuel Smith	Searcy	**	**	**	**
Strother, William	Izard	**	**	**	**
Sutterfield, Ananias J	Searcy	18 Ark Inf, I	61, 12-18	64, 09-02	**
Sutterfield, John R	Searcy	18 Ark Inf, I	61, 12-18	**	**
Sutterfield, Nathaniel	Searcy	18 Ark Inf, I	61, 12-18	**	**
Sutterfield, Peter Moore	Searcy	18 Ark Inf, I	61, 12-18	64, 00	62, 04
Sutton, Logan	Van Buren	18 Ark Inf, K	61, 12-19	**	**
Taylor, Benjamin Franklin	Searcy	**	**	97, 08-04	**
Taylor, Hezikiah	Pope	17 Ark Inf, E	61, 12-21	64, 05-03	**
Thompson, James	Searcy	18 Ark Inf, K	61, 12-19	63, 02-17	(62, 01)
Thompson, John C	Izard	**	**	**	**
Thompson, Pleasant F	Izard	27 Ark Inf, C	62, 07-26	**	63, 09-13
Thompson, Samuel	Searcy	18 Ark Inf, K	61, 12-19	**	**
Thompson, Thomas	Searcy	**	**	**	**
Thompson, William J	Searcy	18 Ark Inf, I *	61, 12-18	**	62, 02
Tilley, James	Searcy	18 Ark Inf, I	61, 12-18	**	**
Tinkle, Michael P	Searcy	**	**	**	**
Tinkle, Robert	Searcy	7 Ark Vols, A	**	**	**
Toney, James P	Izard	8 Ark Inf, H	61, 12-12	64, 01-10	63, 09-27
Toney, Lorenzo D	Izard	**	**	**	**
Treadwell, John F	Searcy	18 Ark Inf, I	61, 12-18	**	**
Treat, James William	Searcy	18 Ark Inf, I	61, 12-18	**	**
Treat, John B	Searcy	18 Ark Inf, I *	61, 12-18	**	62, 06-06
Treece, Benjamin	Searcy	18 Ark Inf, I *	61, 12-18	04, 01-05	63, 01-01
Treece, Daniel	Searcy	18 Ark Inf, I	61, 12-18	62, 01	**
Treece, William	Searcy	18 Ark Inf, I *	61, 12-18	62, 04-06	**
Tucker, John Allen	Searcy	**	**	1896	**
Tucker, John Middleton	Searcy	**	**	62, 12-06	**
Turney, Bowman	Searcy	18 Ark Inf, I	61, 12-18	62, 04-06	**
Turney, Josiah S	Searcy	14 Ark Inf, K	62, 01-21	**	62, 04-03
Turney, Presley B R	Searcy	18 Ark Inf, I *	61, 12-18	**	[65, 04-28
Tyler, Peter A	Searcy	18 Ark Inf ?	61, 01	1862	**
Wainwright, Joseph J	Independence	**	**	**	**
Wallace, William Jasper	Searcy	8 Ark Inf, G	**	**	**
Wallis, James Wiley	Searcy	18 Ark Inf, K	61, 12-19	**	**
Ware, Jahoida J	Fulton	**	**	**	**
Ware, William	Fulton	**	**	**	**
Watson, Samuel W	Van Buren	18 Ark Inf, K	61, 12-19	**	**
Watts, Asa	Searcy	18 Ark Inf, I	61, 12-18	**	62, 04
Watts, Benjamin G	Searcy	18 Ark Inf, I	61, 12-18	**	62, 04
Watts, Samuel	Van Buren	18 Ark Inf, I *	61, 12-18	**	[65, 04-2

Union	Enl	Born	PS Activity	Occupation	POB	M/S	Real	Prop
1 Btn Ark Inf, B	62, 06-10	1818	D, A2	Farm	AR	**	**	200
1 Ark Cav, H	62, 07-30	1840	J	Lab Farm	AL	**	**	**
**	**	1831	A, J, O	Farm	AL	M	300	250
**	**	1807	J	Farm	KY	M	500	300
**	**	1834	X	Cabinet Maker	TN	M	2500	250
3 Ark Cav, M	64, 01-28	1832	B, C	Farm	AL	M	500	300
**	**	1801	B, C	Retired	SC	Wid	**	**
3 Ark Cav, I	64, 01-26	1816	B, C	Farm	TN	M	2000	1500
**	**	1814	B, C	Farm	TN	M	400	400
**	**	1830	D, A2	**	**	**	**	**
1 Ark Inf, K/3 Ark	63, 02-27	1839	J	Farm	TN	M	**	250
**	**	1838	J	Farm	TN	M	300	200
1 Ark Cav, I & C	62, 08-18	1804	D, G, H, P, Q, U, Z	Farm	KY	M	1000	1000
1 Btn Ark Inf, D	62, 07-01	1826	Text	Blacksmith	TN	M	600	600
**	**	1841	Text	LFarm	TN	S	**	**
**	**	1837	D, G, H, P, Q, U, Z	Farm	AR	M	**	300
**	**	1832	G, U, Z	Farm	IL	M	1000	1400
2 Tn Mtd Inf/2 Ark	63, 07-12	1836	B, C	Farm	TN	M	**	20
**	**	1802	C	Farm	TN	M	**	160
**	**	1826	F, G, K, P, Q, U	Farm	TN	S	**	**
**	**	1834	G, H, U	Farm	TN	M	**	75
**	**	1831	I	Farm	IN	M	250	300
Ware's Co G	61, 12-01	1822	A3	Farm	IN	M	200	500
2 Ark Cav, E	63, 09-15	1835	B, C	Farm	TN	S	**	**
**	**	1836	B, C	Lab	IN	M	**	120
*	**	1833	B, C	Lab	IN	M	**	150
*	**	1825	B, C	Farm	TN	M	300	200
*	**	1836	B, C	Farm	TN	M	300	**
*	**	1831	B, C	Farm	TN	M	**	300
*	**	1827	J	Farm	TN	M	500	**
Ark Cav, C	62, 07-24	1836	J	Lab Farm	TN	M	**	**
*	**	1830	B, C	Farm	TN	M	**	150
Ark Inf, K	63, 03-20	1845	J	Farm	TN	M	700	300
*	**	1842	B, C, J	Farm	AR	S	**	**
*	**	1823	G, U, Z	Farm	MO	M	1500	1000
'are's Co G	61, 12-01	1831	A3	**	**	**	**	**
Ark Cav, C	63, 08-12	1837	J	Farrier	TN	S	**	800
'	**	1835	B, C, D	Farm	TN	M	**	**
are's Co, G	61, 12-01	1826	A	Farm	AR	M	3000	1500
are's Co G	61, 12-01	1819	A3	Farm	IL	M	1500	4000
	**	1839	D, A2	Farm	TN	M	**	200
	**	1831	B, C, E	Farm	TN	M	25	480
Ark Cav, M	64, -1-28	1833	B, C	Farm	TN	M	200	708
	**	1844	B, C	Lab Farm	AR	S	**	**

Peace Society Members (continued)

Name	County	CSA	Enl	Died	Desert
Webb, John	Searcy	14 Ark Inf, K	62, 01-06	**	**
Wells, William S	Van Buren	**	**	62, 11-08	**
Whitmire, Jasper J	Van Buren	18 Ark Inf, I *	61, 12-18	**	[65, 04-28]
Williams, Allen	Izard	26 Ark Inf, H	**	**	**
Williams, Jesse	Izard	**	**	**	**
Williams, Wesley	Izard	4 Btn Inf, C	**	62, 09-04	**
Wilson, John	Searcy	18 Ark Inf, I	61, 12-18	64, 01-20	62, 01
Winn, William M	Marion	18 Ark Inf, K	61, 12-19	**	**
Wisdom, William J	Fulton	**	**	**	**
Woodal, William	Izard	8 Ark Inf, I	61, 12-12	62, 06-11	**
Woodrum, Vinsom M	Fulton	**	**	**	**
Woodward, M K	Izard	**	**	**	**
Woodworth, Nathan F	Searcy	**	**	**	**
Wooten, Lorenzo D	Izard	**	**	**	**
Wooten Sr, Lorenzo D	Izard	27 Ark Inf, H	62, 06-14	**	Yes
Wooten, James (J M)	Izard	8 Ark Inf, I	61, 12-12	62, 05	62, 05
Wooten, William	Izard	27 Ark Inf, H	62, 06-10	**	**
Wortman, Christopher M	Searcy	18 Ark Inf, I *	61, 12-18	06, 12-15	**
Wortman, Franklin	Searcy	18 Ark Inf, I	61, 12-18	11, 04-14	62, 04
Wortman, John	Searcy	**	**	62, 04-05	**
Wren, Shadrach H	Fulton	**	**	**	**
Wyatt, Brown	Fulton	**	**	**	**
Yeary, Henry P	Fulton	**	**	**	**
Yeary, Milton	Fulton	**	**	**	**
Yeary, Napoleon B	Fulton	**	**	**	**
Yeary, Nathan	Fulton	**	**	**	**
Yeary, William H	Fulton	**	**	**	**
Young, Bucy	Izard	**	**	**	**
Young, Martin V B	Izard	**	**	**	**
Younger, Alexander	Searcy	14 Ark Inf, K	62, 01-06	1906	62, 03-11
Younger, Thomas	Searcy	**	**	**	**

Union	Enl	Born	PS Activity	Occupation	POB	M/S	Real	Prop
**	**	1826	J, V	Blacksmith	GA	M	**	300
1 Btn Ark Inf, C	62, 06-10	1832	A1	**	**	**	**	**
**	**	1843	B, C	Lab Farm	AR	S	**	**
**	**	1835	I	Farm	IN	S	**	**
**	**	1810	I	Millwright	NC	M	200	2000
1 Btn Ark Inf, A	62, 06-10	1837	I	Farm	IN	S	**	**
**	**	1820	B, C	Farm	SC	M	**	300
**	**	1816	D, P, Q	**	VA	M	800	2275
Ware's Co G	61, 12-01	1828	A3	Farm	IL	M	**	175
**	**	1839	I	**	MO	**	**	**
**	**	**	X, A1	**	TN	**	1000	400
**	**	1832	I	Farm	AL	M	200	100
**	**	1824	J, K	Farm	NY	M	300	1600
Ware's Co G	61, 12-01	1832	A3	Farm	AR	M	**	**
**	**	1808	I	Farm	Unk	M	**	100
**	**	1842	I	Lab Farm	AR	S	**	**
**	**	1844	I	Lab Farm	AR	S	**	**
**	**	1833	B, C	Lab Farm	TN	S	**	**
3 Ark Cav, M	64, 01-01	1822	B, C	Farm	TN	M	**	1000
**	**	1795	A, J	Farm	NC	M	300	**
**	**	1824	X, A1	Farm	KY	M	2700	1075
Ware's Co G	61, 12-01	1843	A3	Lab Farm	MO	S	2000	10000
Ware's Co G	61, 12-01	1833	A3	Farm	TN	S	2000	**
Ware's Co G	61, 12-01	1838	A3	Lab	VA	S	1000	**
Ware's Co G	61, 12-01	1839	A3	Lab Farm	VA	S	**	**
Ware's Co G	61, 12-01	1836	A3	Farm	TN	S	1000	**
**	**	1818	X, A1	Farm	VA	M	1000	500
**	**	1797	I	Blacksmith	VA	Wid	**	**
Ware's Co G	61, 12-01	1838	A3	**	**	**	**	**
6 Mo Inf, F	64, 08-15	1827	U, V	Farm	TN	M	**	300
**	**	1791	U	Millwright	NC	M	**	200

Peace Society Sources

A   Albert W. Bishop, *Loyalty on the Frontier*, St. Louis: A. P. Studley, 1863. Granted that this was published as Union propaganda, the facts seem to be reliable and one can read past the adjectives. It is particularly valuable for Searcy County, with sketches of Searcy Countians Paris Strickland and John W. Morris.

B   Mrs. J. N. Bromley, *Biography of John W. Morris*, Marshall, Arkansas: 1916. John W. Morris's story is typical of many a Peace Society member. He worked with his daughter in the preparation of this biography and it is valuable for the source of the "chain gang" members whom he remembered accompanying him to Little Rock, and when some of them were killed in action. However, it should be noted that forty-five years later he added four names of men whose participation cannot be substantiated with other records.

C   The only extant muster roll of Company I, 18th (Marmaduke's) Arkansas Infantry, which enlisted December 18, 1861, at Little Rock contains the names of the men from Searcy County who were captured and marched to Little Rock by the 45th (Searcy County) Arkansas Militia. This is a useful cross-reference to Morris's list. On January 31, 1862, this unit was joined by two Tennessee companies and, therefore, could no longer retain its Arkansas designation. It was re-designated the 3rd Confederate Infantry. Most of the Peace Society members do not appear on the 3rd Confederate Infantry's rolls.

D   The only extant muster roll for Company K, 18 (Marmaduke's) Arkansas Infantry that enlisted December 19, 1861, at Little Rock contains the names of men arrested north of the Buffalo River from Carroll, Marion, and Searcy counties, and supplemented by men from Van Buren County who had been imprisoned in Little Rock earlier. An asterisk also marks their appearance on the 3rd CSA Infantry rolls.

E   Veda Mae Clemons, editor, *History of Searcy County Arkansas*, Marshall, Arkansas: Retired Teachers Association, 1987. This volume contains a few family recollections about men who were in the Peace Society or chain gang.

F   David Smith, George W. Smith deposition, November 26, 1861, in *Capt. J. R. Homer Scott's Civil War Letters*, J. B. Lemley, editor. Hereafter cited as *Scott Letters*. The Smith boys arrested the Faught brothers, from Tomahawk Township, Searcy County, and brought them before a Carroll County justice of the peace, accusing them of organizing a raid to release jailed Peace Society members.

G   Results of W. C. Faught and Thomas J. Faught interrogation describing sympathies of Tomahawk Township men. Addendum to Smith's deposition, November 26, 1861. *Scott Letters*.

H   Results of investigation by Scott's Battalion and Carroll County JPs. November 1861. *Scott Letters*.

I   Members of Izard County Peace Society Volunteer for Confederate Service. Forty-seven men volunteer for Confederate service under Major Thomas W. Edmondson and Captain Neely C. McGuyre. Ted R. Worley, "Documents Relating to the Arkansas Peace Society of 1861," *Arkansas Historical Quarterly* (Spring 1958). Hereafter cited as Worley.

J   A list of names belonging to a secret order that have not been arrested. Men identified in Searcy County investigations as Peace Society members. December 1861. *Scott Letters*.

K   Nathan F. Woodworth investigation. New York–born Woodworth was accused of Unionist sympathies and a scam was tried to trick him into revealing his sympathies. *Scott Letters*.

L   Carroll County JP investigation of L. D. Jamison, Wesley Hensley, and David Baker. December 5, 1861. *Scott Letters*.

M   Deposition for D. P. Sims, Newton County. December 6, 1861. *Scott Letters*.

N   Testimony of John, Joseph C., J. F. H. Christy, P. M. Hensley, Gilmore Smith, and D. C. Baker before JPs. December 6, 1861. Worley.

O   Thomas J. Slay and Lewis S. Brewer testimony before JPs. December 8, 1861. *Scott Letters*.

P   Carroll County JP orders to commit certain people to further trial and directs Captain Scott to transport them to Little Rock. December 9, 1861. Worley.

Q   Scott orders Lieutenant M. I. Anderson to convey 22 men
        to Little Rock for trial. December 9, 1861. *Scott Letters.*

R   Carroll County JP orders four others to be released on $500
        bond to appear on charges of belonging to the Peace Society.
        December 10, 1861. Worley.

S   Testimony of Slay and Brewer before Carroll County JPs.
        December 10, 1861. *Scott Letters.*

T   Leslie/Scott letter. December 14, 1861. *Scott Letters.*

U   Tyler and Ezell testimony before Carroll County JPs.
        December 18, 1861. Worley.

V   Desmond Walls Allen, editor. *The Fourteenth Arkansas
        Confederate Infantry.* Conway, Arkansas: Arkansas
        Research, 1988.

W   Mitchell/Rector Letter, December 23, 1861. Worley.

X   Testimony of Fulton County Prisoners Before the Military
        Board. December 24, 1861. Worley.

Y   "Correction," *Daily State Journal* (Little Rock), January 9,
        1862, and "The Case of Mr. Edmondson," *Daily State Journal,*
        January 10, 1862—concerns stories about death of Thomas J.
        Edmondson and statements about his alleged PS involvement.

Z   Peter A. Tyler to Evaline M. Tyler letter, January 17, 1862.
        Property of Buffalo National River, NPS, Harrison, Arkansas.

A1   "Confederate Court," *True Democrat* (Little Rock), January
        23, 1862, names of those tried and released by Judge Ringo,
        Confederate Circuit Court, eastern district of Arkansas.

A2   Testimony of Persons Arrested as Members of the Peace
        Society. February 1862. Principally Van Buren County people.
        Worley.

A3   J. J. Ware's Co. G, Phelps's 6-Month Volunteer Missouri
        Infantry. Enlisted for six months in December 1861, initial
        formation December 1, 1861.

A4   Alexander Copeland's Federal Pension File for service with
        Co. M, 3rd Arkansas Cavalry (Union).

A5   Kie Oldham Collection, Item #110d, Arkansas State Archives.

Text   References are in the text.

True Democrat Evaluation and Rebuttal

An exchange in the *True Democrat* in early 1862 sheds some light on Peace Society issues, especially those faced in Izard County.

"The Peace Society: We have received several letters and persons have called upon us to make statements, in relation to the alleged conspiracy, or peace society, formed in the northern part of the state. We confess that we are [at] a loss to know what is the true state of the case, but we fear a great many innocent men and a number of ignorant ones have been shamefully treated. Sometime last summer, Mr. Harvick, of Monroe County, caused the arrest and examination of some members of a self-styled *pro bono publico*; or peace society, but the evidence proved nothing treasonable and the parties were dismissed. Sometime afterwards arrests were made and persons sent here from Van Buren, Izard and other counties. The most of them protested their innocence of any treasonable intent, their loyalty to the Confederacy and when offered a release on condition of service in the army, promptly volunteered. The oath of the society, so far as disclosed has no direct treason in it, but is suspicious as affixing the death penalty on an informer.

"On the other hand, it was charged that this society was instituted for the purpose of giving aid and comfort to the enemy; that upon the approach of the Lincoln's troops, the houses of the members were to be distinguished by a mark on the door facing and were to be unmolested; that arms from the federals in Missouri had been placed in their hands with which to fight against the South; that besides the oath already known, there was another and treasonable one in which the members swore hostility to the Southern Confederacy and that the leaders were abolitionists. It was admitted that the majority of these men were ignorant and had no knowledge of the ultimate objects of the society or designs of their leaders.

"On the other hand, we have been solemnly assured that if such a society existed there was nothing treasonable in it; that there was but one oath; that innocent men were induced to join by being told it promised them protection and that no collusion with abolitionists or Lincoln's army was thought of. It is bitterly denied that any arms or ammunition were received from Missouri, or that any were found. It is asserted that persons without authority commenced making arrests without warrants and upon suspicion, or when an enemy pointed out some person as a member; that there was no security of person; that old men, some of them having three sons in the Confederate army and who had furnished food and clothing to our troops, were seized, ironed and sent to this city, and that others who had responded to Col. Borland's call for troops, upon their return from Pocahontas were seized and imprisoned.

"In the case of Mr. Edmondson, those who killed him say it was done in self defense and while he was resisting arrest. His friends say that Edmondson was a true southron; that in the reign of terror he advised certain persons whom he knew to have enemies to escape until the storm blew over, and for this he was accused of being a member of the society; that they sought to arrest him and because he refused to submit, shot him.

"We do not know which of these stories is true, but if half that is told us is a reality, there is a dread state of affairs there. The power of making arrests without warrant is a dangerous one to put in the hands of any man or set of men and in this case it appears to have been exercised by anybody or everybody. Arrests are being made yet, or were being made until lately and the state has had to pay large sums for arresting, guarding and bringing these men here. While all this was going on, regular orders of regular Confederate officers are pronounced against as conflicting with the civil authority and running counter to the law.

"It has been intimated that no more prisoners will be brought here as it is intended to make short work of those suspected men hereafter. So, if anyone has an enemy in north Arkansas he has only to denounce him as a member of the peace society to ensure his death.

"The governor of the state has sworn to see the laws faithfully executed and if treason exists in that quarter he should see that the accused and arrested men have the advantage of a trial and a defense. The law, in this instance, has been lost sight of or trampled underfoot.

"If the governor will not act in the premises, the Military Board can appoint a commission to proceed to these counties, enquire into these matters, cause the legal arrest of parties against whom evidence is found and restore quiet and order among the people.

"We do not intend to impugn the motives of any person or persons engaged in making these arrests. They may have been actuated by patriotic motives, but there is a limit to all things, and it is high time their power of arresting citizens and killing those who demur, should be superceded [sic] by the strong arm of the law."[315]

Harris Township's William M. Aikin's rebuttal of the *True Democrat*'s article was published in March:

"*The Jayhawkers.* We have no hesitancy in giving place to the following letter. In a former article to which the letter may be termed a reply, we said that from the conflicting statements made to us at the time we were unable to determine how far these men were guilty. That some of them were tories seems now to be clear. Hereafter short work must be made with enemies in our midst. We can excuse the somewhat petulant tone of the letter for the facts it gives. Our only object in referring to the subject was to arrive at the true state of matters.

Sylamore, Izard Co., Jan. 31, 1862
"Editor True Democrat–

"Dear Sir: In your issue of 16th inst., you have an editorial on the self styled Peace Party of North Arkansas. I write this in reply to some reports which are therein set forth, viz: That the men when taken to Little Rock disclaim any treasonable intent and when offered a release on condition of volunteering in the Confederate service, they gladly accepted the same. Of old men who have three sons in the Confederate army and who had contributed food and clothing to the troops at Pocahontas, being arrested, ironed and taken to Little Rock. Of men who had responded to Col Borland's call for thirty day troops at Pocahontas, and on their return were arrested, and that a man who has an enemy in this part of the State, who will just point him out as one of them, will be arrested, etc., etc.

"In reply to the above reports, I can say first, as to their treasonable intent, I was only on one committee and served on that one half day, but during that time, I helped examine some five men and one of them said he understood it to be a movement against secession—that he was attaching himself to a secret society that was in favor of the North and against the South.

"I have lived in this township (Harris) for the last six years, and have a right to know something about the private feelings of these men. When you consider that Harris township with a voting population of forty-eight, turned out thirty-four jayhawkers, you concede that I ought to know something of them. When I and several other gentlemen first raised the *stars and bars*, these very men threatened to come in force and pull them down. When the news came here last summer, as it first did, that Price and McCulloch were beaten at Oak Hills, these very men threw up their hats and hurrahed for the United States of America. When I and others were canvassing this county last summer for volunteers for Col. McCarver's regiment, these men would not come out even to hear us speak nor muster—they swore that they would never muster under the d–d *nigger* flag, but if anyone would just come along with the stars and stripes that they would arise at midnight to go to it, and they would fight for it too when they got there. They plead ignorance now.

"If you will examine your books you will find that I paid Dr. Gaines, when he and Hon. R. W. Johnson and Mr. Newton were canvassing this county last spring, five dollars for ten campaign papers, one of those I ordered to myself and nine of them I ordered to be sent to other names, which I sent you—my object being to inform the people up here. Well sir, three of the **immortal** nine turned out to be jayhawkers, and one of them, B. F. Brantly, swore more men in than any man in the county. I have traded with these men for six years, and I defy any man to over reach them in a trade—no sir, they are not so ignorant as they would fain have you believe, nor their looks indicate. If they were true to the southern cause, why did they try so hard those that ran away, to get to the northern army. When the Hon. J. J. Ware heard in Van Buren county that the secret had been told, he rode seventy-five miles in a day, and only stayed five hours at home as I am informed by good authority, and then he and some forty or fifty left, and are now in the northern army in Missouri. Why not go to Pocahontas to Col. Borland, for it was much nearer?

"They all volunteer readily—well, I am very glad to hear it, for I and others tried last summer every inducement to get them to volunteer, and was told that they would die first. (Old men who have three sons in the Confederate army.) Your informant forgot to tell you that those three sons were first in the Peace Society, and volunteered to get out of the scrape. No, Sir, not one man has been arrested in this county, who had a son in the southern army. The committee who tried these men were our best men—old men who have lived here for years, and who have done all in their power for the South, and who have sons and brothers in the army; and they offered these men a choice to volunteer or take a trial at law, and they, every one, chose to volunteer; and when they were taken to Pocahontas, some of the old men were refused and came home and left their patriotic sons there; and one of them is now absent at Pocahontas, I learn, trying to get his son out of the army. One of these men furnished 199 lbs. of flour and one rifle gun—another furnished one rifle gun to Col. McCarver's regiment, for which they have receipts, but neither of them furnished a gun until the captain sent men to them to bring the guns whether they were willing or not.

"No sir, the true men of my county had tried every plan they could devise, and done everything they could to bring them over to the cause of the South, all in vain; and when they found them banded together in a secret sworn society, they took them up.

"One word about these 'who responded to Col Borland's call for 30 day men.' I went to Pocahontas, acting as commissary of Col. McCarver's regiment, and as all the men who went from this county were first attached to Col McCarver's regiment; I ought to know who they were, and I assure you that only one man amongst them went to Pocahontas and he did not go till they were discovered and several arrested; and when he came home the committee turned him loose. His name is Thos. Kamey [*sic* Carney]— he lives in Rocky Bayou township.

"That a man who has an enemy in this part of the State has only to point him out as one to have him arrested.' No such state of society exists here, and further, there has not been one single man arrested here until after he had been [judged], except one who had acknowledged himself that he was one. I am a law abiding man, as all who know me will bear witness; but, it seems in the latter days that the written law and the law of nations ever ceases to protect the right of the people and in that case what would you do (join the Peace society?) True southern men always know what to do in such cases. I, for one, never **wish to live to see the day when they fail to do it**. No sir, my old county has to bear the stigma of being one of the jayhawker counties, but notwithstanding that, she has a proud record in this war, and the men who arrested the jayhawkers made her proud record for her. Here it is—she with a voting population of 1,500 sends seven companies to the southern army, not counting the jayhawkers.

"She has one company with Col. Borland, Capt. Deason; one with Col. Mitchell, Capt. Adams; five companies in Col. McCarver's regiment, viz: Capt. Lindsey's, Capt Aikin's, Capt Barnett's, Capt Elkins' and Capt. Smith's. Fully one half her voting population is in the field, without counting those patriotic gentlemen who were so ruthlessly stopped in their humane efforts to bring peace to our beloved country.

"I have lived here for twenty years, and I do assure you that there is not a more law abiding people in the South, than the men who arrested and sent those men away from here. I was absent when the thing broke out, at my post in the army, with my wife, two orphan nieces, my two children: one seven and the other five, and my negroes at home, the only white male being my son aged seven. Ought I not to feel indignant at my countrymen for stopping such a humane institution, but such is the ferocity of human nature, that I am not on the other hand. I think they did right. A southern man is as safe here as anywhere in the South.

"As to the case of Mr. Edmondson—he was here on his return from the Legislature and participated with them— he was one of the committee, and took charge of the prisoners and papers, and the men who came for him say it was in regard to that subject they sent for him. In regard to the manner of his death, I was not at home at the time and cannot speak. Notwithstanding the length of this article, I ask for it a place in your valuable journal.

Wm. M. Aikin"[316]

Constitution of the Mill Creek Peace Organization Society

We the undersigned subscribers, agree to form ourselves into an association, to be called and known by the name and style of the 'Mill Creek Peace Organization Society.' Self-preservation being an undisputed, and natural right—and the right of communities to combine together for the mutual protection of themselves, their families, and their property, being well established—this being the sole purpose for which we meet—and for this purpose alone, we do adopt the following resolutions by which we expect to be governed in all our proceedings:

> *Resolved*, 1ˢᵗ. That each member before entering into this society, shall take an oath, as follows:
>
> I, _____, do solemnly swear, before Almighty God, and these witnesses, that I will well and truly keep all the secrets of this society; that I will ever hail and always conceal, and never reveal anything. I will, at the shortest notice, go to the assistance of any brother at the peril of my life, so help me God.
>
> 2d. As it is a matter of life or death with us, any member of this society who shall betray to our enemies the existence of this society shall forfeit his life. And it shall be the duty of each member of this society having received knowledge of any such betrayal, to forthwith inform the brethren, each of whose duty it shall be to pursue such traitor and take his life at the peril of their own.
>
> The matter of admitting members shall be in strict accordance with the foregoing preamble and resolutions, and by such members as may be selected by the society.[317]

Appendix V

Calf Creek Resolutions

WHEREAS, It is reported that many of our peaceable, orderly and law-abiding citizens have been accused of entering into a conspiracy against the secession party, for the purpose of murdering, robbing and plundering the citizens of that party; and *whereas*, many of our citizens have already been arrested and are held in custody, or imprisoned, and denied the right to trial, or to be heard in their own defense, and that all men who are desirous of remaining peaceably at home are considered enemies of the country and guilty of treason—

> *Resolved*, First: That the charge of conspiracy for the above or any other purpose, is a gross and palpable falsehood, and that we are ready at any time to take up arms against any body of robbers, North or South, and to maintain the peace of our country and the liberties of our citizens.

> *Resolved*, Secondly: That we are willing to have a full investigation made of the object and purpose of the society to which we belonged, as we intended only to benefit ourselves, when all other resources failed us, without interfering with any seceder or his property, and claiming for ourselves the right to think and act as independent American citizens.

> *Resolved*, Thirdly: That we will not submit to be taken up and tried for crimes of which we are not guilty; and rather than submit to the high-handed oppression now going on, we will defend ourselves by force of arms and die, if necessarily, in the assertion of our liberties.[318]

Camp Culloden Prisoners Sent to Little Rock

Lieutenant M. I. Anderson, in charge of a seventy-five-man guard detail, started the twenty-two prisoners to Little Rock on December 9. The twenty-two were chained, but it was expected that those under bond to appear before the governor would accompany Anderson.

Captain Scott's orders to the officer in charge of the detail marching the prisoners from Camp Culloden [Valley Springs] to Little Rock were as follows:

> Headquarters Battalion, Arkansas Cavalry Vols.
> Camp Culloden, Carroll Co., Arks
>
> Lieutenant—
>
> You will take charge of the following named prisoners committed by the Honbs Kelly Featherston and William Owens associate justices of Carroll Co. Arkansas and under their order to me safely conduct under guard of 75 men and deliver them into the custody of the Governor of the State of Arkansas with as little delay as possible, Keeping an accurate account of the expenditures incurred by yourself & guard of seventy-five men and the said twenty-two prisoners & presenting the Bill thereof to the State authorities for payment and liquidation adding the expenses of the return of your command back to Head Quarters.
>
> The following is a list of the prisoners, to wit:

George Long	Carroll Co.	United Missionary Baptist Preacher & Farmer
Solomon Branum	Searcy Co.	United Missionary Baptist Preacher & Blacksmith
Joshua Reeves	Searcy Co.	United Missionary Preacher & Farmer
David Curry	Searcy Co.	Farmer
James Latterell	Searcy Co.	Farmer
Samuel Thompson	Searcy Co.	Farmer
Patrick L. Downey	Searcy Co.	Farmer

James Thompson	Searcy Co.	Farmer
James E. Curry	Searcy Co.	Farmer
Charles W. Price	Searcy Co.	Farmer
George Hooten	Searcy Co.	Farmer
William Brown	Searcy Co.	Farmer
Mike Tinkle	Searcy Co.	Farmer
William Dugger	Searcy Co.	Farmer
Mayfield Addison	Searcy Co.	Farmer
Luther Phillips	Marion Co.	Farmer
Thomas Dugger	Marion Co.	Farmer
William M. Winn	Marion Co.	Farmer
James Hollis	Marion Co.	School Teacher
Jasper Dugger	Marion Co.	Farmer
William C. Singletary	Marion Co.	Physician
John M. Carithers	Carroll Co.	Southern Methodist Preacher & Farmer

These men above named are committed. The following named persons have entered into recognizance to appear before the Governor as being somewhat implicated and a part of them upon voluntary appearance without arrest before Esqr Featherston & Owens & will surrender themselves to the Governor at Little Rock and not leave without his orders, To wit: John Christy, Joseph C. Christy, J. F. H. Christy, P. M. Hensley, Gilmore Smith, Carroll Kilburn, E. L. Osborn, Carlton Keeling, George M. Hays, J. W. Kirkham, John McEntire, J. C. McNair.

So soon as you have complied with the orders above you will return to your Company Hd Qrs.

Lieutenant M. I. Anderson
Company "A" Battalion Arks Cav Vol. CSA

Jno. R. Homer Scott, captain
Comdg Battalion, Arks Cavalry Volunteers CSA

[John R. H. Scott Letters & Papers][319]

Captain John R. H. Scott to General Benjamin McCulloch

December 3, 1861

Head Quarters Battalion
Arks Cavalry Volunteers
Camp Culloden
Carroll County, Arks
Decr 3d 1861

General,

I have under arrest (and daily making more) Some thirty-five or Forty-five men positively proven to belong to a secret society held together by secret signs, tokens, pass words and and [sic] under the penalty of "**Death**" should one of their number reveal the same.

I have been enabled from their own confessions upon each other to obtain their oaths, signs, tokens & words &c.

I conclude the organization to be of Northern origin having in view the subjugation of the South!

It breathes treason and insurrection of the most conclusive and positive nature.

Some of the most important signs, tokens, &c are given thus (from their own statements): A member when leaving home was to suspend from his door or window a piece of '**Yellow ribbon, calico** or **paper**' to distinguish them as members and as a token 'that if a friend or Northern Army came along that his property & family would not be molested by seeing and finding **this sign** at his door.'

Another token was to say '**Secession**' which if recognized by a member would be answered by saying 'In the Southern Confederacy.'

Another token or word on riding up to a member's house was to say 'Dark night' if the proprietor was a member he would answer 'It will be darker before day.' But if there was a Secessionist or an enemy in the house he would answer in order to caution his friend of their being there & that he should be on his guard, 'Perhaps it will be darker in the morning.'

There was another to be used in camp which some termed a Camp Signal and by which it appears some members (to blind the South) were to volunteer & go into the army of the South and there work our destruction, this signal, word, noise or token was to 'Hoot like an owl' which was to be answered by the 'Howl of a wolf;' there are several others named.

This Society was called by some of them a 'peace party' or 'peace society' or to unite the friends of 'Peace.'

The first signal was to place the forefinger of the right hand upon the nose twice, & then let it fall to the side of the body. The answer to this was to take and place the two forefingers of the right hand separated on the throat under the chin & draw them down twice to the breast & then letting their hand fall down to the side. The 2nd sign was to 'pull with the two forefingers of the right hand the shirt collar, when buttoned around the throat twice as if to relieve if it bound the neck too tight & then letting the hand fall to the side.' The answer to this was 'To open the palm of the right hand and placing it upon the left breast—then letting it fall to the side.' There are a good many other signs, but these are the main & important ones, all corresponding very well in their statements on examination before the Judge of the County Court and a Justice of the Peace holding their court at my camp especially called to examine into it.

This Society or organization numbers several hundred and extends through Fulton, Izard, Searcy Newton, Van Buren, parts of Conway, Pope, Marion & Carroll Counties. There has been nearly one hundred arrested in Clinton, Van Buren Coy., Burryville [sic] in Searcy county and I have arrested thirty-five or forty in Marion, Searcy, Newton & Carroll Counties. All around my Camp and are daily making them. It seems almost universal; in certain localities.

I do think that the contract ought to have been let out for building our cabins to winter in. We need not go north to find our enemies, thay [sic] are all around me bound together by solemn secret oaths &c. Some of the prisoners have stated it was an understanding that if the Northern Army did drive your command before them that this Squadron would have been attacked or *that they "laid such hints"* & if I made or attempted to arrest persons in certain places after I commenced making them & their plans &c. were detected, that they would "give me a fight" &c.

I think it would be advisable to station some of the companies of my command in Wiley's Cove, Searcy County. There is a camp meeting ground with some good buildings, a very large Harbor [sic] and near or in midst of this secret society &c. I think Capt. Boon is in the vicinity or County of the same kind of men, but fear not able to procure winter Quarters conveniently.

I am in hopes I may be permitted to station the companies, if found necessary, *separately* in the most disaffected and unloyal localities or adjoining counties within reach or days ride from my head Qtrs. It will be better in getting the use of buildings in part now erected at certain points by religious Societies & in neighborhoods where protection would be needed &c.

I shall take this liberty of acting as I have suggested hoping it may meet your approval. Should I receive no answer in time to this application and circumstances shall require it in my judgement.

> I am Sir, Very Respectfully
> Your Obt. Servant
> Jno. R. Homer Scott, Capt.
> Comdg Battalion
> CSA

Brig. Gen. B. McCulloch
Comdg Western Division
CSA
Fayetteville, Arks.[320]

Company I, 18th (Marmaduke's) Arkansas Infantry

Company I, 18th (Marmaduke's) Arkansas Confederate Infantry was formed on December 18, 1861, and was composed almost entirely of Peace Society members who had been arrested by the 45th Arkansas Militia in Searcy County. There were two 18th Arkansas Infantry regiments. This one was commanded by Colonel John Sappington Marmaduke of Missouri, and was sent east of the Mississippi River December 22, 1861. Short two companies of making a full regiment, Marmaduke's unit enrolled two Tennessee companies. Confederate authorities did not permit the regiment to keep its Arkansas designation and renamed it a Confederate (not Arkansas) Infantry. By Special Order No. 25, Adjutant and Inspector General's Office, CSA, dated January 31, 1862, the designation of the regiment was changed to 3rd Regiment Confederate Infantry. At the end of the war the 1st, 2nd, 5th, 6th, 7th, 8th, 13th, 15th, 19th, and 24th regiments of Arkansas Infantry and the 3rd Regiment Confederate Infantry were consolidated and formed the 1st Consolidated Regiment Arkansas Infantry, which was paroled at Greensboro, North Carolina. The 3rd Confederate Infantry served in Kentucky, Tennessee, Georgia, and probably North Carolina, and participated in the battles at Bell Station, Kentucky; Shiloh, Murfreesboro, Chickamauga, Tennessee; Corinth, Mississippi; and Tunnel Hill, Georgia.

Other field grade officers of the regiment, besides Marmaduke, were Lieutenant Colonel J. B. Johnson and Majors H. V. Keep and John F. Cameron. Company I consolidated with Company A (formerly Company L, 1st Battalion Arkansas Infantry) on April 23, 1862. Captain J. J. Dawson resigned March 19, 1862, and returned to Searcy County, where he later served as Commissioner for the Imprest Fund. First Lieutenant Morgan M. Terry was stricken from the roll May 6, 1862, but his resignation was effective June 1, 1862. He later served as private in Company C, 7th Arkansas Cavalry. Second

Lieutenant John H. Bradshaw submitted his resignation on January 27, 1862, at Bell Station, Kentucky, for medical reasons. It was approved February 13, 1862. He scarcely served with the Company, because for part of January he served with the grand jury which released the two Peace Society members who had not enlisted with Company I. When he returned to Searcy County, he served briefly with James H. Love's Company K, Fourteenth (Powers) Arkansas, was wounded at Pea Ridge, and was elected representative to the 14th (1862) Confederate Arkansas General Assembly. He later died in Texas toward the close of the war. Third Lieutenant John Stotts resigned his commission March 31, 1862, and it was forwarded with General T. C. Hindman's notation that Stotts was better suited for peaceful than warlike pursuits. Although the two Peace Society–recruited Searcy County companies were consolidated in April 1862 with other companies in the regiment, they initially acted together. On January 1, 1862, Captain Ira Robertson of Company K requisitioned a three-month supply of medicine for the two companies. Dawson was away escorting a second group of Peace Society men (including Peter A. Tyler and Lindsey Price) to the unit. Company I bore the nickname of the "Burrowville Mountain Guards," one of only two Searcy County company nicknames to come down to us. Burrowville Mountain is probably an alternative name for the Devil's Backbone which overlooks the county seat. The entire Company was enrolled December 18, 1861, in Little Rock for the duration of the war.

John Wortman Morris recalled how they were captured, marched to Little Rock, and forced into Confederate service:

> "A peace organization was formed, which had for its object the protection of life and property. It was composed of loyal citizens, and had divisions in Conway, Pope, Marion, Van Buren and Searcy counties.
>
> "John Holmes of Van Buren, and a Mr. Garrison betrayed the organization and caused a number of men to be reported to the state militia." (*Biography of John Morris*, p. 45.)

"At this time the 'Peace Organization Society' was in operation in Searcy and the adjoining counties, and Mr. Morris connected himself with it. This circumstance was not known at the time, but his conduct had nevertheless made him an object of suspicion with the rebel authorities. He was narrowly watched for some months, and on the 28th of October, 1861 (sic), was arrested at Burrowville, the county seat of Searcy. He had heard of the arrest there, without cause, of Union men, but doubting the accuracy of the rumor in its full extent, determined to ascertain for himself the true situation of affairs. Accompanied by a brother-in-law (Beverly Conley), he had scarcely entered the place when two double-barreled shot guns were thrust in their faces and they were insolently told that they were prisoners. John Smith and Mark Hogan, two notorious rebels of that locality, effected their arrest and took the prisoners at once before a Colonel Alexander Ham, then organizing the militia of the county. By him, Mr. Morris was briefly questioned, and then taken to the Court House, where, with others, he was imprisoned for two weeks. A trial was promised but none had, and after being imprisoned as stated, he, with seventy-six other State prisoners, was marched to Little Rock, a distance of one hundred and twenty-five miles.

"...The seventy-seven were chained together two and two, with an ordinary log chain fastened about the neck of each, and for twenty-four hours prior to their departure from Burrowville were thus guarded, in two ranks, as it were, with a long chain running down the center of the column. But rebel cruelty in this instance was foiled by its own invention, for before the party started on its toilsome march, the brutal guard discovered that this disposition of their prisoners was not at all favorable to pedestrianism. Inclination gave way to humanity, and the prisoners were fastened together by twos only, the odd man bringing up the rear with a chain encircling his neck and thrown over his shoulder, that his walking might not be impeded. Six days were spent in the march to Little Rock, and a guard of one hundred men detailed. Arriving there fatigued, worn

out and still in chains, they were marched into the hall of
the House of Representatives, and addressed by Governor
Rector. He offered them their choice, either to volunteer in
the rebel service or go to jail, and await trial for treason,
giving them the *flattering* assurance that if they accepted
the latter alternative, four or six months might elapse
before trials could be had, and that should they insist upon
them then, he was very confident that they would be hung.

"...After the prisoners had determined their choice, their
chains were stricken off, and before leaving the hall, they
were organized into a company, and a Captain and three
Lieutenants appointed over them. Four days later they left
Little Rock for Memphis. Remaining there two weeks, they
were ordered thence to Bell's Station, in Kentucky, twenty-five miles north of Bowling Green. They had previously
been assigned to a regiment commanded by Colonel, now
General, Marmaduke, and insufficiently fed and poorly
clothed, but well armed, they were thenceforth placed in
active service." [*Loyalty on the Frontier*, pp. 127–130.]

The state press relished the thought of conscripting them into
CSA service:

"A GOOD RESULT—We understand that seventy-five of
the men brought to this city from Searcy County a few days
ago arrested upon a charge of belonging to a conspiracy
supposed to be formed for treasonable purposes, were given
the privilege of volunteering for three years in the Confederate service, which they gladly accepted. They elected
officers from outside of their ranks: good and true men
from their own county, who had accompanied them here
as guards to prevent their escape. This mode of drafting of
these men, whether done through the instrumentality of
the Government or the Military Board, was a humane, and
we think, a wise step, much better than to have hung them
as has been suggested. The evidence against these men was
simply that they were members of a secret organization,
and the most of them were so ignorant that they did not
know what the objects of it were. The sinister designs of

the leaders were evidently not known to the body of the members. The alacrity with which they volunteered and pledged themselves to support and fight for the Confederacy is an evidence that they were not badly corrupted or tainted with treasonable designs. We are glad to note this result of the matter from the fact that sensation articles written and published here have been copied all over the country and doubtless gone into the newspapers of our enemies, giving this movement the character of an insurrection or rebellion against our government when really and in truth, not one man even appears to have known the ulterior designs of the organization, and became members of it through motives of patriotism and a desire to protect their homes. (*True Democrat*, Little Rock, December 19, 1861, p. 2, c. 2.)

Muster Roll

Name	Rank	Age	
Dawson, John J.	Captain	—	(Elected 14 Dec. 1861; appointed 19 Dec. 1861; resigned 19 Mar 1862)
Terry, Morgan M.	1st Lieutenant	—	(Elected 14 Dec. 1861; resigned 1 June 1862; stricken from roll 6 May 1862)
Bradshaw, John H.	2nd Lieutenant	—	(Elected 14 Dec. 1861; dropped 1 June 1862; Lt. Bradshaw dropped from roll for being absent without leave; has never been heard from; tendered resignation on 27 Jan 1862 for medical reasons).
Stotts, John	3rd Lieutenant	—	(Elected 14 Dec. 1861; resigned 31 Mar 1862; "Respectfully forwarded approved. Lt. Stotts' resignation should be accepted, as the interests of the service would thereby be promoted. He is better suited for peaceful than warlike pursuits. T. C. Hindman")
Sanders, John L.	1st Sergeant	45	
Barnes, James J.	2nd Sergeant	47	(Sent to hospital Tupelo, Mississippi 20 July 1862)
Palmer, Benjamin E.	3rd Sergeant	30	
Morris, John W.	4th Sergeant	25	
Sutterfield, Ananias J.	1st Corporal	29	

Muster Roll (continued)

Name	Rank	Age	
Kuykendall, Francis	2nd Corporal	35	
Watts, Asa	3rd Corporal	30	
Watts, Benjamin	4th Corporal	28	
Blasingame, Anderson	Private	35	
Barnett, David	Private	33	
Bartlett, William	Private	21	(Sent from Pittsburg Landing to St. Louis, Missouri, June 1862 by Federal forces. Deserted CSA)
Black, S. B.	Private	30	(At inspection in Baldwin, Miss., 5 June 1862)
Bradshaw, William	Private	48	
Bradshaw, Henry	Private	48	
Bratton, Miliken	Private	30	
Castleberry, John R.	Private	44	
Castleberry, W. C.	Private	20	(Absented himself without leave on march from Corinth to Baldwin 1862; teamster for General Cleburne May 1863)
Cate, William A. J.	Private	48	
Chambers, W. R.	Private	40	(Sent from Pittsburg Landing to St. Louis, MO deserted CSA)
Clark, Lewis	Private	43	
Conley, Beverly S.	Private	40	
Copeland, Alexander N.	Private	30	
Copeland, James B.	Private	26	
Copeland, W.	Private	45	
Davis, William	Private	23	
Fisher, William Thomas	Private	34	(Teamster during period covered by muster roll dated 6 Aug. 1863; deserted at Fynch Station; captured by Federals 4 Aug. 1863 at Bridgeport, Ala. 11 Aug. 1863 at Louisville, Kentucky, was released upon taking oath to remain north of Ohio River)
Forehand, Jonathan	Private	55	
Foster, James B.	Private	31	
Garner, Parrish	Private	55	
Gary, B. H.	Private	29	
Harley, John	Private	23	
Harness, John W.	Private	21	(On 1 January 1862 admitted sick to Overton General Hospital, Memphis, Tenn.)

Muster Roll (continued)

Name	Rank	Age	
Harness, William H.	Private	22	
Harris, William	Private	37	(In May or June 1862 returned to Searcy County on furlough w/John W. Morris)
Hatley, James R.	Private	26	(Appears on register of those killed in battle, wounded or died of disease; last paid 1 Sept. 1862)
Hatley, John W.	Private	38	
Jeffreys, William	Private	34	
Johnson, Robert	Private	48	(In May or June 1862 returned to Searcy County on furlough w/John W. Morris; wounded and subsequently died 15 March 1863)
Jones, Stephen	Private	23	
Kesner, William A.	Private	26	
Ladyman, Richard C.	Private	23	(Captured 2 Oct. 1864 at Atlanta; 6 Apr. 1865 mustered into 5th US Volunteer Infantry; claimed to have been loyal; lived in the State of Arkansas)
Lee, Robert	Private	29	
Lynn, Washington G.	Private	26	(Taken prisoner at Murfreesboro 1 Jan 1863; discharged from Gratiot Street Prison, St. Louis, Missouri, 7 Feb. 1863; took oath of renunciation of the CSA and allegiance to the US)
McDaniel, William F.	Private	45	
McInturff, Thomas W.	Private	34	
McLane, S. Allen	Private	34	
McMillin, E. L.	Private	28	
Marshall, William	Private	21	
Martin, Thomas	Private	20	(Died of measles February 1862 at Bowling Green, KY)
Moody, Jonathan	Private	46	
Morris, John Sr.	Private	60	(Sent by Federals from Pittsburg Landing to St. Louis, Missouri, June 1862; deserted CSA)
Morris, John Jr.	Private	28	
Passmore, Joel H.	Private	28	
Potter, William	Private	23	
Ramsey, Smith	Private	47	(Was wounded and died in 1862)

Muster Roll (continued)

Name	Rank	Age	
Shipman, Matthew	Private	31	
Snellgrove, Gasaway	Private	50	
Sutterfield, John R.	Private	60	
Sutterfield, Nathaniel	Private	45	
Sutterfield, Peter M.	Private	23	
Thompson, William J.	Private	25	
Tilly, James	Private	59	
Treadwell, John S.	Private	26	
Treat, James William	Private	25	
Treat, John B.	Private	28	(1 July 1862 admitted to No. 4 USA General Hospital, Louisville, Kentucky, 4 July sent to Provost Martial Prison as a Rebel)
Treece, Benjamin	Private	36	(Taken prisoner at Murfreesboro 1 Jan 1863; received 21 Jan 1863 at Gratiot Street Military Prison, St. Louis, Missouri; discharged 14 Feb. 1863; took oath of renunciation and allegiance)
Treece, Daniel	Private	25	(Died January 1862)
Treece, William	Private	30	(Died April 1862)
Turney, Bowman	Private	21	(Killed at Shiloh, TN 6 Apr. 1862)
Turney, Presley B. R.	Private	19	(Surrendered and paroled 28 Apr. 1865 as 3rd Corporal)
Wallace, James W.	Private	26	(This name found on Co. K Muster Roll as well)
Watts, Samuel	Private	17	(Sent to hospital 8 Jan 1863; present at other musters; surrendered and paroled 28 Apr. 1865 in Greensboro, NC)
Whitmire, J. J.	Private	18	(Surrendered and paroled 28 Apr. 1865 in NC)
Wilson, John	Private	41	
Wortman, Chris M.	Private	28	(4 Dec. 1862 sent to hospital in Chattanooga; captured at Stone's River)
Wortman, Frank	Private	38	

Desertion, sickness, and death were rampant among the Peace Society men. John W. Morris later related, "At that time (April 6, 1862, at Shiloh), the band of seventy-seven men, marched into Little Rock as related, had been reduced by sickness, desertion and death to ten." *Loyalty on the Frontier*, A. W. Bishop, 131. At Shiloh, Bowman, Turney, and William Treece were killed and five others wounded, including Morris. Company I was consolidated April 23, 1862, with Company A. In the Muster Roll (Co. A) of February 28, 1863 at Beth Page, Tennessee, the following were listed:

Barnes, J. J.	Pvt	Absent. Sent to Hospital Tupelo, Miss., July 20, 1863.
Castleberry, W. C.	Pvt	Present
Fisher, W. T.	Pvt	Absent. Extra duty, teamster.
Ladyman, R. C.	Pvt	Present
Lynn, Washington G.	Pvt	Absent. Taken prisoner at Murfreesboro, January 1, 1863.
Treece, Benjamin	Pvt	Absent. Taken prisoner at Murfreesboro, January 1, 1863.
Turney, Presley B. R.	Pvt	Present
Watts, Samuel	Pvt	Absent. Sent to Hospital January 8, 1863.
Whitmire, J. J.	Pvt	Present
Wortman, C.	Pvt	Absent. Sent to hospital Chattanooga, December 4, 1862.

Lynn and Treece deserted at Murfreesboro. Only Presley B. R. Turney and Samuel Watts and J. J. Whitmire were still with the unit when it surrendered April 28, 1865.

Company K, 18th (Marmaduke's) Arkansas Infantry

Company K, 18th (Marmaduke's) Arkansas Infantry was enlisted December 19, 1861, in Little Rock for the duration of the war by Captain Ira G. Robertson. The company was raised under similar circumstances to those of Company I, but principally from the Peace Society members arrested by Captain John R. Homer Scott in northern Searcy County and Marion and Carroll counties, augmented by Peace Society prisoners from Van Buren County already held in Little Rock. However, there was a difference. Company K's captain, Ira G. Robertson, born about 1822, was not a native or resident of Searcy or surrounding counties and he had unsuccessfully been trying to raise a Confederate company in Little Rock since early November. Hype in Little Rock's *Daily State Journal* of November 9, 1861, portrayed Robertson's recruiting efforts as eminently successful with only a few spaces to fill:

A few more recruits are wanted to fill up the "Rector Guards," an infantry company just organizing in this city [Little Rock] by Lieut. Robertson. We cordially recommend the new corps to the favor of those desiring to serve their country. Lieut. Robertson is an old U. S. soldier, being a graduate of West Point, and has seen many years of service. [Not confirmed]

RALLY. The Rector Guards will meet at the Anthony House on Monday next to elect Captain, 1st and two 2nd Lieutenants. Turn out, gentlemen, and organize. Lieut. Robertson is an old "camp dog" and deserves to be Captain of the Guards.

ATTENTION. A New Volunteer Company is forming in this city called the "Rector Guards," and its ranks are fast filling up. A few more men are wanted immediately to complete the muster. Apply to Lieut. L. [*sic*] G. Robertson, Col. Terry or Capt. Headly.

Six weeks later, the Rector Guards had spaces for several more men—Captain Scott's prisoners and the Van Buren County prisoners. All the officers and most of the non-commissioned officers were not from the Peace Society counties. Eighteen men from Pulaski, Prairie, and Jefferson counties and some whose residence is unknown, or men with no mention of Peace Society affiliation, were the only results of Robertson's recruiting. These were:

Mitchell Ames, 1st Sgt; F. H. Baum, 3rd Lt; Thomas Henry Barrenger (Pulaski County) Pvt; Patrick Broderick, Pvt; George Dyer, Pvt (Lonoke); David Forest Pvt; John W. Fugate, Pvt; John L. Glenn, Pvt; Simson Gray, Pvt; Thomas Holderby (Pulaski County) Pvt; John W. Howard 2nd Lt; Benjamin F. Humphrey, Pvt (Hot Spring County); James Lance, Pvt.; John S. Mendler (Pulaski County) Pvt; Loyd Midgett, Pvt (Prairie County); Green Murray, Pvt (Prairie County); John E. Plunkett, 2nd Sgt (Jefferson County); Samuel Reynolds, Cpl (White County); John W. Shields, Pvt (Prairie County); D. C. Wilson, 1st Lt; James Withurst, Pvt; Andrew B. Zimmerman, Pvt.

Peace Society men with non-commissioned rank were: James E. Curry (Searcy County), 3rd Sgt; William Winn (Marion County), 4th Sgt; John M. Carithers (Carroll County), Cpl; David Curry (Searcy County), Cpl; Thomas M. Dugger (Marion County), Cpl.

The list on page 250 shows the men who appeared before the Senate chamber in December 1861.

Appendix VI contains a list of Captain Scott's prisoners that marched to Little Rock. Once they were in Little Rock, they too were given a choice to enlist or stand trial. Apparently, the list starting on page 251 refers to those who elected to enlist in CSA service.

Senate Chamber – 16 December 1861

Jas E. Curry	39	Ten	Farmer	Blk Hair - Blue Eyes
P. L. Downey	62	Ky	Farmer	
Samuel Thompson	24	Mo	Farmer	
L. P. Phillips	27	Ten	Farmer	
Charles Price	22	Ten	Farmer	
James Thompson	57	Ten	Farmer	
James W. Wallace	25	Ten	Farmer	
Aaron V. B. Brewer	19	Ten	Farmer	
Jonas Brewer	56	NC	Farmer	
William Dugger	42	Ten	Farmer	
F. M. Dugger	20	Ten	Farmer	
W. C. Singletary	32	NC	Physician	
Jasper Dugger	18	Ten	Tanner	
James Luttrell	37	Ten	Farmer	
William Brown	29	Ten	Farmer	
W. M. Winn	45	VA	Farmer	
David Curry	34	Ten	Farmer	
George Hooten	38	Ten	Farmer	
J. M. Hollis	24	Ten	School Teacher	
Carroll Kilburn	45	Ten	Farmer	
John Christy	54	NC	Farmer	
John M. Carithers	32	Ala	Farmer	
Joseph C. Christy	29	Ten	Farmer	
James H. Christy	21	Ark	Farmer	
Gilmore Smith	50	Ten	Farmer	
P. M. Hensley	24	Ten	Farmer	
D. C. Baker	21	Ark	Farmer	

[#110d, Kie Oldham Collection, Arkansas State Archives]

Muster Roll

Name	Rank	Age	
Robertson, Ira G.	Captain	39	(Elected 19 Dec. 1861; resigned 12 April 1862; on 1 Jan 1862 requisitioned medicine for three months for the two companies of Arkansas Volunteers-Rector Guards and Burrowville Mountain Guards.)
Wilson, D. C.	1st Lieutenant	30	(Resigned 6 March 1862)
Howard, John W.	2nd Lieutenant	21	(Resigned 12 April 1862)
Baum, F. H.	3rd Lieutenant	24	(Elected 19 Dec 1862; promoted 2nd Lt. 6 Mar 1862; resigned 12 Apr 1862)
Ames, Mitchell	1st Sergeant	30	(28 Feb. 1863: Absent sick in Bardstown, KY since 28 Aug. 1862)
Plunkett, John E.	2nd Sergeant	35	
Curry, James E.	3rd Sergeant	40	
Winn, William	4th Sergeant	45	
Carithers, John M.	Corporal	32	
Reynolds, Samuel	Corporal	40	
Curry, David	Corporal	34	
Dugger, Thomas M.	Corporal	20	
Baker, David C.	Private	25	
Barringer, Thomas Henry	Private	20	(Captured at Stone's River (Murfreesboro) and paroled 1 Jan 1863; rejoined his unit; deserted 7 Sept. 1863; captured 11 Sept. 1863 by Federals near Chattanooga as a deserter; forwarded to Louisville and there released; took oath of allegiance and on 20 Sept. 1863 joined US Army; discharged as prisoner 22 Sept. 1863)
Brewer, Aron V. B.	Private	56	
Brewer, Jones	Private	21	
Broderick, Patrick	Private	29	(Captured at Murfreesboro and paroled 1 Jan 1863; 28 June 1863 detached to Calvert's Artillery Battery; 1 Feb. 1864 transferred to Keys Battery)
Brown, Thomas	Private	27	
Brown, William	Private	39	
Broyles, James F.	Private	24	
Christy, James F. H.	Private	21	(Sent from Pittsburg Landing in June 1862 to St. Louis, Mo. by Federals; listed by CSA as a deserter)

Muster Roll (continued)

Name	Rank	Age	
Christy, John	Private	50	
Christy, Joseph C.	Private	30	(Sent to St. Mary's Hospital, West Point, Miss.; sent from Pittsburg Landing in June 1862 to St. Louis, Missouri, by Federals; listed by CSA as a deserter)
Cook, Henry	Private	28	
Curl, John W.	Private	25	
Curl, Samuel M.	Private	24	
Dickson, Elijah	Private	30	
Downey, Patrick L.	Private	27	
Dugger, Jasper	Private	18	
Dugger, William	Private	42	
Dyer, George	Private	22	
Forest, David	Private	25	
Fugate, John W.	Private	24	
Glenn, John	Private	29	(Captured at Murfreesboro, paroled and returned to unit)
Grey, Simson	Private	32	
Harness, John	Private	24	
Haynes, William	Private	27	(Wounded 21 July 1864 and admitted to hospital 30 Jan 1865 to Way Hospital, Meridian, Miss., for wound; paroled 10 May 1865 at headquarters, 16th Army Corps, Montgomery, Ala.)
Hensley, Porter M.	Private	24	(Sent from Pittsburg Landing to St. Louis, Missouri, June 1862 by Federals; listed as deserter by CSA)
Holderby, Thomas J.	Private	18	
Holley, Alexander	Private	29	
Holley, Ruben C.	Private	35	
Hollis, James M.	Private	24	
Holy, Absalom	Private	27	
Hooten, George	Private	27	
Humphrey, Benjamin	Private	26	

Muster Roll (continued)

Name	Rank	Age	
Kilburn, Carroll	Private	46	(Absent sick from 20 Aug. 1862 in Chattanooga; captured at Murfreesboro; died 31 Oct. in St. Louis, MO.)
Lance, James	Private	30	
Luttrell, James		38	
McQuerter, David	Private	20	
Mendler, John S.	Private	24	(28 Feb. 1863 Roll listed as absent, wounded at Perryville, Kentucky
Midgett, Loyd	Private	24	
Murray, Green	Private	35	
Null, John B.	Private	29	(Appears on register of Claims of Deceased Officers and Soldiers from Arkansas which were filed for settlement in the Office of the Confederate States Auditor for the War Department; presented by Lydia Null, widow, on October 15, 1863 for his death at Memphis, Tenn.)
Parsley, Abraham	Private	27	
Parsley, Archibald	Private	27	
Phillips, Luther P.	Private	25	
Pierce, Stephen P.	Private	30	
Price, Charles W.	Private	22	
Ridings, James C.	Private	32	(Absent as Hospital Nurse from 24 Feb. 1863. Taken prisoner at Harrodsburg, Kentucky; sent to Vicksburg, Miss. via Cairo, Illinois for exchange)
Shields, John W.	Private	26	
Singleterry, William C.	Private	32	(Absent as Hospital Steward from 18 May 1862 through 31 Aug. 1864; native of Marion Co., AR; deserted at Carter's Station, Tenn. 1 Oct. 1864; signed US oath of allegiance 7 Oct. 1864 at Knoxville, Tenn.; released by US officials on recommendation of loyal citizens)
Smith, George	Private	25	
Smith, Gilmore	Private	50	
Stobaugh, Ananias	Private	29	
Sutton, Logan	Private	31	
Thompson, James	Private	57	

Muster Roll (continued)

Name	Rank	Age	
Thompson, Samuel	Private	24	
Wallace, James W.	Private	26	
Watson, Samuel W.	Private	22	
Whithurst, James B.	Private	29	(Deserted 30 June 1863)
Zimmerman, Andrew B.	Private	45	

In the Muster Roll (Co. G) of February 28, 1863, at Beth Page, Tennessee, the following:

Ames, M.	Pvt	Absent. Sick in Bardstown, Kentucky, August 28, 1862.
Barrenger, Thomas	Pvt	Absent. AWOL December 31, 1862. Prisoner.
Broderick, P.	Pvt	Absent. AWOL December 31, 1862. Prisoner.
Glenn, John L.	Pvt	Absent. AWOL December 31, 1862. Prisoner.
Haynes, William	Pvt	Present.
Kilburn, Carroll	Pvt	Absent. Sick in Chattanooga, August 20, 1862. Captured at Murfreesboro.
Mendler, J. S.	Pvt	Absent. Wounded at Perryville, Kentucky October 8, 1862.
Ridings, James C.	Pvt	Absent. Hospital nurse since February 24, 1863.
Singletary, W. C.	Pvt	Absent. Hospital steward May 18, 1862.

Notes

1   "Oklahoman Recalls 'Chain Gang Story' of Forced Service," *Arkansas Gazette*, September 25, 1941, 1B:3/4.

2   Roberta Watts Ferguson, great-granddaughter of Asa Watts and family genealogist, October 30, 2017; Asa Watts deposition, July 9, 1897, pension file of Benjamin H. Gary, Co. E, 4 Ark. Cav. (U.S.); Hattie Watts Treece interview notes, September 28, 1970; "Duck," "Asa Watts," "John Watts," *Searcy County Arkansas: A History of Searcy County Arkansas and Its People* (Marshall, AR: Searcy County Retired Teachers Association, 1987), 93, 227, 229. Some family members say it was Benjamin Arthur who pretended to call hogs when bushwhackers came upon him delivering food to his father.

3   Benjamin G. Watts deposition on July 8, 1897, pension file Benjamin H. Gary, Co. E, 4 Ark. Cav. (U.S.); Military service record, Benjamin G. Watts, Co. M, 3 Ark. Cav. (U.S.).

4   Ibid.

5   Eddie Watts interview, November 4, 2017, notes in author's collection; Roberta Watts Ferguson interviews, November 4, 2017.

6   John C. Inscoe and Robert C. Kenzer, eds., *Enemies of the Country: New Perspectives on Unionists in the Civil War South* (Athens: University of Georgia Press, 2001), 1–14.

7   Clarence Evans, "Memoirs, Letters, and Diary Entries of German Settlers in Northwest Arkansas, 1853–1863," *Arkansas Historical Quarterly* (hereafter cited as *AHQ*) 6 (Autumn 1947): 237.

8   Georgia Lee Tatum, *Disloyalty in the Confederacy* (Chapel Hill: University of North Carolina Press, 1934), 54–166.

9   *Washington Telegraph* quoted as "Union Men" in *Arkansas State Gazette*, December 12, 1861.

10 Tatum, *Disloyalty in the Confederacy*, vii; Luther E. Warren, *Yellar Rag Boys: The Arkansas Peace Society of 1861 and Other Events in Northern Arkansas—1861 to 1865* (Marshall, AR: 1992), 1; "Oklahoman Recalls 'Chain Gang Story' of Forced Service," *Arkansas Gazette*, September 25, 1941, 1B:3/4; Brooks Blevins email, March 17, 2017, based upon research in Donald R. Deskins Jr., et al., *Presidential Elections, 1789–2008: County, State and National Mapping of Election Data* (Ann Arbor: University of Michigan Press, 2010). Searcy County voted in 1912 for Wilson by a plurality; in 1932 for Roosevelt by over 50%; in 1948 for Truman by a plurality; and in 1976 for Carter by over 50%.

11 Ted R. Worley, "Documents Relating to the Arkansas Peace Society of 1861," *AHQ* 17 (Spring 1958): 82–111; William T. Auman and David D. Scarboro, "Heroes of America in Civil War North Carolina," *North Carolina Historical Review* (hereafter cited as *NCHR*) 58 (October 1981): 327–363; William T. Auman, "Neighbor against Neighbor: The Inner Civil War in the Randolph County Area of Confederate North Carolina," *NCHR* 61 (January 1984): 59–92; Kenneth W. Noe, "Red String Scare: Civil War Southwest Virginia and the Heroes of America," *NCHR* 69 (July 1991): 301–322.

12 Phillip Shaw Paludan, *Victims: A True Story of the Civil War* (Knoxville: University of Tennessee Press, 1981). Other works include: Richard Nelson Current, *Lincoln's Loyalists: Union Soldiers from the Confederacy* (Boston: Northeastern University Press, 1992); Richard B. McCaslin, *Tainted Breeze: The Great Hanging at Gainesville, Texas 1862* (Baton Rouge: Louisiana State University Press, 1994); Thomas G. Dyer, *Secret Yankees: The Union Circle in Confederate Atlanta* (Baltimore: Johns Hopkins University Press, 1999); William W. Freehling, *The South vs The South* (New York: Oxford University Press, 2001); Inscoe and Kenzer, eds., *Enemies of the Country*; Robert Tracy McKenzie, *Lincolnites and Rebels: A Divided Town in the American Civil War* (New York: Oxford University Press, 2006); James Alex Baggett, *Scalawags: Southern Dissenters in the Civil War and Reconstruction* (Baton Rouge: Louisiana State University Press, 2002); Jonathan Dean Sarris, *A Separate Civil War: Communities in Conflict in the Mountain South* (Charlottesville: University of Virginia, 2006); Margaret M. Storey, *Loyalty and Loss:*

Alabama's Unionists in the Civil War and Reconstruction (Baton Rouge: Louisiana State University Press, 2004); and Barton A. Myers, *Rebels against the Confederacy: North Carolina's Unionists* (New York: Cambridge University Press, 2004).

13   James M. Woods, *Rebellion and Realignment: Arkansas Road to Secession* (Fayetteville: University of Arkansas Press, 1987), 177, 180; Samuel Augustus Mitchell, "A New Map of Arkansas with its Counties, Towns, Post Offices, etc.," *New Universal Atlas* (Philadelphia: Cowperthwaite, DeSilver & Butler, 1855), 26.

14   Woods, *Rebellion and Realignment*, Tables 2e, 2d, 177, 178.

15   Thomas A. DeBlack, *With Fire and Sword: Arkansas, 1861–1874* (Fayetteville: University of Arkansas Press, 2003), 2.

16   Woods, *Rebellion and Realignment*, Table 6c, 187.

17   Charles Bolton, *Arkansas 1800–1860: Remote and Restless* (Fayetteville: University of Arkansas Press, 1990), 170; DeBlack, *With Fire and Sword*, 5; Woods, *Rebellion and Realignment*, 39.

18   Michael B. Dougan, *Community Diaries: Arkansas Newspapering 1819–2002* (Little Rock: August House, 2003), 40–41.

19   DeBlack, *With Fire and Sword*, 7, 8.

20   Bolton, *Arkansas 1800–1860*, 181, 182; DeBlack, *With Fire and Sword*, 8–10; Charlie Daniels, *Historical Report of the Secretary of State 2008* (Little Rock: Arkansas Secretary of State's Office, 2008), 596; (Little Rock) *True Democrat*, September 1, 1860, 3.

21   Woods, *Rebellion and Realignment*, 80, Tables 6a, 6e; DeBlack, *With Fire and Sword*, 14, 15.

22   DeBlack, *With Fire and Sword*, 11, 12.

23   Ibid., 12, 13.

24   Woods, *Rebellion and Realignment*, 101, 103–106.

25   Ibid., 106.

26   Woods, *Rebellion and Realignment*, 110, 111. There is a printer's error in the report of Searcy County's votes for Breckinridge in the *Arkansas Gazette* (December 8, 1860), which lists Searcy County's Breckinridge vote as "076." It was "276," which gave a majority to Breckinridge. *The Tribune Almanac and Political Register for 1867* (New York: The Tribune Association, n.d.), 67.

27   Woods, *Rebellion and Realignment*, 91, 115; DeBlack, *With Fire and Sword*, 18–20.

28   DeBlack, *With Fire and Sword*, 18–20; Max Cates, "J. J. Ware," *Fulton County Chronicles* 11 (Spring 1996): 31–34. Ware was Fulton County representative to the Thirteenth General Assembly. 1860 Big Creek Township, Fulton County, Arkansas census 277/10, Ware, J. J., age 34, married and born in Arkansas. Woods, *Rebellion and Realignment*, 117, 118.

29   Jack Scroggs, "Arkansas in the Secession Crisis," *AHQ* 12 (Autumn 1953): 194–200.

30   Albert W. Bishop, *Loyalty on the Frontier, or Sketches of Union Men of the South-West with Incidents and Adventures in Rebellion on the Border*, edited by Kim Allen Scott (Fayetteville: University of Arkansas Press, 2003), 9; Woods, *Rebellion and Realignment*, 114–116; Jack B. Scroggs, "Arkansas in the Secessionist Crisis," *AHQ* 12 (Autumn 1953): 190–192; DeBlack, *With Fire and Sword*, 18–19.

31   "N. V. Barnett to Abraham Lincoln, Mt. Elba [Arkansas] November 30, 1860," *Abraham Lincoln Papers at the Library of Congress*, Knox College Transcription, <http://memory.loc.gov/ammem/alhtml/malhome.html> (hereafter cited as *Lincoln Papers*). Nicholas V. Barnett enlisted February 22, 1862, in Company B, Second Arkansas Cavalry Battalion (C.S.) at Mt. Elba, Arkansas. On April 9, 1864, he took the oath of allegiance to the federal government at Pine Bluff, Arkansas. Desmond Walls Allen, *Index to Arkansas Confederate Soldiers*, (Conway, AR: Arkansas Research, 1990); "Second Arkansas Cavalry Battalion" in "ARKANSAS Edward G. Gerdes Civil War Home Page," <http://couchgenweb.com/civilwar/>.

32   "S. B. Pinney to Abraham Lincoln, December 10, 1860," *Lincoln Papers*. Pinney did not stay long in Arkansas. In the 1860 Little Rock census, his three-year-old daughter, Adeline B. Pinney, was born in Wisconsin. The 1880 Minneapolis, Minnesota, census states his son, Carl Byron Pinney, was born 1864 in Minnesota.

33   Cornelius Burnham Harvey, *Genealogical History of Hudson and Bergen Counties, New Jersey* (New York: New Jersey Genealogical Publishing Company, 1900), 128 (hereafter cited *History of Hudson and Bergen Counties*); Obituary of Col. William D. Snow, *New York Times*, February 12, 1910; 1850 U.S. Federal Census, 27th District City of Detroit, Wayne County, Michigan, 3123/359, Josiah Snow; 1860 U.S. Federal Census, Fifth Ward, Chicago, Cook County, Illinois, 1574/1813, J. Snow; "Wm D. Snow to Lincoln, November 16, 1860," "William D. Snow to Lincoln, November 28, 1860," "William D. Snow to Lincoln, December 25, 1863," "Josiah Snow to Lincoln, February 25, 1864," *Lincoln Papers*. On April 27, Snow's Yankee-operated telegraph sent dispatches from Governor Rector to Colonels Roane, Bell, and McGregor. When the State Convention was re-called on May 6, 1861, the Arkansas State Telegraph Company petitioned for a line from Little Rock to Van Buren and to Fort Smith, pledging to operate and guard the interests of Arkansas and the South and to employ only operators who were known to be Southern in both interest and feeling and would serve their country against the common enemy. *Journal of the Called Session of the Convention of Arkansas*, 135–136, 144–145, 163; *Arkansas State Gazette*, April 20, 1861, 3:2; *House Journal 13th Assembly 1860–1861*, 591, 907.

34   "Wm. D. Snow to Lincoln, November 16, 1860," "William D. Snow to Lincoln, November 28, 1860," "William D. Snow to Lincoln, December 25, 1863," *Lincoln Papers*.

35   Cates, "J. J. Ware"; DeBlack, *With Fire and Sword*, 19; Scroggs, "Arkansas in the Secession Crisis," 194.

36   "William D. Snow to Abraham Lincoln, November 16, 1860," (Report from Arkansas) *Lincoln Papers*, Series I, General Correspondence, 1833–1916; Woods, *Rebellion and Realignment*, 116–117.

37   Scroggs, "Arkansas in the Secession Crisis," 198; Woods, *Rebellion and Realignment*, 119.

38   Scroggs, "Arkansas in the Secession Crisis," 195–196.

39   Scroggs, "Arkansas in the Secession Crisis," 195; *Little Rock Arkansas Weekly Gazette*, January 5, January 12, January 19, February 2, 1860; *Little Rock True Democrat*, April 18, 1861. See Appendix I.

40   *Little Rock Arkansas Gazette*; January 12, 1861; "In Search of Bluff Springs," *Searcy County Ancestor Information Exchange* 13 (October 2003), 56; *Acts of Arkansas* (Little Rock: 1854), 161–162.

41   *Arkansas Gazette*, January 12, 1861.

42   *Arkansas Gazette*, January 5, 1861; *Classified Population of the States And Territories, by Counties on the First Day of June, 1860*, State of Arkansas, 12–21, <www2.census.gov/prod2.decennial/documents/1860a-04.pdf.>; Woods, *Rebellion and Realignment*, Table 6c, 187.

43   *Arkansas Gazette*, January 19, 1861, 2:4; Kenneth C. Barnes, "The Williams Clan: Mountain Farmers and Union Fighters in North Central Arkansas," in *Civil War Arkansas: Beyond Battles and Leaders*, edited by Anne J. Bailey and Daniel E. Sutherland (Fayetteville: University of Arkansas Press, 2000), 155–176; Thomas J. Williams, Compiled Service Records (hereafter cited as CSR) National Archives (hereafter cited as NA), Microfilm M399 Roll 53.

44   Scroggs, "Arkansas in the Secession Crisis," 198–199; Woods, *Rebellion and Realignment*, 121–123.

45   Scroggs, "Arkansas in the Secession Crisis," 195. Pike and Clark counties opposed secession but supported a state convention to form a consensus to cooperate with Southern states. *Little Rock Arkansas Gazette*, January 5, 1861; Mark Bean to David Walker, January 28, 1861, David Walker Papers MS 15, Special Collections, Mullins Library, University of Arkansas, Fayetteville, Arkansas, (hereafter cited as Walker Papers); Depositions of John H. Haslow and Elijah Harbour, James Byrne Case File (Calhoun County), Southern Claims Commission case files, RG217, NA.

46   *Arkansas Gazette*, February 2, 1861, 2:3.

47   Charles F. Gunther, *Two Years before the Paddlewheel* (Buffalo Gap, TX: State House Press, 2012), 34–35.

48   Woods, *Rebellion and Realignment*, 130–131; William W. Freehling, *The Road to Disunion: Secessionists Triumphant 1854–1861* (New York: Oxford University Press, 2007), 504.

49   Scroggs, "Arkansas in the Secession Crisis," 205–206.

50   Woods, *Rebellion and Realignment*, 138.

51   William M. McPherson to David Walker, March 19, 1861, Walker Papers. William M. McPherson was born February 15, 1813, in Boone County, Kentucky, the second of five children. His father, a farmer, died when William was nine years old, and he continued the farm. He became a school teacher, then a lawyer—attending Transylvania University in Lexington, Kentucky. He hung his shingle first in Burlington, Boone County, Kentucky, then in 1836 moved to Helena, Arkansas. In Helena, he became involved in land speculation and became heavily indebted when it failed. He was involved in 1836 with William K. Sebastian in a movement to rid Helena of gamblers. In 1840, he left Helena after suffering financial reverses and moved to St. Louis, Missouri. In St. Louis, he became an extensive and successful real estate operator and, by 1852, had paid off his Helena obligations. He became president of the Missouri Pacific Railroad in 1855. In 1861, Missouri Unionist governor Hamilton R. Gamble sent McPherson to Washington DC to get arms for the state militia. After the July 4, 1863, fall of Vicksburg, Mississippi, he was given the contract to transport military stores and personnel between St. Louis and New Orleans, Louisiana. Walter B. Stevens, *St. Louis: History of the Fourth City, 1765–1909* (Chicago: S. J. Clarke, 1909), 229–230; A. H. Burlingham, *A Sermon Commemorative of the late Hon. William M. McPherson preached in the Second Baptist Church, St. Louis, by Rev. A. H. Burlingham, Sunday Morning, Nov. 24, 1872* (St. Louis: Barns & Beyson Printers, 1873); J. Thomas Scharf, *History of Saint Louis and County*, vol. 2 (Philadelphia: Louis H. Everts & Co., 1883), 1490; Ted R. Worley, "Helena on the Mississippi," *AHQ* 13 (Spring 1954): 3–5, 8–9; Louis S. Gertis, *Civil War St. Louis* (Lawrence: University Press of Kansas, 2001), 158.

52   Woods, *Rebellion and Realignment*, 140–141, 144.

53   Woods, *Rebellion and Realignment*, 141; Bishop, *Loyalty on the Frontier*, 7, 115. The term "Black Republican" had been applied to the Republican Party by the Democrats since its founding to identify them as favoring equality for African Americans. During the 1860 election, Southern Democrats used the term derisively to indicate Lincoln's victory would incite slave rebellions. Patricia L. Faust, ed., *Historical Times Illustrated Encyclopedia of the Civil War* (New York: Harper Collins Publishers, 1986), 63.

54   Woods, *Rebellion and Realignment*, 143–146; James J. Johnston, ed., "Letter of John Campbell, Unionist," *AHQ* 29 (Summer 1970): 170–182.

55   "Union Address to the People of Arkansas," *Little Rock Arkansas Gazette*, April 6, 1861, 2:7; Bishop, *Loyalty on the Frontier*, 129–136.

56   Scroggs, "Arkansas in the Secession Crisis," 217–219; Woods, *Rebellion and Realignment*, 148–150; "Arkansas State Canvass," *Memphis Daily Appeal*, April 16, 1861, 1:1; H. B. Allis to David Walker, March 30, 1861, Walker Papers. In the 1850 census, H. B. Allis, age 36, born in New York, was living in Little Rock, Pulaski County; Manuscript Census Returns, Seventh Census of the United States 1850, population schedules, Dwelling 487, Little Rock, Pulaski County, Arkansas. In 1860, he was living in Vaugine Township, Jefferson County, owning six slaves with $15,000 in real estate and $9,000 in personal property; Manuscript Census Returns, Eighth Census of the United States, 1860, Dwelling 350,Vaugine, Jefferson County, Arkansas; Manuscript Census Returns, slave schedule, Eighth Census of the United States, 1860, Page No. 21, Slave Inhabitants, Vaugine, Jefferson County, Arkansas.

57   James P. Spring to David Walker, April 4, 1861, Walker Papers. Spring and family are found in the 1850 census living in Jackson Township (Jasper), Newton County, Arkansas, an attorney with $800 of real estate, born in Tennessee, age 30. In 1860, he is a lawyer, age 40, with family in Fort Smith, Sebastian County, with $9,000 in real estate and $3,000 in personal property.

58 Woods, *Rebellion and Realignment*, 127; W. M. Fishback to David C. Williams, April 10, 1861, D. C. Williams Collection, Clara Eno Papers, Arkansas State Archives, Little Rock, Arkansas (hereafter cited as Eno Papers).

59 Woods, *Rebellion and Realignment*, 156–158; *Little Rock Arkansas True Democrat*, April 25, 1861, 2:1; Isaac F. Morris, Manuscript Census Returns, Eighth Census of the United States, 1860, Dwelling 177, Prairie, Newton County, Arkansas.

60 Woods, *Rebellion and Realignment*, 155; *Little Rock Arkansas Gazette*, April 20, 1861, 2; Bishop, *Loyalty on the Frontier*, 138, 141–142; *Little Rock Arkansas Gazette*, May 11, 1861.

61 James J. Johnston, "Letter of John Campbell, Unionist," *AHQ* 29 (Summer 1970); Woods, *Rebellion and Realignment*, 159–160.

62 James Troy Massey, ed., *Memoirs of Captain J. M. Bailey* (Harrison, AR: n.d.), 63; T. Lindsey Baker, ed., *Confederate Guerrilla: The Civil War Memoir of Joseph Bailey* (Fayetteville: University of Arkansas Press, 2007), 40.

63 Scroggs, "Arkansas in the Secession Crisis," 223; "Letter of John Campbell to Fellow Citizens of Searcy County," *Little Rock Arkansas Gazette*, May 11, 1861.

64 Johnston, "Letter of John Campbell, Unionist," 181–182 footnote 10; Scroggs, "Arkansas in the Secession Crisis," 223–224; Woods, *Rebellion and Realignment*, 159–160.

65 *Arkansas Gazette*, December 29, 1860, 2:1. Walter Lee Brown, *A Life of Albert Pike* (Fayetteville: University of Arkansas Press, 1997), 349–350; Carl H. Moneyhon, "Albert Pike," in *Arkansas Biography: A Collection of Notable Lives*, edited by Nancy A. Williams (Fayetteville: University of Arkansas Press, 2000), 223–224; James P. Spring to David Walker, April 4, 1861, No. 15, Walker Papers, Letters, Folder 2; H. B. Allis, Pine Bluff to David Walker, March 30, 1861, No. 15, Walker Papers, Letters, Folder 2; Mark Bean, Cane Hill to David Walker, January 28, 1861, No. 13, Letters, Walker Papers, MS W15; Fay Hempstead, *Historical Review of Arkansas* (Chicago: The Lewis Publishing Co., 1911), 453–454; John Hallum, *Biographical and Pictorial History of Arkansas* (Albany: Weed, Parsons and Company, 1887), 103–104; Robert E. Waterman and Thomas Rothrock, eds., "The Earle-Buchanan Letters of 1861–1876," *AHQ* 33 (Summer 1974): 116, 123–124.

66 Johnston, "Letter of John Campbell, Unionist," 179–180, footnote 7; John Campbell, Confederate Compiled Service Records, Arkansas, 14th (Powers) Arkansas Infantry, National Archives; James J. Johnston, "Bullets for Johnny Reb: Confederate Mining and Nitre Bureau in Arkansas," in *Civil War Arkansas*, 68; John Campbell to Governor H. Flanagin, January 26, 1865, No. 1038, Kie Oldham Collection, Arkansas State Archives, Little Rock, Arkansas (hereafter cited as Oldham).

67 Alfred Holt Carrigan, "Reminiscences of the Secession Convention," *Publications of the Arkansas Historical Association* 1 (1906), 309; Bishop, *Loyalty on the Frontier*, 22; *History of Benton, Washington, Carroll, Madison, Crawford, Franklin, and Sebastian County, Arkansas* (Chicago: Goodspeed Publishing Co., 1889), 948; Hallum, *Biographical and Pictorial History of Arkansas*, 252–255.

68 *Journal of the Convention of the State of Arkansas which was begun and held in the capitol, in the city of Little Rock, on Monday the fourth day of March, one thousand, eight hundred and sixty-one* (Little Rock: Johnson & Yerkes, 1861), 90–93; Manuscript Census Returns, Seventh Census of the United States, 1850, 265/265, Jackson Township, Newton County, Arkansas, Schedule 1, Free Inhabitants, and Eighth U.S. Census, 1860, 1471/1424, Fort Smith, Sebastian County, Arkansas, Schedule 1; James P. Spring, "Arkansas and Texas, Confederate Papers Relating to Citizens or Business Firms," National Archives Microfilm Series M346; Goodspeed's *History of Northwest Arkansas*, 1205–1206; John I. Smith, *The Courage of a Southern Unionist: A Biography of Isaac Murphy, Governor of Arkansas 1864–1868* (Little Rock: Rose Publishing Co., 1979), 22; Hallum, *Biographical and Pictorial History*, 244–252; *Biographical and Historical Memoirs of Southern Arkansas* (Chicago: Goodspeed Publishing Company, 1890), 277–278.

69 Hallum, *Biographical and Pictorial History*, 271–272; William D. Snow to Abraham Lincoln, November 16, 1860, Lincoln Papers; Ruth Caroline Cowen, "Reorganization of Federal Arkansas, 1862–1865," *AHQ* 18 (Summer 1959): 137.

70   W. M. Fishback to D. C. Williams, April 10, 1861, Eno Papers; Harry W. Readnour
     "William Meade Fishback (1831–1903)," *Encyclopedia of Arkansas History & Culture*,
     www.encyclopediaofarkansas.net; "Letter from Northwest Arkansas," *Arkansas Gazette*,
     July 20, 1861, 2. Neither Fishback nor Blakemore are found in the Index of Military Service
     Records of Confederate Soldiers from Arkansas. William M. Fishback to James H. Lane
     of Kansas, June 17, 1864, in U.S. Senate, *Senate Miscellaneous*, 1st Session, 38th Congress,
     No. 129.

71   U.S. War Department, *The War of the Rebellion: A Compilation of the Official Records
     of the Union and Confederate Armies*, 128 vols. (Washington DC: Government Printing
     Office, 1880–1901), ser. I, vol. 34, 580–81 (hereafter cited as *OR*); Lyman Bennett,
     "Recruiting in Dixie," edited by James J. Johnston, *White River Valley Historical
     Quarterly* 39 (Fall 1999): 14–15.

72   "A Table, Showing the names of members of the State convention," *True Democrat*, April
     18, 1861, 1:3–5; See Appendix I; Bishop, *Loyalty on the Frontier*, 26–28; Smith, *Biography
     of Isaac Murphy*, 37; Harvey H. Bolinger, assistant surgeon, 1st Ark. Inf., CSR-Arkansas,
     NA M399, Roll 44.

73   "A Table," *True Democrat*, April 18, 1861, 1; Ralph Wooster, "The Arkansas Secession
     Convention," *AHQ* 13 (Summer 1954): 8; Desmond Walls Allen, *Index to Arkansas
     Confederate Soldiers*. The following Unionist delegates became Confederate officers:
     Rufus K. Garland (Hempstead) Captain, 4 Arkansas Infantry; Anson W. Hobson (Ouachita)
     Colonel, 3 Arkansas Cavalry; Burr H. Hobbs (Carroll) Quartermaster, 15 (Northwest)
     Arkansas Infantry; H. Shelby Kennard (Independence) Captain, 1 Arkansas Volunteers
     (30 day); J. N. Cypert (White) Captain, 7 Battalion Arkansas Infantry; Joseph Jester (Hot
     Spring) Captain, 3 Arkansas Cavalry; Milton D. Baber (Lawrence) Colonel, 45 Arkansas
     Cavalry; Jabez M. Smith (Saline) Colonel, 11 Arkansas Infantry; F. W. Desha (Independence)
     Lt. Colonel, 7 Battalion Arkansas Infantry; T. F. Austin (Marion) Captain, 27 Arkansas
     Infantry; Desmond Walls Allen, *Arkansas' Damned Yankees* (Conway, AR: Arkansas
     Research, 1987); Hallum *Biographical and Pictorial History*, 880–882.

74   James Alex Baggett, *The Scalawags: Southern Dissenters in the Civil War and
     Reconstruction* (Baton Rouge: Louisiana State University Press, 2002), 19, 44–45, 77–78,
     104; *Classified Population of the States and Territories, by Counties, on the First Day of
     June, 1860*, Arkansas Table No. 5, page 20. <http://www2.census.gov/prod2/decennial/
     documents/1860a-04.pdf>

75   Nathaniel Cheairs Hughes Jr., *Sir Henry Morton Stanley, Confederate* (Baton Rouge:
     Louisiana State University Press, 2000), 93–96, 113, 139 fn.1; "Deserters," *Arkansas
     True Democrat*, March 25, 1863, 2:4.

76   *Message of Gov. Henry M. Rector to the General Assembly of Arkansas, In Extra Session,
     Nov. 6, 1861* (Little Rock: Johnson & Yerkes, 1861), 5.

77   Georgia Lee Tatum, *Disloyalty in the Confederacy* (Chapel Hill: University of North
     Carolina Press, 1934), 45–49; Anne J. Bailey, "Defiant Unionists: Militant Germans in
     Confederate Texas," in *Enemies of the Country: New Perspectives on Unionists in the
     Civil War South*, edited by John C. Inscoe and Robert C. Kenzer (Athens: University of
     Georgia Press, 2001), 208–221.

78   Clarence Evans, "Memoirs, Letters, and Diary Entries of German Settlers in Northwest
     Arkansas, 1853–1863," *AHQ* 6 (Autumn 1947): 237–239.

79   "Josiah Snow to Lincoln, February 25, 1864," *Lincoln Papers*; *History of Hudson and
     Bergen Counties*, 128; Baggett, *Scalawags*, 119.

80   See Appendix II.

81   Woods, *Rebellion and Realignment*, 163–165; Michael B. Dougan, *Confederate Arkansas:
     The People and Politics of a Frontier State in Wartime* (Tuscaloosa: University of Alabama
     Press, 1976), 64–67.

82 *Ordinances of the State Convention, which convened in Little Rock May 6, 1861* (Little Rock: Johnson & Yerkes, 1861), 12, 20–22, 24–27, 33, 37, 40, 73–74, (hereafter cited as *Ordinances*); *Message of Governor Henry Rector to the General Assembly November 6, 1861*, Arkansas Collections J87.A821861, Special Collections, Mullins Library, University of Arkansas, Fayetteville (hereafter cited as *Message*).

83 Clyde W. Cathey, "Slavery in Arkansas (Part I)," *AHQ* 3 (Spring 1944): 71–76; Raymond Lee Muncey, *Searcy, Arkansas: A Frontier Town Grows Up With America* (Searcy, AR: Harding Press, 1976), 3, 4.

84 1850 U.S. Census, Schedule I, Arkansas, Independence County; Muncey, *Searcy, Arkansas: A Frontier Town*, 34; *American Annual Cyclopaedia and register of the important events of the year 1861* (New York: D. Appleby & Co., 1868), 25.

85 Dougan, *Confederate Arkansas*, 68–69; DeBlack, *With Fire and Sword*, 36; Scott-Boone, November 13, 1861, File 5 Box 1, John Rice Homer Scott Papers A-35, Special Collections, University of Arkansas at Little Rock Library (hereafter cited as Scott Papers); *OR*, ser. I, vol. 8, 726–27, 638, 640; Court-Martial papers, Box 1, File 7, Scott Papers; Scott-McCulloch, November 7, 1861, Box 1, File 5, Scott; Furlough James K. Broadway, October 17, 1861, *Civil War Letters: Scott*.

86 *Ordinances* 12, 20–22, 24–27, 33, 37, 40, 73–74; *Message*.

87 *Ordinances*, 24–27; *Message*.

88 William G. Stevenson, *Thirteen Months in the Confederate Army* (New York: A. S. Burns and Co., 1959), 20–30.

89 *Biographical and Historical Memoirs of Southern Arkansas* (Chicago: Goodspeed Publishing Co., 1890), 877–878. James Shelton was born about 1808 in Tennessee and is found in Ashley County in 1850 census and in Polk County in 1860 census. His two youngest sons, William and John B., both served in the 2nd Arkansas Infantry (U.S.). Desmond Walls Allen, *Second Arkansas Union Infantry* (Conway, AR: Arkansas Research, 1987), 54.

90 "Meeting in Pope County," *True Democrat*, July 4, 1861.

91 Bishop, *Loyalty on the Frontier*, 143; Bosworth-Rutherford, September 4, 5, 6, 1862, Joseph Robinson Rutherford Papers, Special Collections, Mullins Library, University of Arkansas, Fayetteville. Bosworth was born in 1833 in Taunton, Bristol County, Massachusetts, and died October 9, 1862, aboard the gunboat USS *Mound City*. He was a brick mason. He is buried in the Plain Cemetery, Taunton, Massachusetts. The spring was probably Double Spring, Flint Township, Benton County, which became a post office in 1851.

92 "Bloody Affray in St. Francis County," *Des Arc Semi-Weekly Citizen*, May 21, 1861, 2:2.

93 "Newton County," *True Democrat*, April 25, 1861, 2:1.

94 Jesse Weaver-Jefferson Weaver May 13, 1861, Roll 6 Misc., O. J. McInturff Papers Microfilm, Arkansas State Archives, Little Rock, Arkansas. Jesse Weaver is in 1860 Cedar Township, Clark County, Arkansas U.S. census, age 27, born in Tennessee. Jesse is shown on 33rd Arkansas Infantry rolls enlisted May 15, 1862, Company H, deserted June 24, 1862. He rejoined and is present on September–October 1862 Muster Roll, then is listed as deserted August 3, 1863. He then enrolled November 17, 1863, in Company A, 4th Arkansas Cavalry (US) at Benton, Arkansas. Jefferson Weaver is not on the 1860 Marion County census, but he is shown on 14th Arkansas Infantry rolls as enrolled July 8, 1861, at Yellville in Company A. Company A was raised July 8, 1861, from Marion County, William C. Pace Captain. He is listed "deserted" and struck from the rolls in May–June 1862 Muster Roll. Then, on January 17, 1863, he is on a list of prisoners paroled for exchange from Springfield, Missouri, as a private in Co. A, 16th Arkansas Infantry, which was raised September 12, 1861, from Johnson County, L. N. C. Swaggerty captain. Jefferson Weaver may have been added to Swaggerty's company to help with the numbers once it was in north Arkansas. Both the 14th and the 16th were transferred east of the Mississippi River in April 1862.

95 *Civil War Letters: Jno. R. Homer Scott's Squadron of Cavelry* [sic] *in Pope County, Arkansas and Carroll County, Arkansas*, edited by J. B. Lemley (Russellville, AR: J. B. Lemley, Lester Finley & Elaine Weir Cia, n.d.) (hereafter cited as *Scott Letters*). In 1860, Newton County, White Township, U.S. census John McCoy, age 40, born in Tennessee, farmer, with $300 real estate, $300 personal property is in residence #384. Uriah Bush, age 21, born in Tennessee, day laborer, is in Charles Bacchus household residence #397 White Township. McCulloch-Scott Special Orders No. 174, November 13, 1861, Coll A-35, Box 1 File 14, Scott Papers; McCoy-Scott November 15, 1861, Scott Papers: John McCoy Federal Service File, 1 Arkansas Infantry (U.S.). McCoy served as state senator 1854–1855, Newton Co. representative 1858–1859; Newton Co. representative to 1864 Arkansas Constitutional Convention and as president of that body, and as senator in 1864–1865. Walter F. Lackey, *History of Newton County, Arkansas* (Point Lookout, MO: School of the Ozarks Press, n.d.) 354–360; Daniels, *Historical Report of the Secretary of State 2008*, 121, 124, 127; Scott-McCulloch, November 7, 1861, Scott Papers; Scott-Boone November 7, 1861, Scott Papers.

96 McCoy-Scott November 15, 1861, Box 1, File 5, Scott Papers.

97 Scott-Boone November 7, 1861, Scott Papers; Boone-Scott November 12, 1861, Scott Papers; Scott-McCulloch November 7, 1861, Box 1, File 5, Scott Papers.

98 William Monks, *A History of Southern Missouri and Northern Arkansas, Being an Account of the Early Settlement, the Civil War, The Ku-Klux and Times of Peace*, edited by John F. Bradbury Jr. and Lou Wehmer (Fayetteville: University of Arkansas Press, 2003), 621–666.

99 Silas C. Turnbo, *History of the Twenty-seventh Arkansas Confederate Infantry* (Conway, AR: Arkansas Research, 1988), 20–21.

100 *OR*, ser. 1, III, 575–580, 584, 587, 588–598, 609–610.

101 *OR*, ser. 1, III, 638, 671, 672, 687, 689.

102 James J. Johnston, "Reminisce of James H. Campbell's Experiences during the Civil War," *AHQ* 74 (Summer 2015): 151; Co. B, 2nd Arkansas Cavalry (Union), Compiled Military Service Record (hereafter cited CSR), M399 Roll 18 of Andrew J. Garner; *True Democrat*, August 22, 1861, 1:7. Thomas W. Edmondson, age 38, farmer, born in North Carolina, #789/788, Harris Township, Izard County, Sylamore P.O., 1860 Federal U.S. Census. Representative 13th Arkansas General Assembly, Daniels, *Historical Report of the Secretary of State*, 125; 3rd Lt/Lt QM, Co. H, 14th (McCarver's) 14th Ark Inf. Enrolled September 23, 1861, at Pocahontas. Reported died on December 23, 1861. Arkansas, 14th (McCarver) Arkansas Infantry, Compiled Military Service Record of Thomas W. Edmondson.

McCarver's "regiment" lacked three companies of being a regiment and was designated a battalion. It was not until April 1862 that it obtained the additional three companies to become a regiment and was designated 14th (McCarver's) Arkansas Infantry, not to be confused with the 14th (Powers) Arkansas Infantry also raised principally in north-central Arkansas. John F. Walter, *Capsule Histories of Arkansas Military Units in the Civil War*, Special Collections, Mullins Library, University of Arkansas, Fayetteville. William S. Lindsey was mustered in on September 1, 1861, as captain, Co. A, McCarver's Battalion.

103 *OR*, ser. 1, III, 640–641; James J. Johnston, *Searcy County Men in the Civil War: Union and Confederate, A Compilation of Muster Rolls* (Fayetteville, AR: Searcy County Publications, 2011), 5, 9; "Letter from Izard County," *Little Rock True Democrat*, August 22, 1861, 1:7; "The Jayhawkers," *True Democrat*, March 6, 1862, 3:1&2. William M. Aikin, age 36, born in South Carolina, merchant, is in Harris Township, Izard County, 1860 Federal Census. Thomas W. Edmondson, age 38, born in North Carolina, is also in Harris Township, 1860 census, four residences away from Aikin. Mary Cooper Miller, *1860 Federal Census of Izard County, Arkansas* (Batesville, AR: M-F Publications, 1984), 34–35. See Appendix III.

104 *OR*, ser. 1, III, 671–672, 695–698, 700, 708–709, 711; "Proclamation," *True Democrat*, October 3, 1861, 4:3.

105 Burgevin-Rector, October 8, 1861, #38 Burgevin, Oldham.

106 Foster-Rector, October 14, 1861, #52 Foster, Oldham. Foster identified: David White Jr. David White Sr., Henry White, William White, William White Sr., Jackson White, Scott Forester, Francis M. Musgrove, Carney Davis, James Kirke, Jack Putnam, and Elijah Putnam. Scott Forester, Francis M. Musgrove, Elijah Putnam, Jacob Putnam, David White Jr., Henry L. White, William M. White Sr., and William White are found in the federal 4th Arkansas Cavalry along with William H. Walker and a Houston C. Walker whom Foster mentions as knowing about the sham company. It appears from these service records that Peyton M. Epperson, born about 1811, living on Muddy Fork on the Pike–Howard County line, may have led some of these men to a federal recruiter who signed them up on November 19, 1863, in Benton, Arkansas. They first signed in to the 3rd Arkansas Infantry, which was then absorbed by the 4th Arkansas Cavalry. Epperson and some others were mustered out March 28, 1864, because the company in which they had enlisted had been dissolved.

107 Leslie-Rector October 21, 1861, #60b Oldham.

108 *Little Rock Daily State Journal*, November 9, 1861, 2:1&2.

109 Benjamin G. Watts Deposition A, February 23, 1900, Benjamin G. Watts Co. M, 3rd Ark Cav, Pension.

110 Benjamin G. Watts Deposition B, July 8, 1897, Benjamin H. Gary Co. E, 4th Ark Cav. Pension. The returning Confederates were the Arkansas troops who fought at Wilson's Creek on August 10, 1861, then refused to be mustered into the Confederate service and returned home with their arms. They did not organize the militia. It had existed since territorial days and was a requirement enacted by the legislature that all adult males serve in the Arkansas Militia. "Union League" is used in many depositions, statements, and letters after the Civil War in lieu of "Peace Society."

111 Ted R. Worley, "Documents Relating to the Arkansas Peace Society of 1861," *AHQ* 17 (Spring 1958): 89–91, (hereafter cited as Worley).

112 Scott-Governor December 6, 1861, #99 Oldham; Worley, 89–91; "Testimony of Peter A. Tyler December 8, 1861," #102 Oldham; Worley 94–97; "Constitution of the Mill Creek Peace Organization Society," #110c Oldham; Worley, 87–88; "Oath," File 18, Box 1, Coll. A-35, Scott Papers; "Testimony of Persons Arrested as Members of the Peace Society," #110d Oldham; Worley, 107. See Appendix IV.

113 Scott-McCulloch, December 3, 1861, File 6, Coll. A-35, Scott Papers; Leslie-Rector, Worley, 102–104; Kemp-Rector, Worley, 106. See Appendix VIII.

114 "Testimony of Persons Arrested as Members of the Peace Society," #110d Oldham and Worley, 107.

115 "State of Arkansas vs. Nathan F. Woodworth," *Scott Letters*; "State of Arkansas vs. L. D. Jamieson," *Scott Letters*; Scott-McCulloch, December 3, 1861, File 6, Coll. A-35, Scott Papers; Leslie-Rector, Worley, 102–104; Kemp-Rector, Worley, 106; "Twenty-seven prisoners…," *Little Rock Daily State Journal*, November 29, 1861, 2:1; "Some three weeks since…," *Little Rock True Democrat*, December 5, 1861; "Letter from Col. Borland," *Little Rock Gazette*, December 14, 1861, 2:5.

116 "Deposition A-June 12, 1900," Alexander Copeland, Co. M, 3rd Ark Cavalry Federal Pension File; "Deposition C-June 15, 1900" Copeland Pension; "W. A. Kesner Affidavit August 27, 1896," Benjamin H. Gary Co. E, 4th Ark Cavalry Federal Pension File; "Deposition B-July 8, 1897," Gary Pension; "Deposition-C, July 9, 1897," Gary Pension.

117 Albert W. Bishop, *Report of the Adjutant General of Arkansas* (Washington DC: Government Printing Office, 1867), 245 (Senate, 29th Congress, 2nd Session, Mis. Doc. No. 53) (hereafter cited as Bishop, *Report*).

118 Bishop, *Loyalty on the Frontier*, 7, 9–10.

119 "Addendum to David & George W. Smith's Deposition–November 26, 1861," *Scott Letters*; Oliver P. Temple, *East Tennessee and the Civil War* (Johnson City, TN: Overmountain Press, 1995 reprint), 262; *Biographical and Historical Memoirs of Northeast Arkansas* (Chicago: Goodspeed Publishing, 1898), 968–969.

120 "Geo. W. Lee Deposition H-February 23, 1900," Benjamin G. Watts, Co. M, 3rd Ark Cavalry Pension.

121 Bishop, *Loyalty on the Frontier*, 127–140; Mrs. J. N. Bromley, *Biography of John W. Morris* (Marshall, AR: 1916), 45; Scott-McCulloch, December 3, 1861, File 6, Scott Papers; "Fulton County Prisoners' Testimony," #110c Oldham; "William J. Young Deposition D, June 13, 1900," Alexander Copeland, Co. M, 3rd Ark Cavalry Pension; "Lafayette Brashear letter November 27, 1897," Walter W. Brashear, Co. L, 1 Arkansas Cavalry Pension; "John F. Treadwell Deposition May 3, 1897," John W. Lay, Co. I, 3rd Ark Cavalry Pension; "General Affidavit Alexander Copeland," Copeland Pension; "John W. Morris Deposition," Copeland Pension; "Benjamin G. Watts Deposition B July 8, 1897," Benjamin H. Gary, Co. E, 4th Ark Cavalry Pension; Faust, *Historical Times*, 564–565, 772; "Geo. W. Lee Deposition H-February 23, 1900," Benjamin G. Watts, Co. M, 3rd Ark Cavalry Pension; "Testimony of Peter Tyler on the Peace Society." Worley, 95.

122 "Union Cause," *Goodhue Volunteer* (Red Wing, MN), April 22, 1863, 2:1.

123 Robert M. Matthews, *Six Months in the Infantry Service: The Civil War Journal of R. P. Matthews and Roster of The Phelps Regiment Missouri Volunteers*, edited by Jeff Patrick (Springfield, MO: Independent Printing C., 1999), ii, 7–8.

124 "The Conspiracy in the Northwest," *Little Rock Daily State Journal*, November 30, 1861, 2:1&2; "Some three weeks...," *Little Rock True Democrat*, December 5, 1861; Silas Turnbo, *History of the Twenty-seventh Arkansas Confederate Infantry* (Conway, AR: Arkansas Research, 1988), 22.

125 J. William Demby, *The Mysteries and Miseries of Arkansas* (St. Louis: 1863), 5, 8.

126 Job A. Parsley (Griggs Township) said Ananias Stobaugh (Griggs Township) first told him about it, then Chris Denton (Holley Township) did. Moody is the farthest back we can go with the information available. Ananias Stobaugh testified, "A man by the name Moody organized this society in our neighborhood (Griggs Township)." Samuel W. Watson (Holley Township) identified Moody and Henry Bradshaw (Big Flat Township, Searcy County) as the men who swore him in. Watson lived four residences away from Christopher Denton, another prominent Peace Society Unionist organizer. "Testimony of Persons Arrested as Members of the Peace Society," Worley, 107–111; "Testimony of the Fulton County Prisoners Before the Military Board," Worley, 98–102 (#110c Oldham); "Testimony of Peter Tyler on the Peace Society," Worley, 94–97; "Benjamin G. Watts Deposition B-July 8, 1897," Gary Pension.

127 "Testimony of the Fulton County Prisoners," Worley, 98–102; "The Conspiracy in the Northwest," *Little Rock Daily State Journal*, November 30, 1861, 2:1&2; "Some three weeks...," *Little Rock True Democrat*, December 5, 1861.

128 Scott-McCulloch, December 3, 1861, File 6, A-35, Scott Papers. See Appendix VII.

129 Warren, *Yellar Rag Boys*, 1–28; "Testimony of Isaiah Ezell on the Peace Society," Worley, 97; "Testimony of Peter Tyler on the Peace Society," Worley, 95 (#102 Oldham); Scott-McCulloch December 3, 1861, Scott Papers; "Alexander Copeland Deposition A-June 12, 1900," Copeland Pension; "Testimony of Persons Arrested as Members of the Peace Society," Worley, 107–111.

130 Scott-McCulloch, December 3, 1861, File 6, A-35, Scott Papers. See Appendix VII.

131 "We have just received...," *Mountain Wave*, May 3, 1894, 2:4.

132 Faust, *Historical Times*, 420, 564–565; Georgia Lee Tatum, *Disloyalty in the Confederacy* (Chapel Hill: University of North Carolina Press, 1934), 54–166.

133 William T. Auman and David D. Scarboro, "Heroes of America in Civil War North Carolina," *North Carolina Historical Review* 58 (October 1981): 342, 343, 360.

134 Ibid., 328, 331, 358.

135 Ibid., 328, 330, 333, 356.

136 Ibid., 327, 340, 361.

137 "Some three weeks since…," *Little Rock True Democrat*, December 5, 1861; "The Peace Society," *True Democrat*, January 16, 1861, 2:2; *American Annual Cyclopedia* (1861), 25. John A. Harvick, age 42, born in South Carolina is in Cache Township, Monroe County 1860 census. He had served as Monroe County sheriff 1850–1854 and had been county and circuit clerk since 1858. He served as 1st lieutenant, Co. E, and Assistant Quartermaster in 25th Arkansas Infantry.

138 Inscoe and Kenzler, *Enemies of the Country*, 83; *Little Rock Daily State Journal*, November 13, 1861, and November 15, 1861, 3:3; "By Telegraph," *True Democrat*, November 21, 1861, 1:3.

139 *OR*, ser. I, vol. 3, 697–698; "Proclamation," *True Democrat*, October 3, 1861, 4:3.

140 *Arkansas True Democrat*, November 7, 1861, 2:3, 3:3.

141 *Arkansas True Democrat*, November 7, 1861, 3:3; November 14, 1861, 3:4.

142 *Arkansas True Democrat*, November 7, 1861, 3:3; November 14, 1861, 3:4; November 21, 1861, 3.

143 "The Jayhawkers" William M. Aikin letter, *True Democrat*, March 6, 1862, 3:1 & 2.

144 Ibid.

145 Bishop, *Loyalty on the Frontier*, 133–134.

146 Scott's headquarters at Camp Culloden has been identified as near Valley Springs, Boone County, which at that time was in southeast Carroll County. The Van Buren County Clerk at that time was J. T. Bradley (1854–1864). Scott-McCulloch November 20, 1861, File 5 Box 1, John Rice Homer Scott Papers, University of Arkansas at Little Rock (hereafter cited as Scott Papers). Bishop, *Loyalty on the Frontier*, 133–134. John W. Holmes, age 8, in 1850 Federal census is living with his parents, Benjamin and Winsey Holmes in Bear Creek Township, Searcy County, as well as older brother William D. Holmes, age 11. In the 1860 Federal census, John Holmes is living with wife Nancy J. (age 16) in Hartsugg Township, Van Buren County. John Holmes enlisted March 1, 1862, at Clinton in Co. D, 31st Arkansas Infantry. His older brother William D Holmes had enlisted February 1, 1862, in the same company. Both are listed as "deserted" in January 22–August 31, 1862, muster roll. William D. Holmes later enlisted February 1, 1864, in Co. I, 3rd Ark Cav (U.S.) in Searcy County. Civil War Military Compiled Service Records, (hereafter cited CSR) and Desmond Walls Allen, *Third Arkansas Cavalry* (Conway, AR: Arkansas Research, 1987), 58. John W. Holmes is in the Provost Marshal Records for the Batesville Arkansas District under "Bad Characters." He and James McRoberts had "hung an old man" named Grace in a robbery attempt. Union Provost Marshal, vol. 110/360, pp. 22–23, *Department of Arkansas* "Bad Characters" in Van Buren County. Co. D, 31st Ark Inf under Capt. R. S. Hill was mustered January 22, 1862. Ronald R. Bass, *History of the Thirty-first Arkansas Confederate Infantry* (Conway, AR: Arkansas Research, 1996), 108; Affidavit of George W. Lee in Benjamin G. Watts, Co. M, 3rd Ark. Cav. Federal Pension File, indicates some Peace Society members were conscripted into Co. D. John Holmes's widow, Nancy J. married William Aday in 1866 in Van Buren County. They are in Mt. Pleasant Township, Searcy Co. in 1870 Federal Census with her five-year-old son, John W. Holmes. (The voting township in the southwest corner of Searcy County was called "Mountain" in the 1860 census. In the 1870 and later censuses, it is "Mount Pleasant.") *Grooms Marriage Index 1865–1991* (Clinton, AR: Van Buren County Historical Society, n.d.), 1.

147 "The Latest War News," *Reading Times* (Reading, PA), March 1, 1862, 3; Scott-Boone, November 25, 1861.

148 "The Conspiracy in the Northwest," *Daily State Journal*, November 30, 1861, 2:1 & 2; Scott-Boone November 25, 1861, File 18, Box 1, Scott Papers.

149 *Daily State Journal*, November 29, 1861, 2:1.

150 #110, Oldham, published Worley, 107.

151 *1860 U.S. Federal Census of Van Buren Co., Arkansas* (Clinton, AR: Van Buren County Historical Society, n.d.). Prisoners who arrived at Little Rock on November 28 with their Van Buren County township listed in 1860: Bailey, J. F. (Red River); Barns, William (Griggs); Broyles, J. F. (Holley); Cook, Henry (Holley); Curl, John W. (Union); Curl, Samuel M. (Union); Dickerson, Elijah (Union); Gadberry, William (Union); Gilbreath, John (Union); Harness, John (Wiley's Cove, Searcy County); Harness, William (Wiley's Cove, Searcy County); Hensley, Fielding H. (Union); Holley, Absalom (Holley); Holley, Alexander (Holley); Holley, R. C. (Holley); Null, John B. (Griggs); Parsley, A. A. (Griggs); Parsley, Job B. (Griggs); Pierce, S. P. (Turkey Creek); Ridings, James C. (Unknown); Smith, George (Holley); Smith, John (Holley); Stobaugh, Ananias (Griggs); Stobaugh, Edmond (Griggs); Sutton, Logan (unknown); Tackett, W. J. (Unknown); Watson, Samuel W. (Holley), #110d, Oldham.

152 Scott-Boone November 7, 1861, Box 1, File 14, Scott Papers; Boone-Scott, November 12, 1861, File 5, Box 1 Scott Papers.

153 Phelps' Regiment, Infantry 6-months, 1861, Microcopy 405, Rolls 703, 704; 1850 and 1860 Federal censuses.

154 "The Jayhawkers"; Phelps' Regiment, Infantry 6-months, 1861, Microcopy 405, Rolls 703, 704; 1850 and 1860 Federal censuses; James J. Johnston, "Col. John S. Phelps 6-Month Missouri Infantry Volunteers," and "Peace Society in Fulton County," *Fulton County Chronicles* (Fall 1996): 15, 26–44; "The Traitors in Arkansas," *Daily State Journal*, January 26, 1862.

155 Testimony of James A. Baker and Shadrach H. Wren in "Testimony of the Fulton County Prisoners Before the Military Board," #110 Oldham. Shadrach H. Wren, age 36, farmer, born in Kentucky, Big Creek Township, Fulton County, 1860 Federal Census. Wren was a close acquaintance of J. J. Ware; mentioned in Ware's November 19, 1860, letter to his wife to obtain corn from Wren. Wren was Unionist candidate in February 1861 state convention election, which had to be re-run twice, both times without an acceptable result. Cates, "J. J. Ware," 31–34; *Biographical and Historical Memoirs of Northeast Arkansas* (Chicago: Goodspeed, 1889), 981; "Election in Fulton County," *Arkansas True Democrat*, April 25, 1861, 2:2; James Baker, age 32, farmer, born in Tennessee, Bennetts Bayou Township, Fulton County, Arkansas, 1860 8th Federal Census; Worley, "Arkansas Peace Society of 1861," 98–102.

156 1860 8th Federal Census, Benton Township, Howell County, Missouri #260, Gehazi (*sic* Gehuger) B. Ball, age 44, blacksmith, born in North Carolina (spelled Gehuger in "Testimony of the Fulton County Prisoners" file); Milford W. Ball, age 22, farmer, born in North Carolina, #262, Alexander Magbie (*sic* McBee), age 60, farmer, born in Tennessee; James Magbie, age 26, farmer, born in Tennessee. 1860 8th Federal Census, Franklin Township, Izard County, Arkansas #205, William Strother, age 26, cabinetmaker, born in Tennessee. Nunnelie's name is written Nunnelie in 1860 Bennett's Bayou Township, Fulton County Census, but is spelled Nunles in 1870 Wayne County, Tennessee census and Nunelee, Nunnellee, Nunnelee, and Nunnelly in his CSR-Co. G, 31st Ark. Inf.

157 Worley, "Arkansas Peace Society of 1861," 85–87.

158 Worley, "Arkansas Peace Society of 1861," 85–87; Izard County, Arkansas, 1860 Federal Census.

159 #110a, Oldham published in Worley, "Arkansas Peace Society of 1861," 87–88. See Appendix IV.

160 "A Southern Conspiracy–Jayhawkers in Arkansas–Some of Them in Memphis," *Nashville Union and American* (Tennessee), December 20, 1861, 2. This almost exact oath appears in the Kie Oldham Papers and in Worley "Documents Relating to the Arkansas Peace Society of 1861" as "Constitution of the Mill Creek Peace Organization Society." It also appears in "Arkansas Intelligence," *Memphis Daily Appeal*, December 27, 1861, 2 .

161 "The Jayhawkers," *True Democrat*, March 6, 1862, 3:1&2. Addendum B, #137 Oldham. Mary Cooper Miller, *1860 Federal Census of Izard County, Arkansas* (Batesville, AR: M-F Publications, 1984). See Appendix III.

162 Rector-Benjamin December 3, 1861, *OR*, ser. 1, vol. 8, 700–701; Benjamin-Rector December 5, 1861, *OR*, ser. 1, vol. 8, 702; Worley, 88; The 16 prisoners enlisted December 12, 1861, at Pocahontas. "Company H (New), 8th Arkansas Infantry Regiment," www.couchgenweb. com/civilwar/8infcoh (accessed April 22, 2015).

163 *OR*, ser. 1, vol. 8, 709–710; Worley, 106; "Jayhawkers," *Daily State Journal*, January 8, 1862, 2:1. It is interesting that Benjamin F. Brantley of Harris Township., Izard County—who was identified as a major recruiter and Peace Society activist—and his brother and neighbor Thomas Brantley both joined Co. H, 8 Ark. Inf. on January 13, 1862, at Pocahontas. They were the only two men to join on that date, six days after the Izard County prisoners arrived in Little Rock. This leads one to believe that they had been arrested and agreed to join rather than be tried in Little Rock. Both Brantleys (also spelled Brantly) are listed as sick on every muster roll from the time they enroll until August 1864 when muster rolls stop. Both are sent to the hospital from Corinth, Mississippi, on May 12, 1862, by the surgeon. However, Thomas Brantley is paroled at Jacksonport, Arkansas, on June 15, 1865. B. F. Brantley is Izard County Treasurer 1868–1872, but he is not found in the 1870 Izard County Census. Family records indicate he died March 29, 1869, in Izard County, but they are without documents to support this.

164 Leslie-Rector, December 27, 1861, #60a Oldham. In 1860 Searcy County Census, Jesse Cypert, age 46, Bear Creek Township, Henry Bradshaw, age 48, Campbell Township. Locust Grove and Big Flat Townships were on the eastern border of Searcy County adjoining Izard County's Harris Township. These townships are now in Stone and Baxter counties. Burrowville, now Marshall, was the county seat. Mary L. Barnes Deposition L, June 13, 1900, Alexander Copeland Co. M, 3rd Ark. Cav. Federal Pension File.

165 Benjamin G. Watts Deposition A, February 23, 1900, Benjamin G. Watts Co. M, 3rd Ark. Cav., Pension File.

166 Benjamin G. Watts Deposition B, July 8, 1897, Benjamin H. Gary Co. E, 4th Ark. Cav. Pension File. Burrowville, Searcy County seat, was renamed Marshall in 1867. John R. Redwine was captain of Co. E (Locust Grove Township), 45th (Searcy County) Arkansas Militia. William G. Garrison was 3rd Sergeant, Co. E. James Harris and William B. Harris were privates in Co. E. It is not clear which was intended. Abner Smith and Thomas Harness were Peace Society recruiters living in Holley Township, Van Buren County, in the 1860 Federal Census. Johnston, *Searcy County Men in the Civil War*, 16–22. John Berry Treat, born 1835 in Indiana, living in Big Flat Township in 1860. Waddy Thorpe Hunt, private, Co. E, 45th Arkansas Militia, but in May 1862 he was elected captain of Co. F, 27 Ark. Inf. Thomas M. Alexander was sheriff for the 1860–1862 term, and enlisted on February 8, 1864, in Company K, 3rd Arkansas Cavalry (Union).

167 Wilson-Scott November 24, 1861, Box 1, File 18, Scott Papers. Neither J. L. Wilson nor John Berry Treat are found in the service records for the 14th Arkansas Infantry (neither Powers's nor McCarver's). The 14th Infantry is usually referred to as Powers, for Frank P. Powers who assumed command in mid-1862, replacing William C. Mitchell, who was captured March 8, 1862, at Pea Ridge, although Pleasant Fowler and Eli Dodson had commanded in the interim. There are two John Berry Treats living in Big Flat Township, Searcy County in the 1860 Federal Census, one age 26 and the other age 40, both born in Indiana. The younger J. B. Treat served in Dawson's Co. I, 18th (Marmaduke's) Arkansas Infantry composed entirely of Peace Society men.

168 Leslie-Rector, December 27, 1861, #60a Oldham. Johnston, *Searcy County Men*, 16–22.

169 John F. Treadwell Deposition, May 3, 1897, in John W. Lay, Co. I, 3rd Ark. Cav. Pension; Benjamin G. Watts Deposition B, July 8, 1897, Benjamin H. Gary Co. E, 4th Ark Cav. Pension.

170 A. W. Bishop, *Loyalty on the Frontier or Sketches of Union Men of the South-West* (St Louis: A. P. Studley, 1863), 134–135. See Appendix V.

171 "Conspiracy in the Northwest," *Daily State Journal*, November 13, 1861, 3:3; *Daily State Journal*, November 12, 1861, 3:3. *Daily State Journal*, November 15, 1861, 3:3.

172 *Daily State Journal*, November 30, 1861.

173 Leslie-Rector, December 27, 1861, #60a Oldham. Johnston, *Searcy County Men*; Rector-Leslie November 28, 1861, #746 Oldham; Charles F. Gunther, *Two Years before the Paddlewheel*, edited by Bruce S. Allardice and Wayne L. Wolf (Buffalo Gap, TX: State House Press, 2012), 31.

174 *OR*, ser. I, vol. 8, 699.

175 Leslie-Rector, December 27, 1861; Bishop, *Loyalty on the Frontier*, 127–128; Mrs. J. N. Bromley, *Biography of John W. Morris* (Marshall, AR: n.p., 1916) 46; Ebenezer D. Jameson Deposition A, March 5, 1890, Ebenezer D. Jameson, Co. I, 3rd Ark. Cav. Pension; "Probably County's Oldest Citizen Celebrates 94th Birthday Sunday," *Marshall Mountain Wave*, July 14, 1950, 1:5/6.

176 Scott-McCulloch, November 7, 1861, Box 1, File 5, Scott Papers; Furlough of James K. Broadway, October 17, 1861, *Scott Letters*.

177 Scott-McCulloch, November 20, 1861, Box 1, File 5, Scott Papers.

178 "Smith Testimony, November 26, 1861," *Scott Letters*. William Kimbell appears on a list of Secret Society men who had not been captured, probably dated late November. Kimbell, born about 1828 in Tennessee, in 1860 Census, Bear Creek Township, Searcy County. Local lore says he was hanged by Confederates above the spring north of Marshall, i.e., the Zack (or Kimbell) Spring: "I will mention the killing of Bill Kimbell, who was tied to a tree, one mile from Marshall and shot to death. A grave was dug near the tree where the man gave up his life, and the lifeless form was placed in it." Unknown source note in author's collection. Kimbell was taxed in the 1862 Tax Year (Searcy County Tax Records, Arkansas History Commission). John Reeves could not be positively identified.

179 Scott-McCulloch, December 3, 1861, Box 1, File 6, Scott Papers. Author's interview notes with Betty Harris, Marshall, Arkansas, with information from May Keeling Gallegos. Price's wife, Malinda, was the daughter of Peace Society member James P. Thompson and sister to prisoners Thomas and Samuel Thompson. See Appendix VI.

180 Leslie-Rector, December 27, 1861; Johnston, *Searcy County Men*; "State of Arkansas vs. Nathan F. Woodworth," *Scott Letters*. (These collars are identified as tap rings.)

181 James H. Ellis Deposition E, July 8, 1897, Gary Pension. Scott-Brooks January 1, 1862, Box 1 File 6, Scott Papers.

182 Leslie-Scott, December 3, 1861, *Scott Letters*.

183 Bishop, 124; R. D. C. Griffin Affidavit September 16, 1896, Benjamin H. Gary Co. E, 4th Ark. Cav. Pension; Joseph Hurley Deposition E, February 23, 1900, B. G. Watts Pension. Hurley served in Co. C (Wiley's Cove Township), 45th Ark. Militia and in Co. M, 3rd Ark. Cav. (U.S.). Johnston, *Searcy County Men*; Mary Frances Harrell, ed. *History and Folklore of Searcy County Arkansas* (Harrison, AR: New Leaf, 1977), 228; R. D. C. Griffin Deposition B, June 15, 1900, Copeland Pension; Benjamin G. Watts Deposition A, February 23, 1900, Watts Pension; "Conversation with Elsie (Rumley) Hardin," Notes by Pauline H. Madiera, Afton, Oklahoma, in author's collection.

184 Leslie-Rector, December 27, 1861, #60a (2) Oldham.

185 Leslie-Rector, December 9, 1861, #116a Oldham; Bromley, 47–48; Leslie-Ham, December 9, 1861, Oldham. Although Leslie's prisoners' list has not survived, John W. Morris named those of his fellow prisoners whom he could remember in 1916: William Harness, J. W. Harness, R. C. Ladyman, Gasaway Snellgrove, James Foster, William Bartlett, Jeff Chambers, Alex Copeland, James Copeland, Benjamin Passmore, [E. L.] McMillan, J. J. Whitmore [Whitmire], John Hatly, Jim Hatly, John S. Treadwell, Frank Kuykendall, Pete Sutterfield, Mathis Shipman, William Hays, M. Bratton, S. B. Black, Alan McClan [McLane], C. M. Wortman, Frank Wortman, W. F. McDaniel, Jonathan Forehand, Paul Garner, H. Bradshaw, William Bradshaw, Asa Watts, Ben Watts, Sam Watts, P. B. R. Turney, Bowman Turney, Ben Treece, Dan Treece, William Treece, John Treat, James Treat, Joel Passmore, Wash Lynn, Louis Clark, William Davis, William Morris, John Morris Sr., John Morris Jr., Thomas Fisher, Thomas McInturff, William Kesner, William Harris, Anderson Blasingame, William Thompson, William Potter, Jonathan Moody, William Marshall, J. J.

Barnes, J. L. Sanders, John Wilson, Robert Johnson, W. Wallace, [Smith] Ramsey, William Cates, Steve Jones, David Barnett, N. Sutterfield, Ananias Sutterfield, and John Sutterfield. Bromley, 46–47. The only muster roll for Co. I, 18th (Marmaduke's) Ark. Inf. corroborates Morris's list and adds names Morris could not remember. Johnston, *Searcy County Men*, 23–27; Asa Watts Deposition C, July 9, 1897, Gary Pension; Mrs. J. N. Bromley, *Biography of John W. Morris* (Marshall, AR: 1916), 46–47.

186 Thomas J. Archer Deposition D, July 8, 1897 Gary Pension; Johnston, "Reminiscence of James H. Campbell's Experiences during the Civil War," 52. William J. Kelley, Affidavit, December 8, 1897, and General Affidavit, April 16, 1896, Watts Federal Pension.

187 John F. Treadwell Deposition, May 3, 1897, in John W. Lay, Co. I, 3rd Ark. Cav. Pension.

188 Bromley, *Biography of John W. Morris*, 46–47; Bishop, *Loyalty on the Frontier*, 127–130; Johnston, *Searcy County Men*, 23–27; *Daily State Journal*, December. 17, 1861, 2:1. The newspaper reported seventy-eight prisoners, as did Leslie's report, but John W. Morris insisted on seventy-seven, and even named the odd man. Since the only lists of prisoners are Morris's memoirs and the December 18, 1861, Muster Roll of Co. I, 18th (Marmaduke's) Arkansas Infantry, which has seventy-six enlisted men and Morris said there were two who did not enlist, it is unclear whether there were seventy-seven or seventy-eight.

189 "From Memphis," *Times-Picayune* (New Orleans), December 18, 1861, 2; "The Peace Society in Arkansas," *Richmond Dispatch* (Virginia), December 19, 1861, 3; Also in: *Daily Journal* (Wilmington, North Carolina), December 18, 1861, 3, and *Nashville Union and American* (Tennessee), December 18, 1861, 3.

190 Nathan F. Woodworth trial transcript, December 4, 1861, *Scott Letters*.

191 William Caler, No. 13962, Southern Claims Commission; Untitled list, *Scott Letters*; D. P. Sims testimonial, Box 1, File 6, Scott Papers. See Appendix VI.

192 "Claimant's Affidavit July 23, 1900," James F. Homer Christy, Co. H, 1st Ark. Cav. Pension.

193 Arkansas vs. L. D. Jamison, Wesley Hensley, David Baker, December 5, 1861, *Scott Letters*; Scott-Governor Rector, December 6, #89 Oldham; Worley, 91–93.

194 List of Prisoners Sent to Little Rock December 9, 1861, #110a Oldham; Scott-Anderson, December 9, 1861, Box 1, File 6, Scott Papers; Worley, 91–93; "Senate Chamber," December 16, 1861, #110d, Oldham.

195 List of Prisoners Sent to Little Rock December 9, 1861, #110a Oldham; Scott-Anderson, December 9, 1861, Box 1, File 6, Scott Papers; Worley, 91–93; "Senate Chamber," December 16, 1861, #110d, Oldham; Mitchell-Rector, December 23, 1861, #66 Oldham; Confederate CSR-Arkansas: George M. Hays, John W. Kirkham, Eli L. Osborn, Co. H, 14th (Powers) Ark. Inf. The four prisoners who did not enlist were George Long, age 32, United Missionary Baptist preacher from Carroll County; Solomon Branum, age 45, United Missionary Baptist preacher from Marion County (despite his efforts to raise men to free the prisoners); Joshua Reeves, age 41, United Missionary Baptist preacher from Searcy County; and Mayfield Adison, age 38, Searcy County farmer. See Appendix VI.

196 Van Buren County Prisoners, #110d, Oldham; Prisoners to Little Rock, December 9, 1861, #110d, Oldham; "For the War," *Daily State Journal*, December 20, 1861, 2:2; "Rector Guards," *Daily State Journal*, November 9, 1861.

197 Testimony of Thomas J. Slay and others, December 8, 1861, *Scott Letters*. Brantly is Benjamin F. Brantly, Harris Township, Izard County. His name is variously spelled Brantly and Brantley. Perry Strickland is Paris Strickland, Calf Creek Township, Searcy County. Benjamin F. Slay and others, Camp Culloden, December 10, 1861, *Scott Letters*.

198 Arkansas vs. George M. Hays, J. W. Kirkham, John McEntire, and J. C. McNair, December 10, 1861, *Scott Letters*; Scott-McCulloch, November 7, 1861, Box 1, File 5, Scott Papers. Voucher #16, J. W. Kirkham, December 12, 1861, Box 1 File 2, Scott Papers. Scott-Brooks, January 25, 1862, Box 1, File 6, Scott Papers. In this December 14 letter to Scott, Leslie refers to Mount Pleasant Township. It is Mount Pleasant in 1870 as previously noted. Leslie's December 14 letter narrows the time range when the name was changed.

199 Leslie-Scott, December 14, 1861, *Scott Letters*.

200 Scott-Leslie, December 15, 1861, Box 1, File 6, Scott Papers; Headquarters Division, Special
      Orders #181, January 1, 1862, Box 1, File 15, Scott Papers.

201 Smith Addendum, *Civil War Letters: Scott*; Testimony of Peter A. Tyler, #102, Oldham.

202 "The Latest War News," *Reading Times* (Reading, Pennsylvania), March 1, 1862, 3. Adams
      was elected captain of Company E, 3rd Arkansas Cavalry (CSA) on February 22, 1862, at
      Dover, but he failed an examining board and was discharged at Tupelo, Mississippi, on
      August 9, 1862. Then, on December 29, 1862, he was elected captain of Co. A, Hill's 7th
      Ark. Cav., but was dropped from the rolls February 13, 1864, based on information in the
      Inspector General's report.

203 "A List of Names belonging to a Secret Order that has not been arrested," *Scott Letters*;
      Leslie-Rector, December 25, 1861, #116b, Oldham; Leslie-Rector, December 27, 1861, #60a
      (2) Oldham; DuVal-Burgevin, February 13, 1862, Oldham #3402; Samuel Leslie, 45th Ark.
      Militia Service Records, Microcopy M317 Roll 239.

      Names on "A List of Names belonging to a Secret Order" are: Benj Taylor, David C. Ruff,
      E. B. Jameson, Carroll Arter, John Wortman, Sam Strickland, Paris G. Strickland, John
      Strickland, Si Turney, Prisley Turney, Hesaciah Taylor, Nicholas Suton [Seaton], John
      Jinkins, four Slays (There are six possible Slays in 1860 Searcy County census. Five joined
      Co. H, 1st Ark Cav in July 1862. Father Nathan Slay [born 1809] and Levi Slay signed a
      petition December 6, 1861, to release captives who had willingly come in to testify. Others
      are: Benjamin F. Slay, Cornelius D. Slay, Thomas J. Slay, William Henry Slay), L. D. Jamison,
      Benj Hensley, Thomas Forehand, Joseph Cummins, Dink (Theophilus) Parks, Wm Pearce,
      Daniel J. Parks, Clabe Smith, Allen Tucker, Mid Tucker, Yong Macky (Young Macky, i.e.,
      McKey, also Maxey. Henderson G. Mackey, brother-in-law of Claiborn Smith), Joel Baker,
      Ransom Harrison, Bazzel Kimbell, John Kimbell, Thomas Guthrey, Jasper Wallace, B.
      William Kimbell, Green Adams, John Webb, Wm. F. Scott, Levi Cash, ----- Winkle on
      Hampton Ark (sic?), N. F. Woodworth, Peter Reeves, Timothy Arthur Duck, [In box: J. B.
      Jackson, M. P. Hogan, M. (maybe Knox-surname unclear). These names appear to be the
      accusers.], Robert Grinder, Saml Grinder, Josiah Lane, John Brown, Isaiah Ezell, Claiborne
      Manes, Danl Parks, John Ezell, Jo Arter believed to be in it; so says Beverly Conley.

204 Boone-Scott, November 23, 1861, Box 1, File 5, Scott Papers; Wilson/Treat-Scott, November
      24, 1861, Box 1, File 18, Scott Papers.

205 *Daily State Journal*, December 29, 1861, 2:2.

206 Oldham #116b. Peter A. Tyler Letter, January 17, 1862, photocopy in Joan Farris and John
      Ed Fox, *The Wood Family Roots and Branches* (privately printed); Johnston, *Searcy County
      Men*, 30, 123.

207 Oldham #116b. Peter A. Tyler Letter, January 17, 1862, *The Wood Family Roots and
      Branches*; Johnston, *Searcy County Men*, 30, 123; Spencer Adams, Mary Adams
      Confederate Widow's Pension File, Arkansas History Commission; Susie Keeling interview
      notes April 17, 1992, Johnston collection; Wiley Wallis Deposition E, dated June 13, 1900,
      Alexander Copeland, Co. M, 3 Ark. Cav. Pension.

208 "Serious Affray," *Daily State Journal*, January 4, 1862, 2:2; "Jayhawkers," *Daily State
      Journal*, January 8, 1862, 2:1; Worley, "Arkansas Peace Society of 1861," 106.

209 "Murder by Jayhawkers," *Daily State Journal*, December 31, 1861, 2:2.

210 "Correction," *Daily State Journal*, January 9, 1862, 2:1. #881/881 William C. Cole, farmer,
      age 27 born in Tennessee, in Sylamore Township, Izard County, #913/912 John Gilchrist, age
      25 born in Tennessee, in Sylamore Township, Izard County. *1860 Federal Census of Izard
      County*, Schedule 1. Mary Cooper Miller, transcriber (Batesville, AR: M-F Publications,
      1984) 38, 39.

211 "The Case of Mr. Edmondson," *Daily State Journal*, January 9, 1862, 2:1.

212 "The Peace Society," *True Democrat*, January 16, 1862, 2:2.

213 Headquarters 1st Battalion Arkansas Cavalry, January 22, 1862, to Capt. Scott, Box 1, File 16, Scott Papers; Borland-Scott, January 29, 1862, *Scott Letters*; Board of Survey, Camp Leona, Burrowville, Arkansas, January 28, 1862, Box 1, File 6, Scott Papers; Desmond Walls Allen, *The Fourteenth Arkansas Confederate Infantry* (Conway, AR: Arkansas Research, 1988); "A List of Names." Two of the thirty-four were on the "not arrested" list: Josiah S. "Si" Turney and John Webb. Alexander Younger, who enlisted on January 6 with John Webb, was sworn into the Peace Society by Peter Tyler, but this information was not available when the list of those not arrested was compiled. William Caler, who was released upon the pleas of the Morrisons, enlisted on January 22 under pressure.

214 Bishop, *Loyalty on the Frontier*, 132–140; Johnston, *Searcy County Men*, 53–58, 69.

215 "List of Bushwhackers, Guerrillas, etc.," Department of Arkansas, Vol. 110/360, Records of U.S. Army Continental Command, 1821–1920, RG 393, National Archives.

216 "The Peace Society," *True Democrat*, January 16, 1862, 2:2. See Appendix III.

217 "The Jayhawkers," *True Democrat*, March 6, 1862. In the Slave Schedule, 1860 Federal Census, Izard County, Wm. M. Aikin has three slaves: one male and two females. See Appendix III.

218 *Biographical and Historical Memoirs of Northeast Arkansas* (Chicago: Goodspeed Publishing Co., 1889), 264, 918. Toney first served in Ware's Co. G, Phelps's six-month infantry regiment and was discharged May 12, 1862, at Springfield, Missouri. He then enrolled July 1, 1862, at Jacksonport, Arkansas, as captain, Co. D, 1st Battalion six-month Arkansas Infantry.

219 Raymond Lee Muncy, *Searcy, Arkansas: A Frontier Town Grows Up With America* (Searcy, AR: Harding Press, 1976), quoting (Des Arc, Arkansas) *Citizen*, May 8, 1861, 34; "Bloody Affray in St. Francis County," *Des Arc Semi-Weekly Citizen*, May 21, 1861, 2:2; "The Peace Society," *True Democrat*, January 12, 1862, 2:2; "Pro bono Publico," *True Democrat*, December 5, 1861; Warren, *Yellar Rag Boys*, 26.

220 "Pro bono Publico," *True Democrat*, December 5, 1861.

221 Testimony of the Fulton County Prisoners, #110c Oldham; Benjamin G. Watts Deposition A February 23, 1900, Federal Pension File, Benjamin G. Watts Co. M, 3 Ark. Cav.

222 "Jayhawkers," *Daily State Journal*, January 8, 1862, 2:1; "Mr. John Quillin," *Daily State Journal*, January 9, 1862, 2:2; "The Sixty Jayhawkers," *Daily State Journal*, January 12, 1862, 2:2; "Confederate Court," *True Democrat*, January 23, 1862, 2:1.

223 *True Democrat*, January 23, 1862.

224 *OR*, ser. 1, vol. 8, 699; L. Scott Stafford, "Daniel Ringo: 1850–1861," in *United States District Courts and Judges of Arkansas, 1836–1960*, edited by Frances Mitchell Ross (Fayetteville: University of Arkansas Press, 2016), 63–64. (Ringo was re-nominated to the Confederate judgeship on March 26, 1862; this nomination stated that his and other Arkansas judicial appointments for district attorney and marshal were the incumbents.) *Journal of the Congress of the Confederate States of America 1861–1865* (Washington DC: Government Printing Office, 1904) 58th Congress, 2nd Session, Senate Document No. 234, vol. 2, 108; John Hallum, *Biographical and Pictorial History of Arkansas*, Vol. 1 (Albany: Weed, Parsons & Co, 1887), 147; Fay Hempstead, *Historical Review of Arkansas: Its Commerce, Industry and Modern Affairs*, Vol. 1 (Chicago: Lewis Publishing, 1911), 457–458; "Confederate Court," *True Democrat*, January 23, 1862, 2:1; Bishop, *Loyalty on the Frontier*, 129; Mrs. J. N. Bromley, *Biography of John W. Morris*, (Marshall, AR: 1916), 48; Margaret Ross, "Chronicles of Arkansas," *Arkansas Gazette*, December 31, 1961; Garland-Benjamin, January 25, 1862, *OR*, ser. 2, vol. 2, 1917; personal email communication Kathryn C. Fitzhugh, UA Little Rock/Pulaski County Law Library, Little Rock, Arkansas.

225 "Confederate Court," *True Democrat*, January 23, 1862, 2:5. Apart from Bradshaw the jurors were from Pulaski County (two), Jefferson County (two), Saline County (two), and one each from Ouachita, Pike, Desha, White, Prairie, Dallas, Perry, and Polk counties; *OR*, ser. 2, vol. 2, 1417; Garland-Benjamin; *Journal of the Congress of the Confederate States*, Vol. 2, 108.

226 "The Jayhawkers," *True Democrat*, February 27, 1862, 1:3.

227 Beck-Rector March 7, 1862, #585 Oldham; "Items," *True Democrat*, March 27, 1862, 2:5; "Oath" endorsed February 1, 1862, by Military Board, Worley, 107.

228 Desmond Walls Allen, ed., *Turnbo's Tales of the Ozarks: War and Guerrilla Stories* (Conway, AR: Arkansas Research, 1987), 83–84; 1860 U.S. Federal Census, Sched I, Howell County, Missouri, Gehazi R. Ball, 260/260. Gehuger's name is spelled Gehuger in the Military Board's interrogation minutes in the Oldham Collection but is spelled Gehazu or Gehaza in the census and Gehazi in other documents. Gehazi's son Robert E. Ball enlisted December 22, 1863, at Salem, Dent Co., Missouri in Co. E, 11th Missouri Cav. Military service records could not be found for Gehazi or Milford W. Ball. Turnbo said that Gehazi and his sons enlisted in the Union army and that Gehazi enlisted in Captain Robbins's company, Colonel Wammath's regiment. The closest match is 2nd Lt. Alfred M. Robins Co. H, 32nd Mo. Inf. with Lt. Col. Henry C. Warmouth commanding, but there are no Balls listed in that regiment.

229 Johnston, *Searcy County Men*, 23–30; Claims of Deceased Officers and Soldiers from Arkansas filed for settlement in Office of Confederate States Auditor for the War Department, Presented by Lydia Null, widow of John B. Null, Co. K, 18th (Marmaduke) Ark. Inf., on October 15, 1863; Peter A. Tyler to Eveline M. Tyler, January 17, 1862, in Joan Farris and John Ed Fox, *The Wood Family Tree Roots and Branches* (privately printed) in author's collection; Warren, *Yellar Rag Boys*, 25–27; Sarah Gary Deposition, A, July 8, 1897, Benjamin H. Gary, Co. E, 4th Ark. Cav. Pension; Sarah Harness Deposition, April 21, 1893, and Samuel Leslie Deposition, April 24, 1893, John W. Harness Co. M, 3rd Ark. Cav. Pension.

230 Bromley, *Biography of John W. Morris*, 48–49.

231 Franklin Kuykendall Affidavit December 11, 1897, Benjamin G. Watts, Co. M, 3rd Ark. Cav. Pension; Peter M. Sutterfield General Affidavit, Peter M. Sutterfield, Co. M, 3rd Ark. Cav. Pension; David Barnett Affidavit May 20, 1901, David Barnett, Co. M, 3rd Ark. Cav. Pension; Franklin Wortman Affidavit January 1903, Franklin Wortman, Co. M, 3rd Ark. Cav. Pension; Benjamin G. Watts, General Affidavit April 7, 1896, Benjamin G. Watts Co. M, 3rd Ark. Cav. Pension; Mary M. Johnson Deposition K June 13, 1900; Alexander Copeland Deposition A June 12, 1900; Zack T. Johnson Deposition I, June 13, 1900, Alexander Copeland Co. M, 3rd Ark. Cav. Pension; Lt. Col. William K. M. Breckenridge Civil War Daybook, 1862–1863, Tennessee State Library and Archives. William J. Thompson, 2nd Arkansas Cavalry CSR M399, Roll 11.

232 James M. Hollis, Federal Military Service Record, Co. E, 2nd Tennessee Mtd. Inf.; James M. Hollis, Co. E, 2nd Tennessee Mtd. Inf. Pension.

233 Johnston, *Searcy County Men*; CSR: 3rd CSA Inf. & 18th (Marmaduke's) Ark. Inf.; Samuel W. Scott and Samuel P. Angel, *History of the Thirteenth Regiment Volunteer Cavalry, USA* (Philadelphia: Ziegler & Co., 1903), 231, 367–368; *A Reminiscent History of the Ozark Region* (Chicago: Goodspeed, 1894), 253–254.

234 Bromley, *Biography of John W. Morris*, 49–50.

235 Ibid.

236 Bromley, *Biography of John W. Morris*, 49–53; Johnston, *Searcy County Men*. Marmaduke's 3rd Confederate Infantry was part of Hindman's 1st Brigade of Hardee's 3rd Army Corps at the battle of Shiloh. James Lee McDonough, *Shiloh—in Hell before Night* (Knoxville: Tennessee Press, 1977), 143–144. McDaniel died February 8, 1906, after serving in Company I, Third Arkansas Cavalry (U.S.). Johnson died March 15, 1863, in Searcy County; Harris served in Company F, Twenty-seventh Arkansas Infantry and later in Company M, Third Arkansas Cavalry (U.S.) and died on May 9, 1917.

237 Johnston, *Searcy County Men*; "Claimant's Affidavit" July 23, 1900," James F. Homer Christy, Co. H, 1 Ark. Cav. Pension.

238 Desmond Walls Allen, *The Fourteenth Arkansas Confederate Infantry* (Conway, AR: Arkansas Research, 1988); "A list of names belonging to a Secret Order that has not been arrested," *Scott Letters*.

239 S. H. Wren, *Biographical and Historical Memoirs of Northeast Arkansas*, 980–981.

240 Richard Lowe, ed., *A Texas Cavalry Officer's Civil War: The Diary and Letters of James C. Bates* (Baton Rouge: Louisiana State, 1999), 94–95.

241 Bishop, *Loyalty on the Frontier*, 133–140; "A list of names…" *Scott Letters*; Peter A. Tyler Testimony, #102 Oldham; Benjamin F. Slay Testimony, *Scott Letters*; Lowe, ed. *A Texas Cavalry Officer's Civil War*, 95; 9th Texas Cavalry CSR (accessed April 2012) and Federal 1st Ark. Cav. Service Records (accessed May 26, 2015). John W. McDaniel enlisted August 7, 1862, in Co. H, 1 Ark. Cav. (U.S.) by John Morris.

242 "The Call for Troops," *True Democrat*, February 6, 1862; Johnston, *Searcy County Men*.

243 Morris could only remember the names of Jonathan Forehand, John Forehand, Fletcher Strickland, John Strickland, Isaac McDaniel, John H. Ruff, Harden Trammel, James Boyd, and a Mr. Riles. Bromley, *Biography of John W. Morris*, 56–54; Johnston, *Searcy County Men*, 23–27; "Yocum Creek Skirmish," *Searcy County Ancestor Information Exchange*, September 2014, 44–48. Luther Phillips enlisted on July 25, 1862, in Company K, First Arkansas Cavalry (U.S.), about the time that Morris arrived in Springfield. Phillips was killed on November 11, 1862, at the skirmish at Yocum Creek, Carroll County, where Searcy County provost marshal James Shaw, leading the Searcy County home guards, was fatally wounded.

244 James Ervin Shipman Deposition I March 28, 1903, Federal Pension File Paton Drewry Co. L, 1st Ark. Cav. The name Hide-out Mountain south of Snowball reflects its use as a refuge for men avoiding conscription during the Civil War.

245 Benjamin F. Snow Affidavit, October 1, 1895, Benjamin F. Snow, Co. B, 2nd Ark. Cav. Pension.

246 The Home Guard who arrested the Witts Springs men included Shipman, John Russell, Cornelius Bohannon, Robert Casey, and Alf and Jim Holmes. Besides Paton Drewry, they took James E. Drewry, Wesley Roberts, and Joseph Stirman. James Ervin Shipman Deposition I, March 28, 1903, and Paton Drewry Deposition A, March 23, 1903, Federal Pension File Paton Drewry Co. L, 1st Ark. Cav; Benjamin F. Snow Affidavit October 1, 1895, Benjamin F. Snow, Co. B, 2nd Ark. Cav. Pension. Hamilton B. Dickey enlisted on May 4, 1864, in Co. D, 2 Ark. Cav. (U.S.). Desmond Walls Allen, *Second Arkansas Cavalry* (Conway, AR: Arkansas Research, 1987), 45.

247 Jo Apsie Morrison, Campbell, Arkansas, Interview recording and notes in author's collection, July 1861; Union Provost Marshal, Vol. 110/360, 22–23, *Department of Arkansas* "Bad Characters" in Van Buren County.

248 Kenneth C. Barnes, "The Williams Clan," 155–176; *OR*, ser. 1, vol. 48, pt. 2, 841–845, 494, 595; *Report of the Adjutant General of Arkansas*, 272, 273.

249 *Report of the Adjutant General of Arkansas*, 70–72.

250 James J. Johnston, *Tax Lists Searcy County Arkansas 1839–1866* (Fayetteville, AR: Searcy County Publications, 2003); John F. Treadwell Deposition May 3, 1897, in John W. Lay Co. I, 3rd Ark. Cav. Pension; Francis Kuykendall General Affidavit April 1, 1896, and Benjamin G. Watts Deposition A, February 23, 1900, in Benjamin G. Watts Co. M, 3rd Ark. Cav. Pension; Charles Pemberton Deposition A, May 19, 1888, Charles Pemberton, Co. I, 3rd Ark. Cav. Pension; Asa Watts Deposition C, July 9, 1897, Benjamin H. Gary Co. E, 4 Ark. Cav. Pension; Hattie Watts Treece to Roberta Watts Ferguson, October 23, 1978, in author's collection.

251 Arkansas Miscellaneous, Jeptha McGinnis, Co. A, Head's Battalion; Paton Drewry Deposition A, March 23, 1903, Paton Drewry, Co. L, 1st Ark. Cav. Pension. (Drewry is often spelled Drury.)

252 Arkansas Miscellaneous, Jeptha McGinnis, Co. A, Head's Battalion. Court-martial refers only to "Taylor," but B. F. Taylor is the best identification. *OR*, ser. 1, vol. 22, 195; Paton Drewry Deposition A, March 23, 1903, Paton Drewry, Pension.

253 Civil War Union Service Records, 1 Ark. Inf., 1 Ark. Cav. David C. Ruff had an interesting year in 1862. At age 45, he enrolled August 29, 1862, in Co. M, 1 Ark. Cav. in Searcy County from Springfield, Missouri. He deserted October 18, 1862, in Searcy County. This raises two questions: Was he one of Morris's companions on their escape to Springfield? What was he doing in Searcy County in October—recruiting?

254 *OR*, ser. vol. 1, 22, pt. 1, 208; 1850 Federal census, Wayne County, Tennessee, #759/769, Tidings Thompson household.

255 Samuel R. Curtis, "The Army of the Southwest and the First Campaign in Arkansas," *Annals of Iowa* 7, no. 1 (1869): 18, quoted in Robert G. Schultz, *The March to the River: From the Battle of Pea Ridge to Helena, Spring 1862* (Iowa City: Camp Pope Publishing, 2014), 167–168.

256 *Report of the Adjutant General of Arkansas for the Period of the Late Rebellion, and to November 1, 1866*, U.S. Senate, 33rd Congress, 2nd Session, Mis. Doc. No. 53 (Washington DC: Government Printing Office, 1867) (hereafter cited as *Report of the Adjutant General*), 236–245.

257 Samuel R. Curtis Journal, June 15, at State Historical Society, Des Moines, Iowa, quoted in Schultz, *The March to the River*, 166–167.

258 Franklin O. Stobaugh Deposition I, Edmund S. Stobaugh 3rd Ark. Cav. Pension; *Report of the Adjutant General*, 245.

259 *Report of the Adjutant General*, 245.

260 These June 18 recruits included Peace Society members Abner H. Smith and William H. Harness of Leslie's chain gang and the sons and brothers of Peace Society men from Holley, Union, and Turkey Creek townships. Among them were Michael N. Broyles and Jonathan Moody's son Sparling Moody, who were in Peace Society–rich Holley Township with Chris Denton in 1860. Michael, born in 1839 in Tennessee, was next door to his brother James F. Broyles—born 1837 in Tennessee—one of the Van Buren County prisoners serving in Company K, Eighteenth Infantry. The June 19 recruits were Elijah Dickerson of Holley (who had served in Company K, Marmaduke's Eighteenth Arkansas Infantry), John Gilbreath's son David W., and James F. Bailey. (Bailey and John Gilbreath were both tried and released by the January Confederate Court.) One of the two Searcy County recruits was Michael P. Tinkle of Tomahawk Township, who had tried to free the Peace Society prisoners in Burrowville and Clinton. Co. D, 9 Mo. Cav.; *1860 U.S. Federal Census of Van Buren Co., Arkansas* (Clinton: Van Buren County Historical Society, n.d.); *OR*, ser. vol. 13, 64. Union Civil War Service Records, 10th Mo. Cav.; 1850 Federal Census Greene County, Tennessee, Joshua Broyles household; Co. A, 9 Mo. Cav.; 1860 U.S. Federal Census of Van Buren County, Arkansas; Len Eagleburger, *The Fighting 10th: The History of the 10th Missouri Cavalry U.S.* (Bloomington, IN: 2004), Appendix B; Smith family genealogist Lora Kates McDaniel emails September 28, 2013, and December 20, 2015, in author's collection.

On June 18, 1862, the following enlisted in Co. D, Bowen's 9th Mo. Cav. (townships noted in parentheses): Broyles, Michael N. (Holley—brother of James F. Broyles), Hensley, Fielding H. (Union), Harness, William H. (Cove, Searcy County), Moody, Sparling B. (Holley—son of Jonathan Moody), Passmore, George W. (Turkey Creek), Smith, Abner H. (Holley), Smith, Elias D (Union—Abner's brother), Smith, George W. (Holley—Abner's brother), Smith, John T. (Holley—Abner's brother), Smith, Joseph W. (Holley—Abner's brother), Work, Thomas J. (Holley).

On June 19th, the following enlisted in Co. D; Bailey, James F. (Red River), Gilbreath, David W. (Union), Hart, William (unknown), Honeycutt, Phillip (Holley), Lott, James (Hartsuggs), Copeland, Joab (Griggs), Copeland, John R. (unknown), Weir, John W. (Holley), Dickerson, Elijah (Union), Denton, Martin Van Buren (Prairie, Searcy County), Tinkle, Michael P. (Tomahawk, Searcy County).

On June 24, 1862, the following enlisted in Co. A, Bowen's 9th Mo. Cav.: Berry, John (Union), Hawkins, Calvin R. (Giles), Martin, Jonathan (Turkey Creek), Tyler, James B. (Turkey Creek).

The Ninth consolidated with the Tenth Missouri Cavalry in December 1862 and was transferred to Tennessee.

261 Union Civil War Service Records, 10th Mo. Cav.

262 Confederate Civil War Service records, Arkansas, 14ᵗʰ (Powers) Ark. Inf. and Union
     Arkansas 2ⁿᵈ Ark. Cav.; Johnston, *Searcy County Men*, 5–14, 74–77.

263 *Report of the Adjutant General*, 93.

264 Congressman Thomas Boles, letter to Charles Lanham, March 26, 1868, Lanham Papers,
     Arkansas State Archives, Little Rock, Arkansas; *Biographical and Pictorial History
     of Arkansas*, Vol. 1, (Albany: Weed Publishers, 1887), 435, 436; William H. Pruden III,
     "Thomas Boles (1837–1905)," *Encyclopedia of Arkansas History & Culture*, www.
     encyclopediaofarkansas.net.

265 Thomas Boles, Co. E, and Unit Information, Union Civil War Service Records, 3rd Ark.
     Cav. M399 Roll 25.

266 *OR*, ser. 1, vol. 22, pt. 2, 690–691; *Report of the Adjutant General*, 94; 1860 Federal Census,
     Arkansas: Burk Johnson lived in Magazine Township, Yell County; William H. Stoutt lived
     in Gum Log Township, Pope County. Burk Johnson enlisted October 14, 1863, in Co. F,
     3ʳᵈ Ark. Cav. (U.S.). Desmond Walls Allen, *Third Arkansas Union Cavalry* (Conway, AR:
     Arkansas Research, 1987), 60; William H. Stout enlisted December 26, 1863, in Co. H, 4ᵗʰ
     Ark. Cav. (U.S.). Desmond Walls Allen, *Fourth Arkansas Union Cavalry*, (Conway, AR:
     Arkansas Research, 1987), l, 86. Desmond Walls Allen, *Second Arkansas Union Cavalry*
     (Conway, AR: Arkansas Research, 1987). Of thirty-eight men who enlisted in the 2ⁿᵈ Ark.
     Cav. (U.S.) at Dardanelle, twenty-three went into Co. F, the others into Companies E and M.

267 Leander S. Dunscomb, Co. G, 3ʳᵈ Ark. Cav. M399 Roll 26 NA.

268 *OR*, ser. 1, vol. 48, pt. 2, 844. Barnes, "The Williams Clan"; Jo Apsie Morrison Interview
     Notes, Marshall, Arkansas, July 1961, author's collection.

269 David C. Ruff, Jarrett Reeves, Alexander Younger, Co. F, 46 Mo. Inf., CSR M405, Roll 681.

270 John W. Morris, CSR-Arkansas M399, Roll 9, National Archives Microfilm. *OR*, ser. 1,
     vol. 13, 64.

271 Bromley, *Biography of John W. Morris*, 70–79. William F. McDaniel and Robert McDaniel,
     Co. I, 3 Ark. Cav. (U.S.), CSR-Arkansas, M399 Roll 30, National Archives Microfilm.

272 David C. Ruff, Benjamin F. Taylor, Co. I, 1 Ark. Inf. (U.S.) CSR-Arkansas, M399, Rolls 50, 51;
     Lorenzo D. Jameson, Co. H, 1 Ark. Cav. (U.S.) CSR M399 Roll 6; Johnston, "Reminiscence
     of James H. Campbell's Experiences during the Civil War," 157–158, footnotes 20, 21.

273 *OR*, ser. 1, vol. 34, pts. 3, 8.

274 Lyman Bennett, "Summer of 1863," edited by James J. Johnston, *White River Historical
     Society Quarterly* 38 (Spring 1999): 6. Johnston, *Searcy County Men*, 74–77.

275 Joseph S. Arter, Andrew J. Bratton, John B. Hinchey, Ebenezer B. Jameson, John H. McElroy,
     Nicholas Seaton, and Hezekiah Taylor joined Co. E, Lemoyne's 17 Inf. with Walter Brashear.
     Lafayette Brashear: H. Clay Evans letter November 27, 1897, Walter W. Brashear, Pension;
     Johnston, *Searcy County Men*, 31–33, 74–77; Lyman Bennett, "Recruiting in Dixie, Part
     II," edited by James J. Johnston, *White River Valley Historical Quarterly* 39 (Winter 2000):
     5. Mortimer M. Brashear (misidentified by Bennett as both William and Walter) was killed
     August 5, 1863, in Searcy County. He was born November 18, 1817, in Kentucky and was
     living with his family in the 1850 U.S. Census in Campbell Township, Searcy County.
     He moved to northern Pope County, where his son Walter W. was married in 1857. "Hon.
     Walter W. Brashear," *Biographical and Historical Memoirs of Western Arkansas* (Chicago:
     Southern Publishing Co., 1891), 215–216; *Report of the Adjutant General*, 44–51.

276 Lafayette Brashear-H. Clay Evans letter November 27, 1897, in federal pension file of
     Walter W. Brashear, Co. L, 1ˢᵗ Ark. Cav.; Johnston, *Searcy County Men*, 31–33, 74–77.

277 Johnston, *Searcy County Men*, 31–33, 74–77.

278 Johnston, *Searcy County Men*, 74–77; *Report of the Adjutant General*, 70–71; James
     J. Johnston, "Brashears/Cassell Connection?" *Searcy County Ancestor Information
     Exchange*, April 1999, 14–17.

279 *OR*, ser. 1, vol. 34, pt. 1, 85–86; Johnston, *Searcy County Men*, 85–88; 2nd Ark. Cav. (US), CSR M399, RG 94, Rolls 0016-0024.

280 Interview with Ben Henley Jr. and Jessie Smith Henley, St. Joe Arkansas, 1962, author's notes; *A Reminiscent History of the Ozark Region* (Chicago: Goodspeed Publishing, 1894), 297–298; 2nd Ark. Cav. (U.S.),Unit Information, Field and Staff, January & February 1864, M399, RG 94, Roll 0075; Dan Allen, "A Family Story from the Civil War," *Searcy County Ancestor Information Exchange*, March/April, 2016, 90–91; Roger McNair, *From Daniel McNair to Us* (N.p.: 2015); *Arkansas Tract Book, Searcy County. 16N, 17W*, Commissioner of State Lands, Little Rock, Arkansas; W. C. Faught and Thomas J. Faught testimony addendum to David Smith and George W. Smith deposition, November 26, 1861, *Scott Letters*.

281 "Reports of Articles and Persons Hired," (Report #1691; Lieut. J. C. Thompson, 1864), Records of the Quartermaster General RG 92, Entry 238, NA; William Monks, *A History of Southern Missouri and Northern Arkansas*, edited by John F. Bradbury Jr. and Lou Wehner (Fayetteville: University of Arkansas Press, 2003), xxi, xxii, xiv, xxv.

282 "Public Meeting in Fulton County," *Unconditional Union* (Little Rock), March 11, 1864, 1:2; Reports of Articles and Persons Hired (Report #1691; Lt. J. C. Thompson, 1864), Records of the Quartermaster General, RG92, Entry 238, NA.

283 "Public Meeting in Fulton County," *Unconditional Union* (Little Rock), March 11, 1864, 1:2; Reports of Articles and Persons Hired (Report #1691; Lt. J. C. Thompson, 1864), Records of the Quartermaster General, RG92, Entry 238, NA; *Report of the Adjutant General*, 272; Treadwell affidavit, of May 3, 1897, in John W. Lay, Co. I, 3 Ark. Cav. Pension; "Co. G, Cocke's Ark. Inf. (6th Trans-Miss.)" in Johnston, *Searcy County Men*.

284 "Testimony of the Fulton County Prisoners Before the Military Board," in Worley, "Documents Relating to the Arkansas Peace Society of 1861," 98–102; "William S. Richardson," *Biographical and Historical Memoirs of Northeast Arkansas* (Chicago: Goodspeed Publishing, 1889), 968–969; Thomas F. Richardson, CSR M405 Roll703, NA Microfilm.

285 U.S. Civil War Draft Registration Records 1863–1865—Schedules I (and II) Consolidated List of all persons of Class I (and II) subject to military duty in the Second Congressional District, consisting of the Counties of Saint Louis and Others, State of Missouri, enumerated during the month of July (June, July, August), 1863, under direction of C. C. Manwaring, Provost Marshal.

286 Daniels, *Historical Report of the Secretary of State 2008*, 127–132, 533–534, 428; "Address," *Phelps County New Era* (Rolla, Missouri), October 12, 1878, www.cdm.sos. mo.gov/cdm/search/cosuppress/ (accessed January 6, 2016). John Bradbury-J. J. Johnston letter August 9, 2005, with *Phelps Co. New Era* clippings; "Richard Parks Bland" http:// history.house.gov/People/Detail/9477 (accessed July 19, 2018); *Reminiscent History of the Ozark Region* (Chicago: Goodspeed Brothers, 1894), 69–70. Brantley may not have completed his term, although the *Historical Report* does not indicate that he did not. He is not in the 1870 Izard County Census, and Ancestry Family tree on www.ancestry.com indicates he died March 26, 1869, at Sylamore Township, Izard County.

287 Monks, *A History of Southern Missouri and Northern Arkansas*, xxxviii–xl; Members of the Fulton County Union League with a Peace Society connection were: Peace Society members Joshua Richardson, James A. Ball, and John Rand. Others were Richardson's son, William; Asa Brantley (younger brother of the two Peace Society Brantleys); the Rands (John's father Edward and brother Nicholas); and J. J. Ware's son, William and Shadrach Wren's nephew William Wren. Brooks Blevins communication April 24, 2018, based on Record of Fulton Council No 1 U.L.A., Folder 5, George W. Dale Papers, Martha McAlmont Vaughn Collection, Arkansas State Archives. Desmond Walls Allen, *Index to Arkansas Confederate Soldiers*, Vol. 3, *P–Z*, 135; J. H. Tracy, J. H. Tracy Jr., N. H. Tracy, Co. G. 8th Ark. Cav. CSR-Arkansas M317 Roll 27; Tony Garrison, "The Murder of Simpson Mason," *Independence County Chronicle* 32 (April/July 1991): 39–47.

288 James J. Barnes, CSR-Arkansas, Co. I, 18 Ark. Inf. (Marmaduke) M317 Roll 159 & 3 Confederate Infantry, M258, Roll 62; Co. I, 3 Ark. Cav. (U.S.), CSR- M399, Roll 24.

289 Benjamin F. Taylor, Co. M, 3 Ark. Cav. (U.S.), CSR M399, Roll 32; "Two Killed, Deputy Marshals Ambushed," *Arkansas Gazette*, August 31, 1897, 1; "Like a Romance," *Mountain Wave* (Marshall, Arkansas), September 24, 1897, 1; "William Harvey Bruce," *History of Pope County, Arkansas*, Vol. 2 (Topeka, KS: Josten Publishing for Pope Co. Historical Association, 1981), 239.

290 "The State-Searcy," *Daily State Gazette* (Little Rock), November 20, 1872, 1:2. Lane's term is only documented as 1866–1872, but he probably served to 1874 as the record shows VACANT for 1872–1874. Daniels, *Historical Report of the Secretary of State 2008*, 533–534.

291 J. William Demby, *The Home Aegis and Monthly Review, Devoted to the Interests of the People* (Little Rock: published by author, 1864), 69.

292 Depositions of John H. Haslow (Hashem in 1860 census) and Elijah Harbour, James Byrne Case File (Calhoun County), Southern Claims Commission case files, RG 217, NA; J. H. Hashem, 341/335, Locust Bayou Township, Elijah Harbour, Caswell Township, 183/179, Calhoun County, Arkansas, 1860 U.S. Federal census, Sched. I.

293 Scott Forrester Claimant's Affidavit, June 29, 1896, Scott Forrester, Co. D, 4th Ark. Cav. Federal Pension File; Scott Forrester, 16 Ark. Inf. CSR-M3127, Roll 152; Thomas Ellison, Co. H, 16th Ark. Inf. CSR M317, Roll 150.

294 1860 U.S. Census, Pike County, Arkansas, Scott Forester, Thomas Ellison, F. R. Forester, James Kirk, P. T. Musgraves, Elijah C. Putman, Jacob Putman, Harvey Walker, W. H. C. Walker, David White Sr., David White Jr., William White Sr. (Forrester is spelled Forester in the census, and Putnam is spelled Putman.); Desmond Walls Allen, *Fourth Arkansas Union Cavalry* (Conway, AR: Arkansas Research, 1987).

295 Lorenzo D. Jameson, CSR M399, Rolls 6 and 47; Company K, 1 Ark. Inf. (U.S.) "Arkansas Genealogy Project, Civil War," www.couchgenweb.com/civilwar/ (accessed January 3, 2016); *Report of the Adjutant General*, 199–204.

296 "Arkansas Genealogy Project, Civil War," Co. L, 2nd. Kansas Cav. (accessed January 4, 2016); Jan Eddleman, "Muster Roll of Company L, 2nd Kansas Cavalry, United States Army—April 30 to June 30, 1864," *Arkansas Family Historian* 35 (September 1997): 107–115; W. S. Burke, *Official History of Kansas Regiments During the War for the Suppression of the Great Rebellion*, Reprint (Ottawa, KS: Kansas Heritage Press, n.d.), 50–51,53–54.

297 *OR*, ser. 1, vol. 22, pt. 2, 37.

298 Eight were from Boone Township, Scott County, two from Mill Creek, Franklin County, two from Revilee (Reville), Scott County, and one each from Gap, Montgomery County; Union, Hot Spring County; Cole and Sugarloaf townships, Sebastian County; and Lees Creek, Crawford County. (Boone and Revilee [Reville] townships are now in southwest Logan County.) Russell T. Baker, *Arkansas Township Atlas 1819–1930* (Hot Springs, AR: Arkansas Genealogical Society, 2003). *Report of the Adjutant General*, 180–182; 1860 U.S. Census.

299 Wiley Britton, *A Traveling Court, Based on Investigation of War Claims* (Kansas City: Smith-Grieves Co., 1926), 189–190; Desmond Walls Allen, *First Arkansas Union Infantry* (Conway, AR: Arkansas Research, 1987), 57; 8th U.S. Federal Census (1860), Schedule I, Middle Township., Franklin County, AR, 808/774 John Powell.

300 William J. Heppington, Co. I, 1st Ark. Inf. CSR M399 Roll 46. (Heffington's file is under Heppington.); *Report of the Adjutant General*, 203, 204; John Whiteford, Co. I, 1st Ark. Inf. CSR M399 Roll 51.

301 *OR*, ser. 1, vol. 22, pt. 1, 602–604.

302 *Report of the Adjutant General*, 203–204.

303 Affidavits: Jeremiah Hackett, General Affidavit, October 28, 1898, Jeremiah Hackett, Deposition A, December 14, 1901, Benjamin F. Hackett, General Affidavit, October 28, 1898, Benjamin F. Hackett, Deposition A, April 15, 1902, and Benjamin F. Henley, Deposition A, December 25, 1900, Benjamin F. Henley, Co. H, 2nd Ark. Cav. Pension; 1860 Census, Sched I, Arkansas: Tomlinson Township, Scott Co. Wm Henley and Cole Twp., Sebastian Co. Jeremiah Hackett.

304 Carl H. Moneyhon, "Disloyalty and Class Consciousness in Southwestern Arkansas," in *Civil War Arkansas: Beyond Battles and Leaders*, edited by Anne J. Bailey and Daniel E. Sutherland (Fayetteville: University of Arkansas Press, 2000), 121–124.

305 DeBlack, *With Fire and Sword*, 76–78.

306 Moneyhon, "Disloyalty and Class Consciousness," 117–132; Depositions of John H. Haslow and Elijah Harbour, James Byrne Case File (Calhoun County), Southern Claims Commission case files, RG217, NA; Harbour identified one of those hanged as ____ Tibbett, Haslow identified Dick Gammill, Cabet Silliman, and Benjamin Nutt. In the 1860 Census, Locust Bayou Township, Calhoun County, Arkansas, John H. Haslow is identified as Hashem.

307 "Matters in Arkansas," *True Democrat*, February 4, 1863, 1:2.

308 *OR*, ser. 1, vol. 22, pt. 1, 752–754.

309 *OR*, ser. 1, vol. 22, pt. 1, 754. "Arkansas Genealogy Project, Civil War," www.couchgenweb.com/civilwar/, Co. K, 24th Ark. Inf. (accessed January 2, 2016).

310 DeBlack, *With Fire and Sword*, 76–78. Deposition of Roscoe G. Jennings, Gayle H. Kyle case file (Clark County), Southern Claims Commission case files, RG217, NA.

311 Bishop, *Loyalty on the Frontier*, 127, 133; "A Union League in the South," *Daily State Journal*, January 22, 1862, 2:3; *Burlington Weekly Free Press* (Burlington, Vermont), February 15, 1861, 1; *Fayetteville Semi-Weekly Observer* (Fayetteville, North Carolina), September 5, 1861, 2.

312 Scott-McCulloch, December 3, 1861, File 6, (Coll-A-35), Scott Papers.

313 William M. McPherson, to Abraham Lincoln, December 25, 1862, Lincoln Papers. McPherson's comment on "being dragged by Hindman's guerrillas" refers to Hindman's General Order No. 17, of June 17, 1862, in which he authorized the formation of independent companies of ten or more to annoy the enemy on the rivers and in the mountains, effectively forming guerrilla units. *OR*, ser. 1, vol. 8, 835.

314 Michael Feldman, Leslie J. Gordon, and Daniel E. Sutherland, *This Terrible War: The Civil War and its Aftermath* (New York: Longmans, 2003), 326–327; Madison Anderson (no date Reel F1217), Gabriel G. Brown (July 9, 1863 Reel F1339), J. E. Jewell (March 20, 1863, Reel F1347), William Kingston (May 25, 1864 Reel F1151), and Lindsey Murdock (September 10, 1863 Reel F1202), SOS, Missouri–Union Provost Marshal Papers: 1861–1866, www.sos.mo.gov/records/archives/archives/provost/provostpdf.asp (accessed January 18, 2016). William J. Hammond deposition, Newell J. Brooks case file (Ouachita, then Nevada County), Southern Claims Commission files, R 217, NAQ.

315 "The Peace Society," *True Democrat*, January 16, 1862, 2:2.

316 "The Jayhawkers," *True Democrat*, March 6, 1862. In the Slave Schedule, 1860 Federal Census, Izard County, Wm. M. Aikin has three slaves: one male and two females.

317 Worley, "Documents Relating to the Arkansas Peace Society of 1861," 87–88; "A Southern Conspiracy–Jayhawkers in Arkansas–Some of them in Memphis," *Nashville Union and American* (Tennessee), December 20, 1861, 2. This almost exact oath appears in the Kie Oldham papers and in Worley as "Constitution of the Mill Creek Peace Organization Society." It also appears in "Arkansas Intelligence," *Memphis Daily Appeal*, December 27, 1861, 2.

318 Bishop, *Loyalty on the Frontier*, 135.

319 List of Prisoners Sent to Little Rock Dec 9, 1861, #110a Oldham; Scott-Anderson, December 9, 1861, Box 1, File 6, Scott Papers.

320 Scott-McCulloch, December 3, 1861, File 6, A-35, Scott Papers.

Bibliography

Primary Sources: Manuscripts

Charles Lanham Collection. Arkansas State Archives, Little Rock, Arkansas.

Clara Eno Collection. Arkansas State Archives, Little Rock, Arkansas.

David Walker Collection. Special Collections, Mullins Library, University of Arkansas, Fayetteville, Arkansas.

John Rice Homer Scott Papers. University of Arkansas at Little Rock Center for Arkansas History and Culture, Little Rock, Arkansas

Joseph Robinson Rutherford Papers. Special Collections, Mullins Library, University of Arkansas, Fayetteville, Arkansas.

Kie Oldham Collection. Arkansas State Archives, Little Rock, Arkansas.

Orville J. McInturff Collection. Arkansas State Archives, Little Rock, Arkansas.

Peter A. Tyler to Evaline M. Tyler Letter, January 17, 1862. Buffalo National River Files, Harrison, Arkansas

Primary Sources: Newspapers

Arkansas Gazette (Little Rock, Arkansas)

Arkansas True Democrat (Little Rock, Arkansas)

Daily State Journal (Little Rock, Arkansas)

Des Arc Semi-Weekly Citizen (Des Arc, Arkansas)

Home Aegis and Monthly Review (Little Rock, Arkansas)

Marshall Mountain Wave (Marshall, Arkansas)

Marshall Republican (Marshall, Arkansas)

Memphis Daily Appeal (Memphis, Tennessee)

Primary Sources: Public Documents

Daniels, Charlie. *Historical Report of the Secretary of State 2008*. Little Rock: Arkansas Secretary of State's Office, 2008.

Journal of the Congress of the Confederate States of America 1861–1865. Washington DC: Government Printing Office, 1904.

Journal of the House of Representatives for the Thirteenth Session of the General Assembly of the State of Arkansas, which was begun and held in the capitol in the city of Little Rock, on Monday, the fifth day of November, one thousand, eight hundred and sixty, and ended on Monday, the twenty-first day of January, one thousand, eight hundred and sixty-one. Little Rock: Johnson & Yerkes, 1861.

Ordinances of the State Convention, which convened in Little Rock May 6, 1861. Little Rock: Johnson and Yerkes, 1861.

Provost Marshal Records for the Batesville, Arkansas District. National Archives, Washington DC.

Report of the Adjutant General of Arkansas for the period of the late rebellion, and to November 1, 1866. Washington DC: Government Printing Office, 1867.

U.S. Census Bureau. *Population Schedules of the Eighth United States Census, 1860, Arkansas.* National Archives, Washington DC.

U.S. Pension Bureau. National Archives, Washington DC.

——. James F. H. Christy, First Arkansas Cavalry, Federal Pension File.

——. Alexander Copeland, Third Arkansas Cavalry, Federal Pension File.

——. Peyton Drewry, First Arkansas Cavalry, Federal Pension File.

——. Benjamin H. Gary, Fourth Arkansas Cavalry, Federal Pension File.

——. John W. Harness, Third Arkansas Cavalry, Federal Pension File.

——. John Wesley Lay Jr., Third Arkansas Cavalry, Federal Pension File.

——. John W. Morris, First Arkansas Cavalry, Federal Pension File.

——. Charles Pemberton, Third Arkansas Cavalry, Federal Pension File.

——. Wesley Roberts, First Arkansas Cavalry, Federal Pension File.

——. Benjamin F. Snow, Second Arkansas Cavalry, Federal Pension File.

——. Edmund Stobaugh, Third Arkansas Cavalry, Federal Pension File.

——. Peter M. Sutterfield, Third Arkansas Cavalry, Federal Pension File.

——. Benjamin G. Watts, Third Arkansas Cavalry, Federal Pension File.

U.S. War Department. *Compiled Service Records of Confederate Soldiers Who Served in Organizations from the State of Arkansas.* National Archives, Washington DC.

——. *Compiled Service Records of Union Soldiers.* National Archives, Washington DC.

——. *Index to Service Records of Confederate Soldiers Who Served in Organizations from the State of Arkansas.* National Archives Microcopy No. 376.

War of the Rebellion: A Compilation of the Official Records of the Union and Confederate Armies. 70 vols. in 128 books and index. Washington DC: Government Printing Office, 1880–1901.

Primary Sources: Websites

www.ancestry.com—1860 Census Records Schedule 1 and Slave Schedule

www.fold3.com—Civil War: Compiled military service records, Union and Confederate

www.fold3.com—Civil War: Southern Claims Commission Files

www.newspapers.com—*Burlington Weekly Free Press* (Burlington, VT)
   Daily Journal (Wilmington, NC)
   Fayetteville Semi-Weekly Observer (Fayetteville, NC)
   Memphis Daily Appeal (Memphis, TN)
   Nashville Union and American (Nashville, TN)
   Reading Times (Reading, PA)
   Richmond Dispatch (Richmond, VA)
   Times-Picayune (New Orleans, LA)

http://www.sos.mo.gov/archives/provost/provostPDF.asp—Union provost marshal papers 1861–1866, Missouri State Archives, Columbia, Missouri.

https://memory.loc.gov/ammem/alhtml/—Abraham Lincoln Papers at the Library of Congress.

www.couchgenweb.com—Edward G. Gerdes Civil War Home Page. Muster rolls of Civil War Arkansas units, Union and Confederate and some other units that served in Arkansas.

Primary Sources: Books and Articles

Demby, James W. *Mysteries and Miseries of Arkansas, or a Defence* [sic] *of the Loyalty of the State.* St. Louis: n.p., 1863.

Lemley, J. B., Lester Finley, and Elaine Weir Cia, eds. *Civil War Letters: Capt. Jno. R. Homer Scott's Squadron of Cavelry* [sic]*, in Pope County, Arkansas and Carroll County, Arkansas.* Russellville, AR: J. B. Lemley, n.d.

Matthews, Robert M. *Six Months in the Infantry Service: The Civil War Journal of R. P. Matthews and Roster of the Phelps Regiment Missouri Volunteers.* Edited by Jeff Patrick. Springfield, MO: Independent Printing, 1999.

Temple, O. P. *East Tennessee in the Civil War*. Reprint. Johnson City, TN: Overmountain Press, 1995.

Turnbo, Silas C. *History of the Twenty-seventh Arkansas Confederate Infantry*. Conway, AR: Arkansas Research, 1988.

Secondary Sources: Books and Articles

Allen, Desmond Walls. *Arkansas' Damned Yankees: An Index to Union Soldiers in Arkansas Regiments*. Conway, AR: D. W. Allen, 1987.

Allen, Desmond Walls comp. *Arkansas Union Soldiers Pension Application Index*. Conway, AR: D. W. Allen, 1987.

———. *Fourteenth Arkansas Confederate Infantry*. Conway, AR: Arkansas Research, 1988.

———. *Index to Arkansas Confederate Soldiers*. 3 vols. Conway, AR: Arkansas Research, 1990.

American Annual Cyclopedia and register of the important events of the year 1861. New York: D. Appleby & Co., 1868.

Anderson, Charles C. *Fighting by Southern Federals*. New York: Neale Publishing Co., 1912.

Ash, Stephen V. *Middle Tennessee Society Transformed 1860–1870: War and Peace in the Upper South*. Knoxville: University of Tennessee Press, 2006.

———. *When the Yankees Came: Conflict and Chaos in the Occupied South 1861–1865*. Chapel Hill: University of North Carolina, 1995.

Auman, William T. "Bryan Tyson: Southern Unionist and American Patriot." *North Carolina Historical Review* 62 (July 1985): 257–292.

———. "Neighbor against Neighbor: The Inner Civil War in the Randolph County Area of Confederate North Carolina." *North Carolina Historical Review* 61 (January 1984): 59–92.

Auman, William T., and David D. Scarboro. "The Heroes of America in Civil War North Carolina." *North Carolina Historical Review* 58 (October 1981): 327–363.

Bailey, Anne J., and Daniel E. Sutherland. *Civil War Arkansas: Beyond Battles and Leaders*. Fayetteville: University of Arkansas Press, 2000.

Bailey, Joseph M. *Confederate Guerrilla: The Civil War Memoir of Joseph Bailey*. Edited by T. Lindsey Baker. Fayetteville: University of Arkansas Press, 2007.

Bailey, Joseph M. *Memoirs of Captain J. M. Bailey*. Edited by James Troy Massey. Independence, MO: Two Trails, n.d.

Baker, Robin E. "Class Conflict and Political Upheaval: The Transformation of North Carolina Politics during the Civil War." *North Carolina Historical Review* 70 (April 1992): 148–178.

Barnes, Kenneth C. "The Williams Clan: Mountain Farmers and Union Fighters in North Central Arkansas." *Arkansas Historical Quarterly* 52 (Autumn 1993): 286–317.

Bartolph, Richard. "Confederate Dilemma: North Carolina Troops and the Deserter Problem, Part I." *North Carolina Historical Review* 66 (January 1989): 61–86.

———. "Confederate Dilemma: North Carolina Troops and the Deserter Problem, Part II." *North Carolina Historical Review* 66 (April 1989): 179–210.

Bass, Ronald R. *History of the Thirty-first Arkansas Confederate Infantry.* Conway, AR: Arkansas Research, 1996.

Bates, James C. *A Texas Cavalry Officer's Civil War: The Diary and Letters of James C. Bates.* Edited by Richard Lowe. Baton Rouge: Louisiana State University Press, 1999.

Bennett, Lyman G. "Recruiting in Dixie, Part 1." Edited by James J. Johnston. *White River Valley Historical Quarterly* 39 (Fall 1999): 13–18.

———. "Recruiting in Dixie, Part 2." *White River Valley Historical Quarterly* 39 (Winter 2000): 3–14.

———. "Recruiting in Dixie, Part 3." *White River Valley Historical Quarterly* 39 (Spring 2000): 3–11.

———. "Summer of 1863." *White River Valley Historical Quarterly* 37 (Spring 1998): 3–14.

Biographical and Historical Memoirs of Northeast Arkansas. Chicago: Goodspeed Publishing, 1898.

Biographical and Historical Memoirs of Southern Arkansas. Chicago: Goodspeed Publishing, 1890.

Biographical and Historical Memoirs of Western Arkansas. Chicago: Southern Publishing Company, 1891.

Bishop, Albert Webb. *Loyalty on the Frontier, or Sketches of Union Men of the South-West; with incidents and adventures in Rebellion on the Border.* St. Louis: R. P. Studley and Co., 1863.

———. *Loyalty on the Frontier, or Sketches of Men of the South-West with Incidents and Adventures in Rebellion on the Border.* Edited by Kim Allen Scott. Fayetteville: University of Arkansas Press, 2003.

Boyd, Lina Owens, comp. *1860 U.S. Census, Newton County, Arkansas & Will Books B and C, 1910 to Present*. Dover, AR: L. O. Boyd, n.d.

Blankinship, Gary. "Colonel Fielding Hurst and the Hurst Nation." *West Tennessee Historical Society Papers* 34 (October 1980): 71–87.

Britton, Wiley. *The Aftermath of the Civil War*. Kansas City, MO: Smith-Grieves, 1924.

———. *Civil War on the Border*. 2 vols. New York: G. P. Putnam's Sons, 1899.

———. *A Traveling Court*. Kansas City, MO: Smith-Grieves, 1926.

Bromley, Mrs. J. N. *Biography of John W. Morris*. Marshall, AR: 1916.

Brown, Walter Lee. *A Life of Albert Pike*. Fayetteville: University of Arkansas Press, 1997.

Bryan, Charles F., Jr. "'Tories' Amidst Rebels: Confederate Occupation of East Tennessee." *East Tennessee Historical Society's Publications* 60 (1987): 3–22.

Carrigan, Alfred Holt. "Reminiscences of the Secession Convention." *Publications of the Arkansas Historical Association* 1 (1906).

Cates, Max. "J. J. Ware." *Fulton County* [Arkansas] *Chronicles* 11 (Spring 1996): 31–34.

Crofts, Daniel W. *Reluctant Confederates: Upper South Unionists in the Secession Crisis*. Chapel Hill: University of North Carolina Press, 1989.

Current, Richard Nelson. *Lincoln's Loyalists*. Boston: Northeastern University Press, 1992.

DeBlack, Thomas A. *With Fire and Sword: Arkansas, 1861–1874*. Fayetteville: University of Arkansas Press, 2002.

Degler, Carl H. *The Other South: Southern Dissenters in the Nineteenth Century*. New York: Harper & Row, 1974.

Dougan, Michael B. *Confederate Arkansas: The People and Politics of a Frontier State in Wartime*. Tuscaloosa: University of Alabama Press, 1976.

Dunn, Durwood. *Cades Cove: The Life and Death of a Southern Appalachian Community, 1818–1937*. Knoxville: University of Tennessee Press, 1988.

Dyer, Thomas G. *Secret Yankees: The Union Circle in Confederate Atlanta*. Baltimore: Johns Hopkins University Press, 1999.

Eagleburger, Len. *The Fighting 10th: The History of the 10th Missouri Cavalry US*. Bloomington, IN: 2004.

Farris, Joan, and John Ed Fox. *The Wood Family Roots and Branches.* N.p.: n.d.

Faust, Patricia L., ed. *Historical Times Illustrated Encyclopedia of the Civil War.* New York: Harper Collins, 1986.

Fellman, Michael, Leslie J. Gordon, and Daniel L. Sutherland. *This Terrible War.* New York: Longman, 2003.

Fleming, Walter L. "The Peace Movement in Alabama during the Civil War I. Party Politics, 1861–1864." *South Atlantic Quarterly* 3 (January–October 1903): 114–124.

Fitzgerald, Michael W. *The Union League Movement in the Deep South.* Baton Rouge: Louisiana State University Press, 1989.

Foner, Eric. "The South's Inner Civil War." *American Heritage* 40 (March 1989): 47–56.

Freehling, William W. *The Road to Disunion: Secessionists Triumphant 1854–1861.* New York: Oxford University Press, 2007.

———. *The South vs The South.* News York: Oxford University Press, 2001.

Gunther, Charles F. *Two Years before the Paddlewheel.* Edited by Bruce S. Allardice and Wayne L. Wolf. Buffalo Gap, TX: State House Press, 2012.

Hallum, John. *Biographical and Pictorial History of Arkansas.* Albany: Weed, Parsons and Company, 1887.

Harrell, Mary Frances, ed. *History and Folklore of Searcy County, Arkansas.* Harrison, AR: New Leaf Press, 1977.

Harris, William C. "East Tennessee's Civil War Refugees and the Impact of the War on Civilians." *Journal of East Tennessee History* 64 (1992): 3–19.

———. "The East Tennessee Relief Movement of 1864–1865." *Tennessee Historical Quarterly* 48 (Summer 1989): 86–96.

Hempstead, Fay. *Historical Review of Arkansas.* Chicago: Lewis Publishing, 1911.

History of Benton, Washington, Carroll, Madison, Crawford, Franklin and Sebastian Counties, Arkansas. Chicago: Goodspeed Publishing Company, 1889.

Humes, Thomas William. *The Loyal Mountaineers of Tennessee.* Reprint. Spartanburg, SC: The Reprint Co., 1974.

Inscoe, John C. "Coping in Confederate Appalachia: Portrait of a Mountain Woman and Her Community at War." *North Carolina Historical Review* 69 (October 1992): 388–413.

Inscoe, John C., and Robert C. Kenzler. *Enemies of the Country: New Perspectives on Unionists in the Civil War South.* Athens: University of Georgia Press, 2001.

Johnston, James J. "Arkansas' 1861 Peace Society." *Arkansas Family Historian* 29 (March 1991): 13–29.

———. "Bullets for Johnny Reb: Confederate Nitre and Mining Bureau in Arkansas." *Arkansas Historical Quarterly* 49 (Summer 1990): 124–167.

———. "Letter of John Campbell, Unionist." *Arkansas Historical Quarterly* 29 (Summer 1970): 176–182.

———. "Peace Society in Fulton County." *Fulton County* [Arkansas] *Chronicles* 14 (Fall 1996): 26–44.

———. "Reminiscence of James H. Campbell's Experiences during the Civil War." *Arkansas Historical Quarterly* 74 (Summer 2015): 147–186.

———. *Searcy County Men in the Civil War: Union and Confederate.* Fayetteville: Searcy County Publications, 2011.

Lackey, Walter F. *History of Newton County, Arkansas.* Point Lookout, MO: School of the Ozarks Press, n.d.

Lewis, A. B. "Chasing Guerrillas in Arkansas." *Confederate Veteran* 29 (1921): 220–221.

Lonn, Ella. *Desertion during the Civil War.* Reprint. Gloucester, MA: Peter Smith, 1966.

Lufkin, Charles L. "Secession and Coercion in Tennessee; the Spring of 1861." *Tennessee Historical Quarterly* 50 (Summer 1991): 98–109.

Madden, David. "Unionist Resistance to Confederate Occupation: The Bridge Burners of East Tennessee." *East Tennessee Historical Society's Publications* 51–52 (1980–1981): 22–39.

Maness, Lonnie E. "Emerson Etheridge and the Union." *Tennessee Historical Quarterly* 48 (Summer 1989): 97–110.

McCaslin, Richard B. *Tainted Breeze: The Great Hanging at Gainesville, Texas 1862.* Baton Rouge: Louisiana State University Press, 1994.

McDonough, James Lee. *Shiloh—in Hell before Night.* Knoxville: University of Tennessee Press, 1977.

McInturff, Orville J. *Searcy County, My Dear: A History of Searcy County, Arkansas.* Marshall, AR: Marshall Mountain Wave, 1963.

McKenzie, Robert Tracy. *Lincolnites and Rebels: A Divided Town in the American Civil War.* New York: Oxford University Press, 2006.

McNair, Roger. *From Daniel McNair to Us.* N.p.: 2015.

Miller, Mary Cooper, comp. *1860 Federal Census of Izard County, Arkansas.* Batesville, AR: M-F Publications, 1984.

Monks, William. *A History of Southern Missouri and Northern Arkansas, Being an Account of the Early Settlement, the Civil War, The Ku Klux and Times of Peace.* Edited by John F. Bradbury and Lou Wehmer. Fayetteville: University of Arkansas Press, 2003.

Muncey, Raymond Lee. *Searcy, Arkansas: A Frontier Town Grows Up With America.* Searcy: Harding Press, 1976.

Neal, Diane. "Treason or Patriotism? Union Peace Societies in Arkansas during the Civil War." *Journal of Confederate History* 1 (Fall 1988): 339–350.

Neal, Diane, and Thomas W. Kremm. *The Lion of the South: General Thomas C. Hindman.* Macon, GA: Mercer University Press, 1993.

Noe, Kenneth W. "Red String Scare: Civil War Southwest Virginia and the Heroes of America." *North Carolina Historical Review* 69 (July 1992): 301–322.

Owens, Susie Lee. *The Union League of America: Political Activities in Tennessee, the Carolinas, and Virginia 1865–1870.* New York: New York University Press, 1947.

Patton, James Welch. *Unionism and Reconstruction in Tennessee, 1860–1869.* Chapel Hill: University of North Carolina Press, 1934.

Pope County, Arkansas Historical Association. *History of Pope County, Arkansas.* Vol. 2. Topeka, KS: Josten Publishing, 1981.

Readnour, Harry W. "William Meade Fishback (1831–1903)." *Encyclopedia of Arkansas History & Culture.* www.encyclopediaofarkansas.net

Reminiscent History of the Ozark Region. Chicago: Goodspeed Brothers Publishers, 1894.

Sawyer, William E. "The Martin Hart Conspiracy." *Arkansas Historical Quarterly* 23 (Summer 1964): 154–165.

Scott, Samuel W., and Samuel P. Angel. *History of the Thirteenth Regiment Tennessee Volunteer Cavalry, U.S.A.* Philadelphia: P. W. Ziegler & Co., 1903.

Scroggs, Jack B. "Arkansas in the Secession Crisis." *Arkansas Historical Quarterly* 12 (Autumn 1953): 179–224.

Smith, John I. *The Courage of a Southern Unionist: A Biography of Isaac Murphy, Governor of Arkansas 1864–1868*. Little Rock: Rose Publishing Company, 1979.

Stevenson, William G. *Thirteen Months in the Rebel Army*. New York: A. S. Barnes, 1952.

Sutherland, Daniel E. "The Real War in Arkansas." *Arkansas Historical Quarterly* 52 (Autumn 1993): 257–285.

———. *A Savage Conflict: The Decisive Role of Guerrillas in the American Civil War*. Chapel Hill: University of North Carolina Press, 2009.

Tatum, Georgia Lee. *Disloyalty in the Confederacy*. Chapel Hill: University of North Carolina Press, 1934.

Thompson, George H. *Arkansas and Reconstruction: The Influence of Geography, Economics and Personality*. Port Washington, NY: Kennikat Press, 1976.

Walter, John F. "Capsule Histories of Arkansas Military Units in the Civil War." Manuscript in Special Collections, Mullins Library, University of Arkansas, Fayetteville, Arkansas.

Warren, Luther E. *Yellar Rag Boys*. Edited by Sandra L. Weaver. Marshall, AR: 1992.

Whiteman, Maxwell. *Gentlemen in Crisis: The First Century of the Union League of Philadelphia 1862–1962*. Philadelphia: Union League of Philadelphia, 1975.

Woods, James M. *Rebellion and Realignment: Arkansas's Road to Secession*. Fayetteville: University of Arkansas Press, 1987.

Worley, Ted R. "The Arkansas Peace Society of 1861: A Study in Mountain Unionism." *Carroll County (Arkansas) Historical Quarterly* 3 (March 1958): 9–16.

———. "The Arkansas Peace Society of 1861: A Study in Mountain Unionism." *Journal of Southern History* 24 (November 1958): 445–456.

———. "Documents Relating to the Arkansas Peace Society of 1861." *Arkansas Historical Quarterly* 17 (Spring 1958): 82–111.

———. "Helena on the Mississippi." *Arkansas Historical Quarterly* 17 (Spring 1954): 1–17.

About the Author

Born in Little Rock, Arkansas, in 1936, James J. Johnston is the son of William C. and Capitola Treece Johnston. He graduated from high school in Camden, Arkansas. His father was a civil engineer, and the family moved several times in Arkansas and Oklahoma and also lived on a naval base in California during World War II. Throughout these years and since, he has lived in Marshall in Searcy County, Arkansas. After earning a BA and MA at the University of Oklahoma, he served three years in the U.S. Navy. At his home port in California, Johnston met his future wife, Margaret Grant. He joined the Foreign Service and served in administrative and consular positions, principally in Africa and Latin America. After he retired in October 1988 from the American Embassy, Mogadishu, Somalia, as Counselor of Administration, he and his wife returned to Marshall.

Johnston and his wife then moved to Fayetteville, Arkansas, but he maintains the family home in Marshall and his business, Searcy County Publications, there. Since retirement, he has continued to write about Searcy County history. For the past twenty-five years, he has published a quarterly, the *Searcy County Ancestor Information Exchange*. He has held local leadership positions as president of the Marshall Rotary Club, Scottish Society of Northwest Arkansas, Searcy County Historical Society, and the Ko-ko-ci chapter of the Arkansas Archeological Society. Also, he has served on the boards of the Searcy County Economic Development Council and Fayetteville's First United Presbyterian Church.

In 1989, Johnston organized the North Arkansas Ancestor Fair, with which he remains active. In 2002, he received a Letter of Commendation from the Arkansas Historical Association for celebrating history and family heritage in north Arkansas through a model program of speakers and workshops. In 2007, Johnston received the McGimsey Preservation Award for his outstanding contributions to the preservation of Arkansas heritage from the Arkansas Archeological Society. The Arkansas Historical Association presented Johnston a Lifetime Achievement Award in 2012 for his dedication to the study of the Civil War and the preservation of Ozarks history. James and Margaret reside in Fayetteville, but he still claims Marshall as his home.

Index

Strickland, John Anderson 218, 270 n203, 273 n243

Strickland, Paris G. 85, 128, 137, 154–157, 172, 198, 218, 269 n197, 270 n203

Strickland, Samuel Smith 218, 270 n203

Strother, William 103, 104, 218 266 n156

Sutterfield, Ananias J. 122, 218, 243, 268 n185

Sutterfield, John R. 218, 246, 268 n185

Sutterfield, Nathaniel 122, 218, 246, 268 n185

Sutterfield, Peter M. 148, 218, 246, 268 n185

Sutton, Logan 218, 253, 266 n151

Swaggerty, L. N. C. 261 n94

Sylamore Township, Izard County, Arkansas 84, 105, 106, 134, 228

T

Tackett, W. J. 266 n151

Talbot's Mill, Arkansas 102

Taney County, Missouri 62, 69, 71, 86

tap rings 268 n180

Tatum, Georgia Lee 14

Tatum, William V. 203

Taylor, Benjamin Franklin 9, 140, 160, 161, 172, 173, 182, 188, 218, 170 n203, 273 n252

Taylor, Hezekiah 176, 218, 270 n203, 275 n 275

Temple, Oliver 83

Tennessee 7, 15, 18, 23, 37, 55, 60, 64, 66, 67, 83, 85, 89, 90, 112, 113, 124, 140, 148–150, 158, 165, 183, 239, 247, 254

Terry, Morgan M. 111, 123, 133, 139, 242

Texas 17, 39, 50, 51, 56, 62, 74, 191, 240

Third Arkansas Cavalry (U.S.) 9, 35, 115, 159, 160, 164, 167–169, 172–174, 181–183

Third Confederate Infantry (Marmaduke) 150, 157, 272 n236

Third Iowa Cavalry 195, 196

Thirty-first Arkansas Infantry 98

Thomas, Calvin 137

Thomason, Hugh F. 44, 51, 52, 54, 205

Thompson, General 43

Thompson, Henry H. 161

Thompson, James Patrick 147, 218, 235, 250, 253, 268 n179

Thompson, John C. 105, 106, 218

Thompson, Pleasant F. 105, 106, 218

Thompson, Samuel 117, 218, 234, 250, 254, 268 n179

Thompson, Thomas 134, 218, 268 n179

Thompson, William J. 122, 148, 149, 160, 162, 218, 246, 269 n185

Thornton, Miles 154

Tibbett, _____ 278 n306

Tilley, James 218

Tinkle, Michael P. 116, 117, 165, 218, 235, 274 n260

Tinkle, Robert 125, 218

Tomahawk Township, Searcy County, Arkansas 73, 83, 87, 112, 116–118, 124, 125, 129–131, 156, 177, 178, 223

Toney, James P. 218, 271 n218

Toney, Lorenzo Dow 102, 139, 164, 218

Totten, Benjamin C. 39, 41, 61, 204

Totten, James M. 205

Trammell, Harden 156, 273 n243

Trammell, Jarrett 156

Tracy, J. H. 181

Tracy, Jesse H. 181

Tracy, Nathaniel H. 181

Treadwell, John Franklin 122, 157, 160, 176, 218, 246, 268 n185

Treat, James 109, 110

Treat, James William 218, 246, 268 n185

Treat, John B. 218, 246, 268 n185

Treat, John Berry 110, 267 n166, n 167

Treat, W. F. B. 105

Treece, Benjamin 152, 160, 184, 218, 256, 247, 268 n185

Treece, Daniel 160, 218, 246, 268 n185

Treece, Henry 117

Treece, John 160

Treece, William 151, 152, 160, 218, 246, 247, 268 n185

Trimble, Robert E. 127, 137, 153

True Democrat 20–22, 24, 28, 32, 45, 55, 65, 67, 81, 92, 117, 136–140, 143, 145, 146, 202, 225, 228, 243

Tucker, John Allen 218, 270 n203

Tucker, John Middleton 218, 270 n203

Turnbo, Silas 71, 86

Turner, Hiram 178, 179

Turner, Jesse 43, 48, 51, 52, 205

Turney, Bowman 151, 218, 246, 247, 268 n185

Turney, Jacob B. 124

Printed in the USA
CPSIA information can be obtained
at www.ICGtesting.com
JSHW022222130524
62889JS00001B/3

9 781945 624124